MW01055672

CANNON MILLS AND KANNAPOLIS

CANNON MILLS
AND
KANNAPOLIS

PERSISTENT PATERNALISM IN A TEXTILE TOWN

TIMOTHY W. VANDERBURG

The University of Tennessee Press / Knoxville

Copyright © 2013 by The University of Tennessee Press / Knoxville.
All Rights Reserved. Manufactured in the United States of America.
First Edition.

The paper in this book meets the requirements of American National Standards Institute / National Information Standards Organization specification Z39.48-1992 (Permanence of Paper). It contains 30 percent post-consumer waste and is certified by the Forest Stewardship Council.

Library of Congress Cataloging-in-Publication Data

Vanderburg, Timothy W.
Cannon Mills and Kannapolis: persistent paternalism in a textile town / Timothy W. Vanderburg.
— First Edition.
pages cm
Includes bibliographical references and index.
ISBN 978-1-57233-972-9 (hardcover) — ISBN 1-57233-972-1 (hardcover)
1. Cannon Mills Company—History.
2. Textile industry—North Carolina—Kannapolis—History.
3. Paternalism—North Carolina—Kannapolis.
4. Kannapolis (N.C.)—Social conditions—20th century.
I. Title.

HD9850.5.V36 2013
338.7'67700975672—dc23
2013001469

I dedicate this book to my wife, Marsha, for her loving support
without which this work could not have been completed.
Furthermore, the memory of my grandparents
who were Cannon Mills workers,
Buford and Clemmie Henley, guided this project.

CONTENTS

ILLUSTRATIONS

Figures

Map

ACKNOWLEDGMENTS

My interest in Cannon Mills as a research subject began in the early 1990s during work for my master's degree. The current work, however, developed from my doctoral dissertation, which was directed by Dr. Richard V. Damms at Mississippi State University. As my major professor, Dr. Damms skillfully guided me through the creation of the dissertation on Cannon Mills and in the process made me a better researcher and writer. Many archivists and librarians gave assistance and advice during the research phase of this book, including William Erwin at the Perkins Library at Duke University, Richard Pipes at Wingate University Library, Terry Prather at the Cannon Memorial Library in Kannapolis, and Larry Hayer and the Kannapolis History Associates. Thanks to Wayne and Mary Ann Vanderburg for a place to stay during my many research trips to Duke. The time to develop my dissertation into a book was provided by Gardner-Webb University with a sabbatical in the fall of 2008. Thanks to Dr. Donna Ellington, Chair of the Social Sciences Department, for covering my classes while I was on the sabbatical. Quiet and rejuvenating environments were provided by friends so I could focus on writing. Thanks, James and Valeria Polk, for the use of your condo at Southport, North Carolina, and Cathy Huffman, for the use of your condo at Cherry Grove, South Carolina. For assistance in developing my research into a book, I thank Dr. Bob Carey at Gardner-Webb University for help with photos and illustrations. The comments and suggestions of Dr. George Loveland guided me in focusing on the main themes and thesis of the book. Special appreciation goes to Dr. David Zonderman for his detailed, thoughtful, and encouraging remarks. And lastly, thanks to Scot Danforth and Kerry Webb at the University of Tennessee Press, who saw the potential in this project and worked to make it better than I had imagined. Any shortcomings of this book are solely mine.

INTRODUCTION

Cannon Mills Company exemplified the southern textile firm. From its creation in the late 1880s until the mid-1980s, Cannon Mills operated as a paternalistic company controlled by a small group of insiders. James W. Cannon and his associates on the board of directors ran the firm from its creation until 1921, when Cannon's son, Charles, took over. Charles Cannon led the firm until his death in 1971. While other companies in the textile industry were divesting themselves of mill villages and the vestiges of paternalism, Charles Cannon was running the firm in the fashion established by his father. Indeed, Kannapolis, the firm's mill village, was the largest unincorporated town in the United States.

Outwardly, Cannon Mills resembled a modern corporation, but Charles Cannon and his associates dominated the company with little influence from stockholders. "Uncle Charlie," as Cannon workers called him, maintained control of the firm through his force of personality, through control of the voting shares of stock, and by making sure that like-minded men served on the board of directors. His degree of control in Kannapolis can be characterized as cultural hegemony, defined by historian T. J. Jackson Lears as

> the spontaneous consent given by the great masses of the population to the general direction imposed on social life by the dominant fundamental group; this consent is "historically" caused by the prestige (and consequent confidence) which the dominant group enjoys because of its position and function in the world of production.[1]

The cultural hegemony established by the Cannons in Kannapolis, based on the prestige of the Cannon family and having a Cannon as the firm's leader, was pervasive and persistent. With the death of Charles Cannon, however, the firm entered a pseudo-paternalistic stage with the quick succession of three chairmen. The accelerated decline of paternalism began with the intrusion of federal government policies regarding discrimination in employment and housing. Executive orders, the Civil Rights Act of 1964, and the 1968 Open Housing Act brought pressure on the paternalistic structure of the firm and mill village.

Cannon Mills' entrance into the modern bureaucratic stage of management came with the purchase of Cannon Mills by California financier David Murdock in 1982. In the four short years that Murdock was CEO, the passing of paternalism hastened as he oversaw the sale of mill houses and part of the company town. By the time Fieldcrest purchased the firm in 1986, Murdock had jerked the company and its community into the modern corporate world. The quick and traumatic demise of paternalism and Murdock's restructuring of the pension fund destroyed workers' loyalty and established bad industrial relations at Fieldcrest Cannon. Increasing numbers of workers turned to the union for protection, resulting in a series of union elections. Pillowtex purchased Fieldcrest Cannon in 1997, and the union finally won an election in 1999, declaring it the greatest labor victory in southern textile history. But the long union struggle against Cannon Mills proved futile as Pillowtex declared bankruptcy in 2003 and was liquidated.

Paternalism emerged in the textile mills in the New South as mill villages sprang forth in the southern Piedmont. Mill owners provided services for mill workers in exchange for hard work, loyalty, and deference to the mill owners. The mill village was self-contained to a degree, as southern industrialists "protected" their workers from the outside world and served as a conduit between the village and the world beyond. This geographic isolation, similar to parents protecting their children from the dangers outside the home, was part of the mills' paternalism.

Life in a mill village was much different from life on a farm. Farmers did their planting and cultivating however they saw fit with little or no supervision. In contrast, mill workers were supervised, had rigid work regulations, and possessed little work autonomy. Farmers controlled their own time and pace of work, while textile workers did not. Mill workers were told when to appear for work, when to have meals, when to take breaks, and when to go home. In addition, workers did not control the speed of their work or how tasks were preformed.

For economic reasons, mill owners often constructed their mills away from town limits, enabling mill owner to avoid paying municipal taxes.[2] In addition, mill owners took advantage of cheap farmland on which to build their mills. Because that farmland lacked housing, stores, churches, and essential public services, the mill owners had to provide these for their workers. Mill owners, therefore, had to build entire communities.

Paternalism in the textile mills of the South developed with the construction of mill villages and may be defined as "a form of traditional authority [which]. . . . involves hierarchical differentiation between classes, concentration of power, and the identification of the subordinate class with members of the dominant class." Furthermore, in the textile villages paternalism included "company control of land, buildings, goods, and services" and an ideology of labor relations.[3]

Economic historians point to the economic necessity for paternalism in the postbellum South. Gavin Wright argues that mill owners placed mills in areas of economic advantage and had to provide services for poor workers. The system, he notes, evolved out of economic need and mill owners did not create it for social control. Cathy McHugh agrees with Wright. She believes that structural changes in the southern economy after the Civil War led to the displacement of farm workers who migrated to the mills. Mill owners responded to the availability of a ready labor source by building mills and mill villages.[4]

Southern textile mill paternalism was not entirely new in that it resembled the paternalism of northern textile mills, which was modeled after English textile practices. By the early 1800s, for example, textile firms in Rhode Island and Massachusetts were providing an elaborate array of services for their workers. Pioneered by two companies in Waltham and Lowell, Massachusetts, this paternalist approach to manufacturing became known as the Waltham system. Both firms used the Waltham (sometimes called the Lowell) system to attract and manage their work forces. Other northern textile companies later used the Waltham system.[5]

Northern industrial paternalism influenced the development of the textile industry in both the antebellum and postbellum South. Eventually paternalism declined in the North and industrialists replaced it with bureaucratic authority.[6] In this pattern, too, the southern textile industry followed the North. Restructuring in the textile industry from the 1920s through the 1940s resulted in many firms selling their mill villages.[7] By the 1970s, textile companies had become modern corporations with bureaucratic management structures and had sold their mill villages.[8]

Historian Donald Roy described this change as moving away from a paternalism marked by "shirt-sleeved informality toward impersonal business relationships."[9] As companies' headquarters moved to distant towns, along with top-level management, the personal touch of industrial paternalism disappeared. Midlevel positions were filled by college-educated managers with modern bureaucratic management styles, and the benevolent paternalism of the mill owner was replaced with either a pseudo-paternalism or a coercive relationship. The pseudo-paternalistic management style harkened back to the paternalism of the former mill owners. It sought to cultivate a personal relationship between management and workers along with a degree of consensus and friendship. In contrast, the coercive (bureaucratic) management relationship sought an impersonal and professional relationship between management and workers.[10] While all textile firms went through this process of management change, Cannon Mills was distinct.

Cannon Mills' paternalism did not fit the standard southern mold. Its paternalism was of a different type and degree than found at other firms. It was much stronger and more persistent. As historians Oliver Dinius and Angela Vergara note,

> The definition [of a company town] emphasizes the company's status as dominant property owner and the town's dependence on a single industry. Other conventional definitions highlight the town's isolation, residential segregation, and company control over urban services, education, and leisure activities. Historically, company towns often met several of these criteria, but only a few model towns met all of them.[11]

Kannapolis certainly met all of these criteria. And while Roy described two alternative management styles that could replace benevolent paternalism, Cannon Mills went through all three stages of management styles. While the story of Cannon Mills Company and Kannapolis is somewhat unique, it does not necessarily revise past studies of paternalism in textile mills or mill villages. Instead, it contributes an additional, overlooked layer of complexity to the story of southern industrial paternalism.

The fate of Cannon Mills was tied to the rest of the textile industry in the South. The same forces that weakened southern textiles also weakened Cannon Mills. If the once conservative, well-managed textile firm with a dominant market share in the towel segment of the textile industry could decline due to textile imports and structural changes in the economy, how could the southern textile market survive?

PART I

The Founding of
Cannon Mills and Kannapolis:
Paternalism Established

CHAPTER 1

————◆→»×←◆→●————

James William Cannon:
Early Influences and the Emergence of a New South Industrialist

James William Cannon, a business leader who represented the spirit of the New South, brought industrial progress to Piedmont North Carolina. Along with other such leaders, Cannon worked to rebuild the South after the Civil War. These leaders believed in a diversified economy but felt the South had distinct advantages in the textile industry. By building mills near cotton fields, for example, the South could save on transportation costs and under-cut northern prices. In addition, the South had a cheaper labor force that was not significantly unionized.[1] Enthusiasm for the textile industry culminated in the tidal wave known as the Cotton Mill Campaign, during which large numbers of textile mills were built.[2]

Cannon exemplified the typical southern textile industrialist, looking forward to the future but strongly influenced by the past. Although indus-trialization was changing the nature of work and human relations in the workplace, Cannon and other southern industrialists continued to have a strong belief in the role of a genteel upper class. This New South upper class included merchant/industrials who continued the traditions of paternalism and deference. Wilbur Cash argued that the paternalism of the Old South plantation system was evident in the mill towns of the New South: Just as the plantation owners supplied their slaves with necessities, so too did the mill owners provided for their operatives. Deference and fear, he noted, were key elements of paternalism in both periods. Nevertheless, attractive as this comparison is, it must not be taken too far. Cotton mill operatives, unlike slaves, could always demonstrate their displeasure with their employer by leaving. Unfortunately, if they did so they usually found themselves working in another cotton mill under a similar paternalistic relationship.[3]

New South industrialists also held a strong belief in individualism and the sanctity of contracts. These beliefs led to a strong anti-union bias. Workers, they thought, should present their grievances to mill superintendents and owners personally, without the odious specter of collective bargaining or the influence of outside agitators—northerners.

Yet New South industrialists still lived under the burden of noblesse oblige. While they reaped profits, they also became benefactors to numerous social, religious, and educational organizations and provided tangible improvement to their communities. A tenuous balance existed between their desire for profits and their social obligation to improve the community. Enlightened self-interest often settled this conflict. Industrialists financed groups or projects that helped the community and simultaneously provided personal or business benefits in the short or long term.

Mill village paternalism demonstrated the tension between profits and community interest. The emergence of the mill village was an economic necessity which helped poor whites to transition from ailing farms to industrial work. It was designed to take advantage of the family labor system that already existed on farms and provide jobs for whites who had lost their farms or were doing poorly in an era of depressed cotton prices. Industrialists thus helped the community by economically uplifting poor whites, increasing their income, and providing better housing and educational opportunities for their children, all while reaping a profit. In operation, therefore, the mill village represented both enlightened economic self-interest and community improvement.[4]

In addition, many new mill owners of the Postwar period, Cannon included, had backgrounds as merchants. Historian David Goldfield noted that "industrialists usually possessed the same values as merchants (frequently they were former merchants), especially if they were engaged in some aspect of staple crop processing."[5] The merchant/industrialist was often the "small town rich man" as characterized by journalist Ralph McGill of the *Atlanta Constitution*. McGill noted that the "small town rich man" was a merchant, usually a bank director, and often a "pillar" of his church. In addition, he was influential in politics.[6] Cannon epitomized this New South industrialist.

James William Cannon was born on April 25, 1852, to Eliza Long Cannon and Joseph F. Cannon. He was the fourth of six children. Although his family was from Cabarrus County, North Carolina, Cannon was born in Mecklenburg County, off Derita Road near Sugaw (Sugar) Creek Presbyterian Church. James's education at the Session House at Sugar Creek ended when, at thirteen or fourteen years of age, he left home to clerk at a store in Charlotte.[7]

In 1869 Cannon went to Concord to work at the mercantile establishment of Phifer and Cannon, where his older brother, David, was co-owner. He made forty-eight dollars his first year at the mercantile.[8] James became a full partner of the mercantile when he was nineteen years old, at which time the firm became Cannons and Fetzer.[9] James was a very capable merchant and soon became a cotton buyer. For more than ten years he purchased cotton from local farmers for Cannons and Fetzer, which became the largest firm on Union Street in downtown Concord.[10] By 1888, Cannons and Fetzer was the second largest buyer of cotton in Cabarrus County, and the Concord papers carried the local cotton quotes from the mercantile.[11]

James Cannon became a prominent businessman in Concord during a time of change and development. Concord was transforming into a commercial and manufacturing town with a new group of leaders—mill men. The town's business leaders had been merchants and craftsmen, predominately from the Presbyterian Church, but this business hegemony began to break down for two reasons. First, newcomers came to Concord with different ideas, and second, these newcomers became industrialists.[12]

Cannon's older brother David had moved to Concord from Mecklenburg County, and in 1869, the year James Cannon started work at Phifer and Cannon, John Milton Odell and his sons also arrived in Concord. The Cannons and Odells changed Concord by challenging the business order of the town. The Odells brought with them their brand of pietistic Methodism, which combined their religious and business beliefs. The Cannons remained with their Presbyterian Church, but like the Odells they challenged the unity of their denomination.[13]

A young James William Cannon, circa 1870.
Courtesy of the Kannapolis History Associates.

Many people living in Concord believed that society's morals had been slipping since the end of the Civil War. Church discipline among Presbyterians was weakening. The local congregations censured members for un-Christian conduct with greater infrequency and David Cannon commented on the declining observation of the Sabbath. The Odells, followed by the Cannons, championed the cause of prohibition as a method of moral uplift for the community.[14]

What the Odells and Cannons represented was what historian Gary Freeze called the emergence of the "paternalistic ethos of the New South." J. M. Odell sought to reform the citizens of Concord and to protect the town's growing number of mill workers from the evils of alcohol. As the Cannons became more involved in the mill industry, their religious and business concerns coincided with those of the Odells. Concord soon had the state's most active Women's Christian Temperance Union chapter and a prohibition club. Both families became politically active in fighting the sale of alcohol within the city limits. David Cannon even ran and won a seat on the city commission as a dry candidate in 1876.[15]

For a brief period the two families were able to keep Concord dry, but soon the wet forces came back into power in city government. In 1887, the dry forces finally won a permanent victory and Concord witnessed saloons moving out of the city. Even the local newspaper had taken up the cause of prohibition. The Odells had lead the way toward a dry Concord and a safer work environment for their mill workers, and James Cannon had learned the lessons of and necessity for New South paternalism.[16]

The Cannons' vision of moral purity did not stop with the issue of alcohol. While the Cannons were willing to split with local Democrats over the alcohol issue, they rallied behind them in battling North Carolina's so-called fusion government, which came to power in 1894. The fusion government was an alliance of Republicans and Populists that ran against the state's powerful Democratic Party. The Cannons viewed the inclusion of blacks in the alliance as contrary to their view of social harmony and their business interests. Furthermore, the fusion government gave much less support to the importance of industry than did the Democratic Party. Populists in Cabarrus County viewed the Cannons as a business interest not aligned with the interest of farmers. Rumors even spread that David Cannon had given one thousand dollars to fight the Populists.[17]

The Cannons worked with the White Government Union and supported the white supremacy campaign of 1898 against the fusion ticket. The victory of the Democrats in the state election of 1898 secured the dominance of the party in the state and ensured that white supremacy would be saved and the industry would be supported. The mill workers of Concord voted overwhelmingly for the Democrats, and Populists charged that the mill hands were afraid to vote against their employers.[18] The power and prestige of the new industrialists became increasingly apparent.

J. M. Odell proved to an excellent teacher to James Cannon on the nature of the textile mill village and its accompanying paternalism. Odell's mill village of Forest Hill was the model for industrial paternalism in the New South, and he once employed more textile workers than any mill owner in the state. James would prove to be an ample student of paternalism, for his legacy would long outlive him.[19]

It is not surprising that when James Cannon decided to build his own cotton mill he turned to John Milton Odell for assistance and guidance. On August 24, 1887, investors met to organize the Cannon Manufacturing Company. The investors included James Cannon and his brother David, John Odell and his son William Odell, along with the town physician and several local merchants. Leaning heavily on his experience in the textile industry, J. M. Odell became president of the firm, and Jim Cannon served as secretary and treasurer. David Cannon, William Odell, physician W. H. Lilly, and merchants P. B. Fetzer and J. W. Wadsworth became the board of directors.[20]

A month later, on September 24, 1887, the Superior Court of Cabarrus County issued the charter for the Cannon Manufacturing Company, which authorized the firm to "conduct, transact, and carry on in all of its branches the manufacturing and sale of cotton goods, yarns, threads, and all textile fabrics out of cotton and woolen goods." Capital was initially set at seventy-five thousand dollars with authority to raise it to two hundred thousand dollars in capital stock.[21]

Thirty-five-year-old Jim Cannon had twelve thousand dollars to invest in the venture, a large sum for that day. The remaining capital came from local and northern investors, including some of Cannon's business associates from New York, Boston, and Philadelphia. In addition, the Philadelphia firm of McGill and Wood invested in the new Concord mill.[22] Costs of construction of the mill, however, ran higher than estimated. The stockholders voted in March 1888 to increase the capital stock to ninety thousand dollars to finish the textile plant. The total cost for the forty-acre tract of land, the mill, superintendent's house, wells, thirteen houses, and equipment came to $88,348.[23]

Built on Franklin Street, adjacent to the tracks of the Richmond and Danville Railroad, the mill housed twenty spinning frames of 280 spindles and 130 looms. The mill was two stories high and had electric lights, a "Morse elevator," a fire pump, and a 150-horsepower steam engine. The surrounding mill village became known as Cannonville.[24]

Among the early workers of the mill on Franklin Street was the Freeze family. Mr. Freeze and his family lived in Gold Hill, sixteen miles from Concord. He moved to Concord to work on the mill homes as a carpenter and bricklayer. Freeze's son Jones remembered the trip:

> We started out before daylight and hit [sic] was way after dark when we go here. Hit don't look like it could take that long to come sixteen miles, but back then there jest wasn't anything you'd call a road; why two teams always went together so if one got stuck the other could pull it out. I was six year old whenever we moved.[25]

When the mill became operational, Freeze and his family worked as mill hands. When Jones Freeze turned nine years old, he began working at the mill as a doffer, making ten cents a day working from six o'clock in the morning until six fifty-five in the evening (child labor was common in the mills during this period). Aline Caudle also worked in the Franklin Mill. "Yessir," she recalled, "when I started down here to plant No. 1 [Franklin Mill], I was so little I had to stand on a box to reach my work. I was a spinner at first, and then I learned to spool."[26] Both Jones Freeze and Aline Caudle moved from farms and worked for the Cannon family for over thirty years.

James Cannon's attitude toward his workers in his first mill was evident in the employment contract workers had to sign. His paternalistic beliefs were reflected in the rules of employment in Cannonville. While some rules made good business sense, others reflected a paternalistic attitude toward workers. The rules included the requirement that mill hands give ten days' notice before leaving or they world forfeit any pay due to them. Supervisors had to give thirty days' notice on the same condition. Workers were required to be at their job five minutes after the signal was sounded and were not allowed to leave the plant without the permission of the supervisor, who was "instructed to grant such a request if it is possible to do so without stopping any machinery." The superintendent was responsible for seeing that equipment was maintained and in proper working order and for regulating the quality and quantity of goods produced. Supervisors were authorized to punish workers by docking pay or dismissing them. Workers who damaged machinery were charged the repair fees at the discretion of the president.[27]

Several rules demonstrated an especially paternalistic disposition. First, swearing and profanity were forbidden on the mill property, a rule that reflected Cannon's conservative Presbyterian beliefs and an attempt to reform the coarse manner of the farmers who worked for him. Second, workers were required to "pledge ourselves that we are not now a member of the Knights of Labor or will not join the order while in the employ of Cannon Manufacturing Company." Cannon preferred to deal with workers as individuals and not as union members. This pledge set the tone for labor-management relations in his future mills.[28]

Operations at the Cannon Manufacturing Company began on April 1, 1888, with spinning and yarn production. Cannon celebrated the operation of the mill with his family. His wife, Mary Ella, and the children rode from their home to the mill in their carriage. Once the family had assembled in the mill, Cannon started the steam engine and the machinery came to life. With the assistance of Joseph Bacon, the first overseer, Mrs. Cannon made the first yarn at the new factory.[29] Weaving began in the mill on August 1. By the end of the first four months of operation, the mill had produced 122,045 yards of sheeting and 109,141 pounds of yarn.[30]

To learn every aspect of textile production, Cannon held the position of supervisor of the mill as well as secretary and treasurer. He maintained an office on the mill's second floor and often donned overalls and strolled through the plant, learning the operation of the machinery. After two years of serving as supervisor, he had learned enough about cotton production and hired Louis Duval for the position of supervisor.[31]

The Cannon Manufacturing Company was a revolutionary textile plant for the South. Most textile mills produced yarn or were set up for weaving. Yarn mills sent their product to weaving plants to be made into cloth. Weaving plants did not produce yarn but merely wove yarn manufactured at other mills. The Cannon Manufacturing Company incorporated both processes, yarn production from raw cotton and the weaving of yarn into cloth. Raw cotton entered the mill and cloth exited.

In the first four months of the mill's operation, the company made a profit of $1,255. President Odell credited Cannon's management for the strength of the firm.[32] Under the leadership of Odell and Cannon, the company was put on a healthy financial basis that set the course for the mill's future fiscal soundness.

The year 1889 was an important one for the Cannon Manufacturing Company. With business going well, the directors decided to expand the plant. Improvements to the mill included the addition of 3,120 spindles, twenty-two cards, forty looms, and miscellaneous equipment.[33] In addition, the firm introduced its first widely recognized and highly successful product—Cannon Cloth. This popular sheeting product became known for its versatility. Appearing in stores on bolts and sold by the yard, it was heavy enough to be used for sacks yet light enough for women's dresses. James Cannon branded this product to differentiate it from other cloth, an uncommon practice for the time. Soon housewives were asking for Cannon Cloth at stores instead of buying unbranded cloth by an unknown manufacturer. Cannon's decision to brand one of his products reflected his experience as a merchant. He knew that customers would ask for a quality product made by a particular manufacturer if the product could be differentiated from other products in the same line. In a retail world of unbranded bulk products, Cannon Cloth was revolutionary. Eventually product branding became the normal retail practice.[34]

Also in 1889, the firm manufactured its first towels, the product that later became synonymous with the Cannon textile empire. Cannon's first towels were crash towels, which had a flat weave, were sold on bolts (similar to Cannon Cloth), and were made to be finished at home. These first Cannon towels could be used for either towels or table linens. Cannon's crash towels marked a major turning point for the towel market for a couple of reasons. First, the production of crash towels represented a manufacturing innovation. James Cannon was willing to take a risk with his mill and experiment with a product line that no one else in the South was manufacturing. He realized that if the venture were successful, the Cannon Manufacturing Company would carve out its manufacturing niche and secure its future.[35]

Second, the manufacture of the crash towel represented a marketing innovation. At the time, only the wealthy used towels. Average housewives dried with whatever type of cloth was available, including the versatile Cannon Cloth. The introduction of the crash towel made towels affordable for the average household. Although crude and unfinished, crash towels were absorbent and could be dyed at home.[36] While stores sold crash towels on the bolt, Cannon tried another method of marketing his firm's new product: He sold crash towels packaged by the dozen. The editor of the *Concord Standard* reported on the packaged Cannon crash towels in a story that appeared on April 12, 1889. Cannon towels were quality goods, absorbent, and sold for seventy-five cents per dozen.[37]

With the success of the Cannon Manufacturing Company, James William Cannon decided to build another mill. In 1892, Cannon and his brother David organized the Cabarrus Cotton Mills in Concord. The new mill produced yarn and cotton sheeting. James Cannon served as president of the new firm.[38]

Cannon's mills weathered the Panic of 1893 quite well.[39] While the years 1893 to 1898 "may be considered a period of depression almost unknown in the history of this country," Cannon's infant textile empire flourished for several reasons.[40] Overseas trade helped to shelter southern textile companies from domestic fluctuations. Between 1887 and 1897, U.S. textile exports to China increased by 120 percent, with most of these shipments being from southern mills.[41] The value of uncolored cloth traded with China increased during the depression from $5,321,500 to $9,277,112.[42] The southern share of the textile trade in China grew at the expense of both northern and British manufacturers. Mills in the Piedmont of North and South Carolina, such as Cannon's, were generally immune to the national economic crisis because they were heavily involved in exporting to foreign countries.[43]

Cannon's success during the problems of the 1890s also reflected the popularity of Cannon Cloth. The high demand for this product led to the establishment of the Cabarrus Cotton Mill and improvements to the Cannon Manufacturing Company. The new equipment added to the original Cannon plant brought it to 255 looms and 9,800 spindles. In 1893, Cannon's mills produced 4.3 million yards of Cannon Cloth.[44] Business was so good that Cannon organized another textile mill, the Patterson Manufacturing Company, in the adjacent town of China Grove.[45]

In spite of the depression, Cannon continued to innovate and take his business in new directions. The manufacturer decided to concentrate his mills' production on towels. Cannon believed that the demand for Cannon Cloth would soon wane and that his mills could make higher profits in producing towels. Having manufactured crash towels in limited numbers, Cannon shifted the production of his mills to larger quantities of a new type of towel. In 1894, Cannon began manufacturing "huck" (short for huckaback) towels. Huck towels had a plain weave like the earlier crash towels but were made of thicker yarn and were thus more absorbent. Six years later, the company began to manufacture the terry, or Turkish, towel. The terry towel, the company explained, had a looped weave, unlike the flat-weave crash and huck towels:

> To understand how terry is woven, picture first the average plain weave fabric: two sets of threads—one warp (lengthwise) and one filling (crosswise). Interlacing, the threads pass over and under each other to form a plain weave. The difference between plain weave and terry weave is that terry weave has three set of threads . . . an extra set of warp (lengthwise)

threads which, during weaving, are loosened to form the loops or pile. The crosswise threads pass over and under the lengthwise yarns in alternate rows. At the same time, the second set of lengthwise yarns, being loosened or slackened, forms the pile on both sides. This, briefly, is the basic principle of terry weave.[46]

The looped weave or pile made terry towels more absorbent than both crash and huck.[47]

Cannon's knowledge of merchandising was evident in his line of towels. Not only did he manufacture different types of towels, but he produced different price points of the same type of towels. Customers could choose between high- and low-end towels of the same type, such as huck or terry towels. Of course, high-end towels were more expensive than low-end towels. Thus, through segmentation of the towel market, Cannon could broaden demand for his products by catering to the entire social spectrum, from the lower middle class to the wealthy.

After 1894, the Cannon textile empire grew phenomenally. In quick succession the Cannon holdings purchased and constructed four mills between 1895 and 1899: the Kesler Manufacturing Company of Salisbury, the Efird Manufacturing Company and Wiscassett Mills Company of Albemarle, and the Gibson Manufacturing Company of Concord.[48]

Stable leadership characterized the first ten years of the Cannon Manufacturing Company. John Odell served as president and James Cannon as secretary and treasurer. In 1897, Odell resigned as president but remained on the company's board of directors. David Cannon became the new president of the firm, while his brother James remained in his office. John and William Odell sold their Cannon stock in 1899 and resigned from the board of directors.[49] David and James Cannon now ran the company alone.

Concord was by now an important industrial town of Piedmont North Carolina. The cotton mills of both Odell and Cannon attracted destitute farmers from the surrounding counties. The Panic of 1873 and especially the Panic of 1893 inflicted a heavy toll on North Carolina farmers. For many farmers who lost their land due to debt, the cotton mills of Concord, and later Kannapolis, offered a way out of farming and a new life. So many came to Concord for "public work" that one Stanly County resident noted that "if you don't see a man for two weeks, you can just say he has gone to Concord's cotton mills."[50]

After the turn of the century, Cannon continued his program of vertical integration at the Cannon Manufacturing Company. The firm built its own bleaching and finishing plant in 1902. Erected at the Cannon Manufacturing Company, the new plant was five stories tall and used the Kier bleaching method, which soaked towels in chemical vats two stories tall. Now the textile firm could bleach many towels, but the results could be uneven and the chemicals could eat holes in the fabric if it was soaked too long. Kier bleaching remained the industry standard until Cannon Mills, the descendant of the Cannon Manufacturing Company, developed continuous bleaching in the 1930s.[51] Another process in the manufacturing of towels had come under the control of the firm.

A year after building the bleaching and finishing plant, Cannon positioned his mills for sales and distribution on a national scale and furthered the process of vertical integration. Reflecting his knowledge of merchandising and his determination to sell his company's own product, Cannon created his own selling agency. Cannon Mills, Inc., or "Inc." as it later became known, sold the goods of the Cannon Manufacturing Company and Cannon's other mills, avoiding independent sale organizations. Traditionally, textile manufacturers sold their products through "commission merchants and independent textile sales organizations."[52] Cannon established a sales office in New York City in 1904 and sent John C. Leslie, a Concord native and secretary and treasurer of Wiscassett Mills Company, to operate the New York office.[53] John Fairfield worked in the New York office and described the Cannon sales operation in the early days as "unique" among textile manufacturers.[54] A year or two later, Cannon opened a commission house in Boston, followed by houses in Philadelphia, Chicago, San Francisco, and St. Louis.[55] With the addition of the sales agency, Cannon now controlled all aspects of towel manufacturing, from cotton buying to manufacturing to sales.

While Cannon created national distribution for his firm's products, another change occurred among the officers of Cannon Manufacturing Company. President David Cannon died on May 29, 1904, and James Cannon became president. Although James had served as secretary and treasurer, he was the true driving force behind the firm. Everyone recognized that the Cannon Manufacturing Company was really his company and deferred to his remarkable skill and vision as a businessman. James Cannon's knowledge of the textile business was unquestioned as he now owned outright or was a partner in several other successful mills. Cannon's son, James W. Cannon Jr., filled the position of secretary and treasurer.[56]

Cannon's business success was due to his ingenuity. He was a visionary businessman who applied his knowledge as a merchant to the textile industry. Cannon's decision to brand name his multipurpose sheeting was an attempt to differentiate it from the nondescript bolts of cloth then sold in stores. Customers requested Cannon Cloth by name. This was the beginning of brand loyalty in the textile industry.

The packaging of his towels represented another textile innovation, as Cannon was among the first textile firms to sell towels precut from the bolt. Packaging and brand naming were two market strategies that would move Cannon's products out of the nondescript bulk textile category. The combination of brand naming and quality packaging would help to ensure strong customer loyalty in the future.

CHAPTER 2

———————◆◆▶◀◆◆———————

THE FOUNDING OF KANNAPOLIS:
Expansion and Paternalism

To facilitate expansion of his towel manufacturing, James Cannon sent Concord real estate agent John K. Patterson to Glass, North Carolina, to purchase six hundred acres of land. Glass was a small community north of Concord along the Southern Railway line that consisted of a general store owned by John Peter Triece, a post office, and a rail depot. Patterson secured options on only three hundred acres in the vicinity of Glass, so he traveled farther north along the unpaved Salisbury Road and obtained options on twelve hundred acres in Cabarrus and Rowan counties. In 1905 and 1906, Cannon exercised his options and purchased 1,009 one-sixth acres at an average price of $26.22 per acre.[1]

According to a newspaper report, the first load of lumber—twelve hundred feet—was delivered November 20, 1906, by a mule named Trim and her mate, owned by W. E. Bostian. The mule team hauled lumber over a dirt road between China Grove and the construction site, a journey that took over an hour, delivering it to the first three carpenters on site: Walter Dayvault, Mr. Simpson, and Mr. Noval. Captain Price supervised the carpenters. Later, other carpenters came to work in the growing mill village.[2]

A year later, James Cannon began construction on two new facilities, a second Cannon Manufacturing Company mill and another bleachery and finishing plant.[3] The firm invested $1.5 million in the facilities, which produced both huck and terry towels. Both plants used electricity provided by the Southern Power Company.[4]

The early name of the new mill village was Cannapolis (meaning "Cannon Town"), paralleling Cannonville, the name of the mill village in Concord.[5] The spelling of the name changed in 1907 when James Cannon referred to the village as Kannapolis in a letter to the Cabarrus County Board of Commissioners. In a request to the board to pave the road between Concord and the new mill village, Cannon stated, "It is no doubt known to each one of you that we are now erecting two (2) large mills at a point seven miles from corporate limits, at a place on the main road from here to Salisbury which has been christened Kannapolis."[6]

Besides the plants, Cannon also constructed housing for the operatives as well as the infrastructure of Kannapolis. Eventually, Kannapolis became the nation's largest unincorporated town, a distinction it retained until 1984. James Cannon was intimately involved in the details of building the new town.[7]

The mill owner was also concerned with the uplift and reform of the residents of Kannapolis, including the children of the mill village. While progressives sought to tighten child labor laws and provide an opportunity for the education of all children, James Cannon linked the education of mill children to his idea of paternalism. As in Cannonville, young children could work with their parents' consent or attend school. Many mill families needed the wages of their children to make ends meet, but as child labor laws slowly tightened, more children attended school. By providing schools, by being concerned about the education and moral development of the children living in their mill villages, mill owners fit the mold of the businessman progressive. Yet many mill owners had other reasons for providing schools. Mill schools were designed to prepare the next generation of mill workers by instilling "industrial discipline" as well as "punctuality, regularity of attendance, reliability, and respect for authority." Some overseers went to the school when extra labor was needed in the mill. Thus schools reformed the habits of the children of poorly educated parents, served as a labor pool when necessary, and kept children out of trouble when they were too young to work or not needed in the mills.[8]

Cannon offered land to the Cabarrus County school board in 1907 to build a school. He gave two thousand dollars for its construction and loaned the county the balance of the twenty-five hundred dollars needed for its completion. The new five-room school, McIver School, was on South Main Street. Because of the growth of the community, Cannon built a second school, Woodrow Wilson School, a decade later.[9] The schools of Kannapolis were among the better mills schools in the state. Offering grades one through

Early Cannon Mills Carpenters. Lr - Sam Cavin, ?, Scott, ? John Dayvault, Charlie Mark
Dayvault, Sid Elliot & Dave Dayvault. Courtesy of Kannoplis History Associates.

eleven, the Kannapolis school system provided a broader education than did
most mill schools in the state. Furthermore, the school term was 180 days,
longer than most. By 1925, with more than fifteen hundred students enrolled,
Kannapolis had the second largest mill school system in North Carolina.[10]

The new mill village grew rapidly. The new post office opened in 1908
and the Cabarrus County commissioners approved the building of a hard-
surfaced road from Concord to Kannapolis. Cannon was also involved in
establishing the town's police department, building its railroad station, and
offering assistance and encouragement in the creation of volunteer organizations and parks.[11]

Another paternalistic aspect of the developing mill village was the establishment of churches. In 1908 First Baptist Church and the local Methodist
Episcopal church were created, followed by the Presbyterian church in
1909. More churches followed, including the First Wesleyan in 1910 and
the local Church of God in 1913, and others came later as the population
of Kannapolis grew. Cannon followed the pattern of encouraging church
membership to control workers. Mill owners subsidized pastors' salaries to
ensure that sermons focused on the morals and manners of the congregation

and not on social justice issues. Some mill workers understood the close relationship between management and the mill churches. One mill worker from
Gastonia stated that "management wanted the workers to be in churches
because they felt the churches domesticed [sic] the workers and that . . . they
would keep them from getting too uppity, and so that's why there seemed
to be a hand-in-glove relationship between management and many of the
churches."[12]

In addition to religion, Cannon placed a great deal of emphasis on recreation for his employees. The company sponsored a baseball team and a
band.[13] Cannon's largest expense, however, was for the YMCA. He built one
of the most elaborate YMCAs in the nation. Cannon described the facility in a letter to an inquiring mill owner from Georgia: "Our building and
equipment stands us about $40,000.00. We have a seating capacity of 750
Opra [sic] Chairs, Gymnasium, Swimming Pool, Shower Baths, Bowling-
Alley, Billiard and Pool Room, and also room with equipment for Boys and
a hall with seating capacity of about 900 with the stage." The facility had a
full-time supervisor, a gymnasium instructor, and a janitor. Total operating
expenses ran at three thousand dollars a year after figuring in the yearly two-
dollar fee to mill operatives. The Kannapolis YMCA eventually grew to ten
thousand members, and the firm claimed it was the largest in the world.[14]

Recreational activities, along with schools and churches, helped to
anchor workers to the mill village. Athletic competitions between mills fostered a mill identity unique to each mill village, and the mill village identity
"fostered solidarity and cohesion with particular mill communities." The
creation and maintenance of a mill village identity fostered loyalty and a

The first loom delivered to Kannapolis. Courtesy of the Kannapolis History Associates.

community history/memory based on the paternalistic bond between workers and management.[15]

Besides recreational opportunities, Cannon provided other benefits for his employees. Operatives received life insurance, occasional free house rent, and a day nursery for the care of young children. To provide housing for young single females, Cannon built dormitories capable of accommodating 350 women.[16]

Welfare work, however, gave mill owners an excuse to pay lower wages. Southern mill owners were sensitive to criticism that they paid lower wages than northern textile manufacturers, but they usually justified the wage differential by pointing out that the cost of living was lower in the South and they provided welfare services the northern manufacturers did not offer. The National Industrial Conference Board dealt this defense a severe blow in a report issued in the early 1920s. The report compared the cost of living in Lawrence and Fall River, Massachusetts, with that in Greenville and Pelzer, South Carolina, and Charlotte, North Carolina, in 1919 and 1921. It found that the cost of living was higher in Charlotte and Greenville than in Fall River and Lawrence. These costs included the lower rent and fuel rates offered by southern mills to their operatives. The report estimated the cost of living to be $1,393.60 in Greenville, $1,438.03 in Charlotte, $1,267.76 in Fall River, and $1,385.78 in Lawrence. The average annual textile wage of $730.00 a year in 1919 or $624.00 a year in 1921 in North Carolina would therefore not cover the cost of living, necessitating that more than one family member work. Cannon's wages averaged $15.60 a week, or approximately $795.00 a year in 1922. The national average hourly wage for textile workers in 1920 was forty-eight cents (this included the wages in New England). Cannon, however, paid an hourly wage of twenty-eight cents.[17]

Starting a mill town had many advantages for Cannon. According to historian James Cobb, the unincorporated town provided "a tax-free haven for the area's dominate employer." Cannon and the company owned the business district, selected and paid the Kannapolis police force, and controlled the local water resources. Control of the local water supply became an important means of "keeping out other industries that might bid up wages."[18]

James Cannon's success as a businessman came partly from his strong work ethic. In a letter to a young mill executive, the Concord mill owner revealed his business philosophy. Mill executives must always, according to Cannon, "maintain a rigid control" of themselves, pay close attention to the details of the business, control costs, and never let anyone doubt their integrity.[19]

Part of James Cannon's commitment to "maintain a rigid control" of his new mill village was to keep Kannapolis dry. Reflecting upon his earlier battles to keep alcohol out of Concord to foster sobriety in Cannonville, he forbade any alcoholic beverages in the mill village and disciplined workers who violated the prohibition. Cannon prohibited alcohol in the village because he realized that drunken workers increased accidents and lowered the production and quality of goods. In addition, alcohol abuse could lead to domestic violence and affect more than one worker since both husbands and wives usually worked in the mill. Supervisors acted on the complaints of neighbors and visited the offending male worker to stress the importance of abstinence. Repetitive offenders were fired and discharged from mill housing, essentially kicked out of Kannapolis. Moral uplift had limited patience.

The paternalism established in Kannapolis was all encompassing. The mill provided everything workers needed, from recreation to spiritual needs to education for their children. James Cannon and his firm supplied everything but autonomy. The paternalistic covenant was set. Workers provided labor for the mill, with deference to management, especially the Cannon family, and the mill provided a salary, housing, recreation, education, and other amenities. Many workers accepted the compact, understanding that their lack of control over their work was the price to pay for the benefits of paternalism. As sociologists Vincent Roscigno and William Danaher noted, many workers understood that "the costs associated with mill-owner control were outweighed by the stability, structure, and amenities that the mill village provided."[20]

Paternalism was particularly strong when the mill owner lived near the mill and his presence was common. Even though his home was on Union Street in Concord, James Cannon routinely traveled to Kannapolis to oversee the mill. In addition, he was a vital part of the economic and business world in Concord. He was a force in the community and had a long history in the county. On one level Cannon seemed to be like one of the workers. Along with his history in the community, his mercantile establishments had done business with many of the families there and he knew many of them. His roots in the community and his familiarity with many families established an aura of family between the mill owner and his workers. This was an essential element of successful paternalism.

Furthermore, Cannon's paternalism contained elements that are viewed by some as crucial aspects of modern management: trust, legitimacy, reciprocity, and organizational justice. Many workers trusted James Cannon because he was known in the community and was a successful businessman.

His reputation was widely known in Cabarrus County and the surrounding area and gave an air of legitimacy to his leadership style.[21]

Sociologist Randy Hodson stated that "workers are more compliant if they view the use of power by management as legitimate."[22] While modern management theory argues that legitimacy comes from a management system based on shared norms (or a work system agreed upon by both workers and management), Cannon's wealth, reputation, and prestige lent legitimacy to his management structure. In other words, deference to his status gave his activities legitimacy.

In addition, the reciprocity in the workplace is also different. In the modern workplace, management expects greater effort from employees in exchange for "rights, privileges, and inducements."[23] With Cannon's

James William Cannon, New South industrialist and businessman.
Courtesy of the Kannapolis History Associates.

paternalistic structure, he had invested heavily in the paternal compact before the workers could fulfill their obligations, spending a considerable amount of money building the mills and village of Kannapolis before the workers were even hired. Once the mill village was built, workers were obligated to obey all rules of the mill village, show deference to management, and be compliant. The reciprocity of the paternalism was mostly front loaded for the mill owner, while workers had to work constantly to demonstrate respect and loyalty for what the mill owner had provided them. Yet James Cannon did provide some aspects of modern work reciprocity with a degree of job security and opportunity for some workers to advance in position and pay.

The weakest aspect of industrial paternalism compared to modern management deals with organizational justice. Workers believed in equal treatment and opportunities at work and were less compliant or loyal when they perceived that factors other than merit determined pay and advances in position. The perception of nepotism, unfair treatment, arbitrary decisions, and any deviation from customary procedures weakened workers' compliance. While this is still true in the modern workplace, paternalistic management styles have a greater problem overcoming perceived organizational injustice. Paternalism was based on the power and prestige of the mill owners, who ultimately defined the nature of the paternal compact. They could change it anytime they wanted, unlike managers in the modern management structure, which tends to be more collective and collaborative in nature. Modern firms are inclined to adhere to a management system and workplace norms that transcend management changes and allow a degree of worker input. Cannon's paternalistic management style was not designed to consider worker input, and some workers would lose trust in him when they believed that the workplace was not based on justice.[24]

In response, some of Cannon's workers would turn to unionization in an attempt to gain a degree of workplace decision making and to correct perceived injustice. What kept more of his workers from organizing was the degree of power that paternalism gave Cannon and the lack of laws to protect workers' rights. Fear became a tool in keeping most workers in line. Many more workers would perceive injustice in the mill village than became active in organizing, and the main reason was they knew the consequences of violating the paternal pact upon which Kannapolis was based. When trust waned, legitimacy was questioned, workers' concept of reciprocity changed, and workplace justice was lacking, fear and the absence of power kept many workers from organizing.

CHAPTER 3

———————◆♦❂♦◆———————

CANNON MILLS, KANNAPOLIS, AND BLACKS:
A Reflection of Racial Attitudes in the South

The exclusion of blacks in the paternalistic structure at Cannon Mills reflected broader attitudes regarding race in the South. Literature, recent events, and science seemed to confirm the view held by most white southerners that blacks were inferior to whites and not suited for industrial work. The writings of North Carolina author Thomas Dixon Jr. reinforced this racial stereotype and had a profound impact on race relations at the beginning of the twentieth century. Dixon's trilogy, The Leopard's Spots (1902), The Clansman (1905), and The Traitor (1907), made the search for a solution to the race problem a national issue. The author did not believe that in the long term blacks could live with whites in the United States. He favored repatriation to Africa. In the immediate term, Dixon believed that white supremacy was needed to control the animalistic instincts of blacks. He was dubious that blacks could be educated and develop to the level of whites, hence the title of the first novel. The second novel had the greatest impact because it was made into the first full-length motion picture, The Birth of a Nation, directed by D. W. Griffith and released in 1915.[1]

Dixon's writings reflected attitudes toward race as seen in then-current events in North Carolina. Earlier attempts by Populists to form a biracial alliance between black and white farmers had fallen apart. There had been a strong reaction to the fusion (Republican and Populist parties) state government of 1896, and the Democrats came back into office using white supremacy as their main campaign theme in the election of 1898. A violent race riot had broken out in Wilmington in 1898, leaving eleven blacks dead, twenty-five injured, and many ultimately choosing to leave the city. Soon Jim Crow laws were passed in North Carolina that greatly restricted the rights of black males to vote or hold office.[2]

Social Darwinism had also appeared as a powerful force in Europe and the United States. Believing that science demonstrated the intellectual superiority of whites, advocates of social Darwinism reinforced the existing racial beliefs of many white southerners, who now relished the idea that science had finally proved what they had been taught for decades. This theory even permeated universities and influenced the educated southerners of the era.[3]

It is not surprising that white southern businessmen were a product of their times when it came to racial attitudes. Many southern businessmen believed that segregation was necessary and that it actually protected blacks by limiting white violence against them. This view was considered moderate for the time, as the alternatives were either full equality or allowing the situation to erupt into a race war. Jim Crow laws brought a degree of stability to the economic and social order in the South. Northern businessmen did not object to Jim Crow because (1) it did not threaten their investments in the South and (2) they viewed it as a progressive way of dealing with race.[4]

Racial views of whites in the South did not differ much from that of Europeans during this period of imperialistic expansion. Writer Erin Clune noted that policies on race were similar in "South Africa, the United States, and Brazil, and especially because the theories themselves often drew from contemporary colonialism to advance conclusions about African evolution or origins." In other words, globalization had not taken place in the realm of economics exclusively, but also in the realm of ideas on race.[5]

The great textile industry advocate Daniel Tompkins thought that blacks were only suited for agricultural work and even then were only productive under white supervision. He believed that they could not hold production jobs in textile mills. Tompkins was aware that 75.3 percent of black farmers in 1900 were sharecroppers or tenants and he believed that the only way to maintain a cheap supply of cotton was to keep blacks from moving up into the ranks of the middle class.[6]

Textile mill historian Holland Thompson's work on the textile industry also furthered racial stereotypes of blacks. Published in 1906, Thompson's important book *From the Cotton Field to the Cotton Mill*, was largely based on the time he lived in and taught school in Concord. He was a friend of J. M. Odell and an acquaintance of James Cannon. Thompson was a keen observer of the textile industry around Concord, and his notations became the basis of his book. He wrote about a black-owned textile mill in Concord that employed black mill workers. Concord black merchant Warren Coleman, whose father was believed to be a local, prominent white leader, constructed the mill in 1901, employing black mill workers and a white supervisor from Massachusetts. Coleman equipped the mill with secondhand machinery from England. The experiment ultimately failed. Thompson recounted that the mill failed due to the installation of secondhand equipment, "a lack of working capital," problems with the black overseers, and the temperament of the black workers:

> Negroes as a class do not work except under direct compulsion. They do not like monotonous labor. They do not like to be alone nor to engage in any employment where they cannot communicate with their fellows. In the small Southern tobacco factories, the negroes talk and sing at their work as there is little machinery and no tension. Whether enough negroes are to be found in a community who will keep up the monotonous routine of a cotton mill week after week, is the question to be solved. The negro was not long enough in slavery to make the willingness instinctive. He has not been long enough out of slavery to develop those ambitions which hold one to distasteful employment for the sake of ultimate satisfaction. Few have developed a pride in doing the given work as well as possible.[7]

Furthermore, Thompson wrote, blacks did not like to work regularly, and he cited the need to grant domestics numerous "afternoons and evenings out." He argued that the strict work roles followed by whites would absolutely fail if applied to black workers. Yet Thompson believed that only through work could blacks be kept from being "an habitual criminal."[8]

The prevailing attitude about blacks restricted their employment in the textile mills. Even if mill owners wanted to hire blacks, white mill workers would not tolerate blacks working in production jobs. When a textile mill in Rome, Georgia, replaced a white female worker with a black one in 1890, it was forced to reverse this action under pressure from the rest of the white workers. White operatives walked out when Fulton Bag and Cotton Mill Company hired twenty black women to spin. The firm later fired the black workers.[9]

The low numbers of blacks working in the textile industry reflected prevailing racial attitudes. In 1890, total textile employment was at 482,110, yet only 5,538 blacks, representing a mere 1.2 percent of the work force, were employed in the industry. Black employment actually dropped in 1900: U.S. census data noted that while the total number of textile jobs had increased to

597,059, the number of blacks working for the mills had dropped to 2,744, or 0.5 percent. By the time the mills in Kannapolis became operational, black employment had returned to the 1890 level.[10]

When James Cannon sent John Patterson to purchase land for a mill and village, few blacks owned land in the area north of Concord that Patterson considered. Of all of the land owners in Cabarrus and Rowan counties Patterson contracted for options for land, only one was black. Of the more than one thousand acres that James Cannon eventually purchased, only nine acres came from a black owner. Lucindy Stepleton and her son signed an option with John Patterson on April 13, 1906. Lucindy's son Frank actually owned the land, it having passed to him after the death of his father, Rodger. Rodger Stepleton had purchased the land in 1874. The Stepletons received $350.00 for their land and moved to the black community of Texas (also known as Little Texas) in Cabarrus County. Frank attended Mount Calvary Lutheran Church and later worked for Cannon Memorial YMCA in Kannapolis and a boardinghouse in the mill village.[11]

Before the creation of the mill village of Kannapolis, the area around George Rose's farm was known as Roseville. The area later became known as Centerview once the mill town was built.[12] In 1908 a mission church was established in the community, sponsored by Bethel African Methodist Episcopal (AME) Zion. "Little Mission Church" later became Marable Memorial AME Zion Church in 1928, named after Elder M. I. Marable.[13] By the 1940s the business district in Centerview along Huron Street included two barbershops, the only black doctor's office in Kannapolis (that of Dr. Levi Gibson), Red Roger's café, a beauty parlor, a dry cleaners, an ice cream shop, a funeral home, and a pool hall.[14] Furthermore, there arose a community band lead by Dolph Foster. It practiced in Bob Park's barbershop and played on special occasions and at picnics.[15]

Two other areas of Kannapolis, Bethel and Texas, were predominantly black communities. The Bethel community was originally known as Dog Trot, a name that came from the number of stray dogs that strolled along the dirt roads and trails in the community. It later became more widely known as Bethel after the Bethel AME Zion Church. Bethel was subdivided into three smaller neighborhoods known as Tin Top Alley, the Pines, and Cartersville. Tin Top was connected to Bethel with a dirt path—no road—and was so named after the tin roofs of the duplexes. The Pines was named after the pine forest that surrounded it, and Carterville came from the Carter family. Carterville's three roads were named after important figures for the blacks of the community: Lincoln; Washington, after Booker T. Washington; and Douglas [sic], after Frederick Douglass.[16]

The last of the major black communities was Texas, which had been settled since at least 1893. Mount Calvary Lutheran Church, founded in 1898, was an important church for those who lived in the area. The church established a school for black children in 1902.[17]

The initial black population in the town limits of Kannapolis was rather small by 1910. The 1910 census counted 1,576 residents, which included 267 households, only 4 of which were black households. Thirty blacks were enumerated, with seven young black females working as cooks or servants and living in the houses of their white employers, perhaps in the home of supervisors or overseers. One household was headed by a widow who had two sons, and the other three black households were headed by men. Most of the black males were listed as laborers or yard hands. One was described as an operator and another as a fireman (boiler operator).[18] No mills jobs were held by black females, and the jobs for black males were all labor intensive and outside of the mill buildings.

To "stay on the lot" presented another harsh reality for some black workers. If they lived too far from their employers to go home each day, they would live during the week with their employer. The worker—a domestic or cook, for example—would then travel home for the weekends. This, of course, meant having their children looked after by a relative or older child during the week. Jobs were scarce, however, and this arrangement was necessary for some families.[19]

As the mill village grew, so did the black population. Black workers came to Kannapolis from surrounding black communities such as Fishertown, several miles from the mill village toward Mooresboro. New black communities arose to meet the demand for housing. The neighborhood of Tin Cup was created by the mill in the 1920s with no electricity or running water. The origin of the neighborhood name has been lost.[20] Georgiatown was so named for the number of blacks who had moved to Kannapolis from Georgia.[21]

A dairy farmer sold property to the mill for a community for black workers. At first this neighborhood was called Nigh-Town because it was near Kannapolis, but later, when new houses were constructed, it became known as Newtown. As workers were settled into the new houses, the community was called Happy Holler. The origin of that name is in dispute. One account states it came from the real estate developers who gave a happy holler after each house that was sold. Another tale states that black residents who moved there from older houses gave a happy holler over moving into their new houses. Yet another story recounts that the children of the community played in a holler nearby and they were happy while playing in the holler.[22]

Besides Bethel AME Zion Church and Mount Calvary Lutheran Church there were several other black churches in the area. One of the oldest black congregations was a Presbyterian church that eventually became known as Bethpage United Presbyterian. It was created after the Civil War when the black members of the white Presbyterian church withdrew to form their own church.[23] The Church of the Brush Arbor was established in 1915 and received its name because it held meetings "at a brush arbor in the Centerview section of Kannapolis." The church moved several times and built larger facilities because of it growth.[24]

The black population in Kannapolis continued to grow, and the school at Mount Calvary Lutheran Church moved to Colored Baptist Church in 1912. Leaders of the Baptist church appealed to the school board for the establishment of a black public school. After a census of black residents in and around Kannapolis, the black public school was created and continued to meet in the church. The need for a dedicated school building for black students was so great that H. J. Peeler, Kannapolis superintendent, appealed to the Cabarrus County Board of Education in 1920 for assistance in building a new school. The school board did not provide any concrete assistance and the school continued in the church with three black teachers. Finally, the construction of the new school was facilitated by a donation of two acres of land from the Cannon Manufacturing Company. The new school, completed in 1923,

Centerview School. Courtesy of the Kannapolis History Associates.

The black neighborhoods of Kannapolis. From Brewington, "The 'Colored Page,'" 3.

became known as Centerview Colored School. Growth of the black population necessitated the construction of yet another building in 1927, and the students moved to the new location. The student population at Centerview grew to 339 with eight teachers.[25]

The school continued to grow, and a new brick addition was constructed in 1937. Centerview was renamed George Washington Carver and increased in size to 575 students and seventeen teachers in 1940. This single school, housing both an elementary and high school, serviced the black community in Kannapolis until integration in 1967. Forty-nine students graduated from Carver in 1967, and the student body was integrated in the next school year. High school students from Carver went to the formerly all white A. L. Brown School, and Carver became the integrated middle school.[26]

The driving force behind Centerview Colored School was its principal, William Lee Reid. Holding a bachelor's degree from Livingstone College and a master's degree from Columbia University, he came to Centerview in 1933. Reid was the men and women's basketball coach as well as the principal. He made the transition from Centerview to George Washington Carver, and under his direction the school added a nicely uniformed band, which included elementary through high school students. Reid served as principal in Kannapolis for thirty-two years.[27]

As Kannapolis grew, blacks were attracted to the mill village for employment. Unlike South Carolina, North Carolina had no Jim Crow laws outlawing the employment of blacks in the textile mills. Custom and racial attitudes, however, limited black employment. So-called Negro jobs confined black males to labor-intensive jobs in the mill yard handling and opening the cotton bales and in the picking room, where ninety-pound laps of cotton were loaded into machines for the next process. Other jobs included work disliked by white men, such as preshrinking, dyeing, and bleaching, which came after weaving. These jobs were difficult because they involved chemicals and heat.[28]

The opening room. Courtesy of the Kannapolis History Associates.

The men of the Georgiatown neighborhood worked for the mill "trucking cotton," a typical Negro job. As one resident recalled,

> The cotton would come in on the freight cars and they'd put a gangplank into the car. The workers would take bales of cotton, put them on a two-wheel truck and push 'em and stack 'em three and four bales all day. Now in the early days, most black people could not work inside the mill, only a few worked inside. I remember there was on Black man who worked as a fireman in the boiler room. But black people didn't work in places like the loom fixers, weavers, cutters, seamstresses and things like that.[29]

Blacks were on the lower end of the pay scale at the Dan River Mills, earning nine to ten cents an hour. Company president Fitzgerald noted that black workers were used as "sweepers, scourers, truck drivers, and in the dyehouse and pickerroom: we do not have them in the mills proper except in the above-mentioned menial capacities."[30]

Jobs were few for black females, aside from doing domestic work for whites. While some cooked and cleaned, some black women specialized in doing laundry. One resident of Texas described her work:

> They went out on the yard and around and washed people's clothes. I've walked up to North Kannapolis with mama in the winter to wash clothes and sometimes before we could get them on the line, they'd be froze. We washed beside an old shed outside. And we washed those clothes—would build a fire around the pot and put them in, chunk 'em, boil 'em, take them out then put them in another wash water, rinse them and hang them on the line. Mama would have to boil water in another pot to put in the rinse water because it was so cold. Sometimes it would be so cold we would almost freeze. There wasn't a lot of things Black women could do. Some of them would work for white people and "stay on the lot."[31]

Katie Geneva Cannon, interviewed in the 1980s, came from a long line of domestics in Kannapolis. She remembered working for the Chapman family. She cleaned the floors, cleaned cabinets, and washed clothes (which included hanging them out on the clothes line and ironing them).[32]

Billie Parks Douglas viewed working in the mill as a step up in life. In the 1940s she made one dollar a week babysitting for white mill workers who worked the second or third shift. As an adult, she worked as a domestic. For black women living in Kannapolis there was not much alternative. "See that was what you did. We didn't have any other choices." Douglas recalled. She resented the higher income white mill workers made and the mill homes they lived in. The mill let "no black women in there. I remember we used to walk by the mill and we'd think, you know, if I was in there we could get well. If I could bring home a check like that home we could all get well." She wished she could provide more for her children. Her daughter commented on how she wished she could dress like the mill people and go on vacations to the beach.[33] There existed a clear economic division between whites and blacks in the mill village.

Employment opportunities in the textile industry for black men were higher than for black women. This fact stems from the greater number of nonproduction jobs that needed greater physical labor or involved hazards that whites sought to avoid. From 1900 until 1960, black male employment greatly outnumbered that of black females in the textile industry. As noted earlier, the low point of black employment during that period was 1900, with 2,744 blacks employed, 2,005 of which were male and 739 female. By 1960, black employment had risen to 43,136, with 33,592 males and 9,544 females employed.[34]

Until the Civil Rights Act of 1964, few textile mills even attempted to hire black workers for production jobs. Textile management gave justification such as "they're happy where they are" and "they're not qualified."[35] In addition, some mill management believed that blacks were more likely to support unions.[36] Trouble erupted when blacks were brought into some mills during the labor shortages of World War II. White workers at Muscogee Mill in Columbus, Georgia, and Fairfax Mill in Alabama protested against the introduction of black workers into the mills. In Danville, Virginia, white spinners and doffers walked off the job when Dan River Mills hired black females as spinners in 1944. Dan River Mills had segregated the black spinners in a separate room, but the white workers demanded that they be placed in a separate building. The union backed the white workers.[37]

Cannon Mills had employed a few blacks inside the mills as janitors and unskilled maintenance. Robert Lee Gill worked as a janitor in the 1950s. Gill cleaned an office, the number 7 spinning room, the card room, and a supply room. Yet when he had to use the restroom he could not use the whites-only restrooms in his section of the mill. "You had to walk out of there, leave all your stuff over there, and go way down up under the waste-house at plant seven," he recounted. And if he wanted some water, he could not use the whites-only water fountains that he routinely cleaned. Gill had to "go down on the cotton platform." Not only were the facilities for blacks not located in the section where he worked, but they were located outside of the mill.[38]

For the blacks living in Kannapolis, the economic opportunities were limited. Before the Civil Rights Act of 1964 Cannon Mills had not attempted to hire many blacks and the bonds of industrial paternalism did not encompass them. The consequence of this situation would be evident as blacks were eventually hired under pressure from the federal government. Black workers were much less loyal to the mill, however, and less intimidated by company pressure during unionization campaigns.

PART II

The Growth and Maturity of
Cannon Mills and Kannapolis:
Paternalism Solidifies Amid Challenges

CHAPTER 4

———◆◆✖◆◆———

A TIME OF UPHEAVAL:
Progressivism and World War I

The period from 1908 to 1921 was a time of change and upheaval for the Cannon Manufacturing Company. Cannon's textile company expanded operations and firmly established itself as the premier towel manufacturer in the world. Simultaneously, the firm battled progressive child legislation and dealt with the problems and opportunities of World War I. Industrial peace did not follow the end of the conflict, however, as the textile firm aggressively combated unionization efforts. After successfully squelching the union, the firm experienced its greatest crisis with the death of its founder.

In addition, the Progressive movement reached its height during this period. Reformers, known collectively as progressives, sought to soften the hard edges of laissez-faire capitalism. Committed to the capitalist system, unlike socialists, progressives viewed government as an ally in reforming the economic system. They shared the antimonopoly sentiment of the Populists and were concerned with the plight of workers. Progressives became particularly concerned about child labor.[1]

Like most textile mill owners, Cannon employed children and battled progressive child labor reformers in North Carolina from the turn of the century. Before 1900, little support for a child labor law existed. Indeed, most textile workers were women and children. Manufacturers justified their employment and low pay on various grounds: women and children's hands and fingers were smaller and more suited to fixing severed threads; the prevailing wage system was based on the "family wage," as all members of the family worked and together they made more than an average farm family;

and by paying women and children less than men, owners could hold down production costs.[2]

Progressives, however, worked to regulate child labor. A progressive groundswell arose in North Carolina with the election of Charles B. Aycock as governor in 1900. Aycock advocated education and child labor reform. Compulsory school attendance and lengthening the school term, along with legal limitations on the age and hours of child workers, threatened the profitability of child labor. Textile manufacturers were so worried the state might enact child labor reform that they met on January 16, 1901, in Greensboro to discuss the situation. In exchange for an understanding that the state legislature would not enact a child labor law in its current session, the cotton mill owners drew up voluntary guidelines regarding child employees. Concord industrialists J. M. Odell and J. W. Cannon served on the manufacturers' committee to investigate voluntary child labor measures and recommend guidelines. The committee eventually urged that mills not employ children younger than twelve years of age during a school term, unless a disabled parent needed that child's income, and not hire children under ten years of age. More than eighty mills accepted the guidelines.[3]

In spite of the assurance by the industry that it could regulate itself, the North Carolina legislature passed child labor reform in 1903. The legislation was essentially the same as the manufacturers' agreement of 1901, and most mills endorsed it. Reformers continued to press for stricter child protection, and again in 1907 and 1913 the North Carolina legislature passed child labor laws. The textile industry steered these laws through the legislature with only minor deviations from the original 1901 agreement.[4] By World War I, North Carolina had banned children under the age of twelve from working and had limited the number of hours per week that children under fourteen could work. Enforcement, however, proved difficult. The Bureau of Labor discovered that 75 percent of mills violated restrictions on child labor.[5] Nevertheless, child labor in the South did decline. From 1914 to 1919, the number of children under age sixteen working in North Carolina declined from 13.3 percent to 6 percent of all wage earners. A similar decrease occurred in Alabama, Georgia, and South Carolina.[6] Thoroughly effective child labor laws did not emerge, however, until the period of the New Deal.

Southern textile manufacturers were glad to have Woodrow Wilson, a southern Democrat, as president, but they did not appreciate all of the progressive reforms advocated by his administration. Child labor was a case in point. The leading advocates of child labor laws were the National Child Labor Committee, led by Alexander McKelway, a North Carolinian and

Presbyterian minister, and Edgar Gardner Murphy, an Alabama reformer. The National Child Labor Committee pushed for a national child labor law, and Murphy supplied Congress with information on child labor provided to him by the American Federation of Labor (AFL). The knowledge that in his own state children worked in the textile mills as much as seventy-two hours a week for as little as thirty cents a day kindled Murphy's activism. Convinced by child labor advocates of the need for national legislation, Congress passed and Wilson supported the Keating-Owens Act in 1916, which prohibited from interstate commerce products made by workers under the age of fourteen or under the age sixteen if they worked more than eight hours per day.[7]

Many in the mill community viewed the child labor law as federal meddling in areas where it did not belong. Mill owners lamented more federal intrusion into their business operations. They worried that the law could negate the wage advantage that southern textile producers held over their northern competitors. Most mill workers also disliked the law. Mill families often needed the additional income provided by their children, and mill work kept children out of trouble and gave them a valuable skill that they likely would use in adulthood.

Furthermore, the law proved difficult to understand and observe. Cannon expressed his confusion to David Clark, secretary of the Southern Cotton Manufacturers association. Could mills continue legally to work children younger than the age set by the law as long as they sold the product within the state? Would it be legal for one mill that employed underage workers to sell yarn to another mill that manufactured cloth to sell outside the state? What liability would mills have if an underage worker worked six hours at one mill and then worked six hours in the same day at another mill?[8] Such questions demonstrated the complexity of the law.

While not successful in keeping the Keating-Owens bill from becoming law, the textile industry organized to test the law in court. The Southern Cotton Manufacturers retained the services of Philadelphia attorney John G. Johnson.[9] After Johnson died, Cannon suggested that the manufacturers' association retain the law firm his New York office used, Hughes, Rounds, Sherman, and Dwight. In particular, he recommended former Supreme Court justice Charles Evans Hughes.[10] Instead, the executive committee of Southern Cotton Manufacturers retained the services of O'Brien, Boardman, Parker and Fox of New York. This firm agreed to fight the child labor law in the Supreme Court for a fee of $5,000. David Clark solicited the sum from the mills,[11] and Cannon's mills contributed $495.[12] The case made its way to the Supreme Court from the U.S. District Court for the Western District of North Carolina. In the case of Hammer v. Dagenhart (1918), attorney Morgan O'Brien represented a Charlotte textile employee who sued to allow his two sons, one under age fourteen and the other under sixteen, to work in a Charlotte mill. On June 3, 1918, the Supreme Court declared the Keating-Owens Act unconstitutional and overturned the law since it was not a regulation of commerce, it contravened the Tenth Amendment, and it conflicted with the Fifth Amendment.[13] The southern textile industry had won an important victory against the forces of progressivism.

This period also represented a time of growth and profitability for James Cannon's textile firm. Earnings had increased from $40,364 in 1897 to $191,355 in 1907.[14] The establishment of the mill town of Kannapolis exemplified a major expansion program for the firm. To pay for the new town, stockholders approved in 1907 an increase of the amount of capital stock from two hundred thousand dollars, set in 1896, to six hundred thousand.[15] Yet the unexpected costs of the facilities at Kannapolis forced the board of directors to ask for another increase in capital stock. Stockholders voted to increase capital stock to $1 million, the maximum allowed by the charter, at its September 24, 1908, meeting. The firm reported that the total costs of Kannapolis would be approximately $1.6 million and that the reserve fund of $925,000 would take care of the excess over the new capitalization.[16]

James Cannon usually had his way at stockholders' meetings. He was president of the firm and his sons were officers. James W. Cannon Jr. served as secretary and treasurer and Joseph Franklin held the office of vice president. Cannon served on the board of directors along with his sons and friends.[17] Besides, out of 5,350 outstanding shares, the Cannon family owned the

Cannon Mills and lake, circa 1913. Courtesy of the Kannapolis History Associates.

largest block of stock, 2,196 shares, of which James Cannon owned 1,658.[18] There was little dissension among the stockholders because of Cannon's unquestioned leadership and the consistent payment of dividends, 5 percent paid semiannually.[19]

While work continued on the mills in Kannapolis, cotton prices rose to levels damaging to the textile industry. Cannon decided to postpone the startup of the new facilities. As textile prices fell in 1908, the Cannon Manufacturing Company temporarily halted production, and Cannon instituted a 10 percent wage cut for all employees from the president down. Production began in Kannapolis in the summer and proceeded slowly as the workers learned the new machinery.[20] Earnings for the firm fell to $176,350.[21] Business conditions remained depressed in 1909 and 1910. Cotton prices stayed high and the demand for textile products dropped further.[22] Earnings fell to $159,456 for 1909 and $142,730 for 1910. In spite of the worsening market conditions, the firm continued to pay a 5 percent semiannual dividend.[23]

The business climate improved between 1911 and 1913. As cotton prices fell and demand for textile products grew, earnings improved for the firm. Cannon's earnings increased from $150,150 to $261,621 during the period. To meet demand, Cannon added 22,700 spindles and 600 looms to the plants in both Concord and Kannapolis. Cannon Manufacturing now possessed 82,000 spindles and 2,600 looms.[24]

Because of improving business conditions, the firm's charter needed amending to allow continued growth. The bulk of Cannon's operations had shifted from Concord to Kannapolis, and the new mill town was constantly undergoing construction and expansion. In 1914, the board of directors recommended amending the charter to permit the move of the firm's headquarters to Kannapolis. In addition, the board voted to amend the charter to allow an increase in capital stock from $1 million to $5 million. Stockholders approved these recommendations.[25]

The distant war in Europe brought opportunities for Cannon Manufacturing. Demand for textile products increased. Earnings for 1915 rose to $381,858 on sales of $5,085,378.[26] By 1916, Cannon's mills were operating at full capacity. Writing to the superintendent of the Paola Cotton Mills of Statesville, North Carolina, Cannon stated that "most of our mills are now running above theoretical production."[27] To meet the increasing demand for textile products, the firm increased its capital stock to $2.5 million to fund the construction of a new mill in Kannapolis and to purchase Cannon and Company of York, South Carolina. James W. Cannon, who owned Cannon and Company, received $411,851 from Cannon Manufacturing. In

addition, the firm paid Cannon $142,392 for an additional 474.64 acres of
land in Kannapolis for the new mill.[28] James Cannon resigned as president
of Cannon Manufacturing before receiving payment on the transactions,
perhaps to avoid accusations of conflict of interest. Martin Cannon became
president of the firm and Charles Cannon was named vice president. J. W.
Cannon Jr. remained secretary and treasurer.[29] Sales and profits continued to grow throughout 1916, with profits reaching $1,186,335 on sales of
$7,278,496.[30]

While the firm made record profits, Cannon worried over the cotton market. The price for cotton was dependent on the laws of supply and
demand. If demand exceeded supply, prices for cotton rose. Cotton prices
fell if supply exceeded demand. The main variable that affected cotton production was weather. Too much or too little rain lowered cotton yields and
caused the price of cotton to rise. Mill owners wished for good weather and
abundant yields so they could purchase cotton at cheaper prices. In the summer of 1916, James Cannon was concerned over the possibility of higher
cotton prices because of dry conditions in the cotton-growing states west of
the Mississippi River.[31] Weather, however, was not the only factor influencing the price of cotton. The boll weevil was an increasing problem. It arrived
in Texas in 1892 and had infested the rest of the Deep South by 1917.[32]

The war added another variable to the cotton equation. Germany's
efforts to limit trade with the Allies threatened to disrupt the American cotton market. German submarine warfare had the potential to restrict or end
American exports of cotton, resulting in a glut of cotton in the United States
that would drive down its price. While lower cotton prices would initially
benefit the textile mills, the blockade would keep American textile firms
from finding costumers overseas. Cannon was concerned that "this kind of
war-fare [sic]" could be successful "and destroy the shipping" of the United
States.[33] In such uncertain times, Cannon remained committed to growing
the firm and meeting the demand for textile products as much as possible.

As Cannon struggled with the unsettled business conditions of 1916,
the Wilson administration proposed, and Congress debated, military preparedness. The House majority leader, Claude Kitchin, Democrat of North
Carolina, opposed preparedness. He believed that the "big Navy and big
Army" programs were pushed by "the jingoes and war traffickers."[34] In spite
of Kitchin's influence, preparedness bills passed Congress, including a bill
for enlarging the navy supported by fellow a North Carolinian, Secretary of
the Navy Josephus Daniels.

Once military preparedness became U.S. policy, Congress turned its
attention to raising revenue for the programs. The Revenue Act of 1916

raised the income tax and imposed new taxes on corporations.[35] Although Kitchin was a Tarheel, Cannon did not view him as an ally in fighting corporate taxes. Writing to fellow textile industrialist Fuller Calloway in Georgia, Cannon acknowledged he did "not like Claude Kitchen [sic]" because "he is antagonistic to corporations."[36] Cannon worked with other mill men to gain the sympathy of the House majority leader.[37] Furthermore, the mill owner worked through the Cotton Manufacturers' Association of North Carolina (CMANC) to kill or modify wartime corporate tax bills. Cannon served on the Committee on Taxation, Commerce, and Labor of the CMANC to guide legislation beneficial to the industry.[38]

The entry of the United States in the war created more problems for the textile industry. Under the burden of transporting hundreds of thousands of troops and supplies, the rail system nearly collapsed. Transportation of goods via rail became a problem for Cannon. The company had difficulties securing cars for receiving and shipping goods. In a May 1917 letter, James Cannon noted that "we have to fight all the time without any let up to get cars and material."[39] Of particular concern was the delay in building the new mill in Kannapolis. Because of the delay in receiving building material, the firm had to store the new textile machinery in warehouses until the mill was ready. Cannon knew that the company was losing money on purchased machinery that sat idle while the firm strained to meet government contracts.[40] After a massive traffic jam during the winter of 1917–18, the Wilson administration created the Railroad Administration to manage the nation's railroads. Headed by Treasury Secretary William McAdoo, the Railroad Administration ran the railroads efficiently through the remainder of the war.[41]

In spite of transportation problems, sales of Cannon textiles increased in 1917. Sales grew to $9,885,171 and brought profits of $922,371.[42] The lower ratio of profit to sales was probably due to higher outlays for transportation and materials.

Government contracts for textile goods increased in 1918. The Cannon Manufacturing Company now had monthly sales to the government greater than the yearly sales in the prewar years. Army and medical contracts totaled more than $1 million in February.[43] Military contracts rose to $2,431,604 in May and to $3,539,029 in August.[44] Besides the specific orders, the government had requested that the textile firm give it the total production of its huck looms, totaling approximately three million towels per month.[45] Because of government demand for textiles, Cannon Manufacturing had another record year of sales in 1918. Sales totaled $16,105,591 with profits of $1,715,247.[46]

Another change occurred among the officers of the firm in 1918. Having served as secretary and treasurer since 1904, J. W. Cannon Jr. resigned. Charles Cannon, serving as vice president, now also accepted the job of treasurer. G. B. Lewis became secretary.[47]

During 1917–18, the textile industry experienced a shortage of male workers. Patriotism spread in Kannapolis as male workers quit the mill to join the military. On July 20, 1917, the Cannon Mills Band traveled to Charlotte to enlist with James Cannon accompanying it. Cannon marched with the band from the depot to enlistment center. Yet such acts of patriotism caused problems for the manufacturer.[48]

With male workers joining the military, Cannon Manufacturing depended on women to fill textile jobs. The textile firm built a dormitory in Kannapolis to house single female workers. Mary Ella Hall, named after Mrs. James Cannon, had 120 rooms, housed 180 women, and had a staff of 20. Meals in the hall were served three times per day. One early tenant, Carrie Bogle, moved into the dormitory in 1918 and lived there for over thirty years. Families could rest assured that dormitory manager Ruth Shields would provide a wholesome environment for their daughters.[49]

By the end of the war in November 1918, a pronounced shift in consumer preference had occurred. The military had ordered all of the flat-weave huck towels that the firm could manufacture. Huck towels were easier to ship than terry towels because more of them could be packed per box. Faced with a shortage of huck towels at home, consumers bought terry towels and soon

Cannon Mills band, 1917. Courtesy of the Kannapolis History Associates.

learned that terry towels were more absorbent than huck towels and did not have to be ironed after laundering. Commercial customers, such as barber shops, railroads, and hotels, also enjoyed the advantages of terry towels. By the time huck towels became available again, Americans had changed their preference to terry. The market for huck declined after the war.[50]

The war had other affects on the textile industry. While profits seemed high, the costs for material and labor had increased greatly. Cannon realized that the war produced an abnormal market in which costs seemed irrelevant. Military contracts caused usually high demand that the mills strained to meet, and that abnormally high demand allowed firms to spread the increased costs of material and labor over greater units of production, so textile manufacturers made profits in spite of higher costs for material and labor.

Cannon seemed troubled by the increased costs. He noted in June 1917 that the cost of coal had risen to four times the level it had sold for one year earlier. In that same month, Cannon recognized that a labor shortage had developed in the industry as a result of male mill workers reporting for military service.[51] By September 1918, the shortage of labor had pushed wages to more than three times the prewar level.[52] Cotton also increased in price. The increased price for cotton stemmed from four years of lower crop yields and higher demand.[53] Cotton had risen three times over the prewar level by November 1918.[54]

The labor shortage was exacerbated by the flu epidemic of 1918. A schoolteacher had the first recorded case of the flu in Kannapolis. As the disease spread, the YMCA was used as a hospital. Eventually, fifty people died of the flu in the mill village, including the undertaker and a druggist.[55]

High taxes also concerned Cannon. The federal government instituted an excess profits tax for corporations with the Special Preparedness Fund Act of March 3, 1917. After the United States entered the war, the War Revenue Act of October 3, 1917, provided additional funds to fund the war effort. Corporations paid even higher excess profit taxes under the War Revenue Act. Cannon wrote to a colleague that "while profits have been good, taxes have been exceedingly high."[56] The textile manufacturer believed that the amount of taxes collected from corporations was "a great mistake."[57] Further, Cannon worried that after the war ended the excess profit tax would hurt businesses as the government canceled war contracts and the economy returned to normal conditions.

In hindsight, the two forces that had a great impact on the textile industry during this period, market forces and the growth in power of the federal government, would lead to the downfall of the Cannon's paternalistic structure in the distant future. The war had introduced market forces that the mill owner could not control. Government war contracts created a temporary increase in the demand for Cannon manufactured goods while the war also increased the price for cotton. Furthermore, a labor shortage drove up wages. Cannon was helpless to control these external economic forces.

In addition, the federal government represented a threat to Cannon's paternalistic structure. James Cannon became leery of government action that would place limits on the management of his mills and Kannapolis. The battle over the Keating-Owens Act demonstrated the complexity of mitigating harmful federal legislation. The mill owner's influence was much less in dealing with the federal government than it had been with the state government. Much more effort, cooperation, and organization were needed to have an impact on federal legislation. In addition, federal management of the railroads and rising taxes had a negative effect on Cannon's businesses.

Unknown to James Cannon at the time, the parameters and limitations of his paternalism were being established. Stable market forces and a weak federal government provided a climate favorable to the continuance of the mill village. The status quo was desired but was impossible to maintain. Yet the management structure established in Kannapolis was so strong that it would continue, with some modifications, long after Cannon's death.

CHAPTER 5

———————

POSTWAR DOWNTURN, LABOR UNREST, AND NEW MANAGEMENT

Soon after the armistice, demand for textiles declined as the government canceled contracts. The War Industries Board announced that when possible, the government would not cancel contracts, and that certain criteria would be considered before orders were canceled. These included the effects of the cancelation on the industry, labor, the community, and the textile firm. In spite of some reassuring words, the government immediately began to cancel orders placed after October 1, 1918. Furthermore, the War Industries Board announced that modifications or adjustments could be made to contracts amounting to more than $100,000.[1] Cannon's firm soon had more than $3.5 million in canceled government contracts. The consumer market failed to take up the slack.[2] By 1919, the industry had entered what Cannon called a "depression." Cannon Manufacturing received few new orders as the firm sold existing inventories. Profits fell to $848,051, a loss of more than $860,000 from 1918.[3] Taxes for the year 1919, totaling more than $850,000, were more than the year's profit.[4] Cannon bitterly complained, "I think our friends in Washington went just a little too far in their tax record. In my opinion it is going to hurt the industries in our country insomuch as it leaves them so little with which to follow the decline downward."[5] Congress did repeal the excess profits tax in November 1921, three years into a decline for the textile industry.

In the immediate postwar business environment, cost became an important issue for textile mills. Profits were being squeezed by the high costs of labor and material. Of particular concern were the high wartime wages. The costs for raw materials would drop after the war because of lower demand, but lowering wages would be a different matter. Workers were accustomed to the higher wages and would resist wage cuts. Textile mills could not maintain the bonuses and continue paying the high wages workers had acquired during the labor shortages of the war.[6]

With few orders being placed with the mill, the Cannon Manufacturing Company, along with most of the mills in the area, went to a four-day work week.[7] The textile manufacturer knew it was not "wise to continue the present high bonus under the conditions of trade today."[8] James Cannon and other manufacturers considered how to reduce wages without causing labor unrest. He believed that the best course of action was to work in concert with other mills of the area. Workers would be less likely to quit Cannon Manufacturing Company after wage cuts if the surrounding mills also cut wages. Following the lead of the Cone and Spray mill owners, who reduced their bonuses on January 1, 1919, Cannon reduced the bonuses to his workers by 50 percent for full-time and 25 percent for part-time workers.[9] Cannon kept in communication with H. R. Fitzgerald of Riverside Cotton Mill and Dan River Cotton Mill in Danville, Virginia, because Cannon believed "we should work as closely together as possible in arriving at adjustments that are vital to us all."[10] Fitzgerald informed Cannon that Riverside and Dan River planned to reduce bonuses to their workers in March.[11] In addition, the two mill men shared information on bonuses and wages for various jobs in their mills. Cannon also worked with other mills in reducing wages since his mill workers seemed to "keep well posted as to what other mills are doing."[12]

In addition to working in concert with other mills, Fitzgerald took another step to forestall labor unrest at Riverside and Dan River. In 1919 he introduced industrial democracy, a scheme involving the writing of a constitution and the creation of a cabinet composed of company executives, a senate comprised of supervisors, and a house of representatives chosen from among the workers. "Bills" or proposals had to be approved by both the house and senate but could be vetoed by the cabinet. Based on John Leitch's ideas in his book *Man to Man*, Fitzgerald believed that a more evenhanded treatment of his workers would smooth out relations between management and labor and lessen strife at his mills.[13] Since industrial democracy weakened the paternalistic structure in the mill village, Cannon had no interest in instituting it in his mills.

In spite of the effort to avoid labor unrest, the years immediately following the war witnessed unprecedented union activity among textile operatives. The United Textile Workers of America (UTW), organized in 1901 and affiliated with the American Federation of Labor, became the voice of textile labor. The UTW had some success organizing and striking against northern textile mills, but it was not very successful in cracking the anti-union South. A renewed attention to the South began in 1918. Late that year, the union decided to concentrate its effort on the forty-eight-hour work week and called for a general strike on February 3, 1919, to support this objective.[14]

The spark behind the UTW was its president, John Golden. Born in 1863 in Lancashire, England, Golden had become a cotton mill operative as a young boy. He came to the United States in 1884 after being blacklisted for his activities with the Mule Spinners' Union. Settling in Fall River, Massachusetts, he obtained employment in the textile trade and continued his labor activity, joining the National Mule Spinners' Organization of the United States and Canada. In 1902, he became the president of the United Textile Workers of America. Golden led the union through successful strikes in 1912 in Lawrence and Lowell, Massachusetts, and by the outbreak of the war in Europe, his UTW had over of two hundred thousand members. He successfully sought federal mediation in a strike in Manchester, New Hampshire, in 1918.[15]

In February 1919, heeding the UTW call, textile workers went on strike in Georgia and South Carolina. The strikes spread to Charlotte, North Carolina, in late February. Workers' grievances included the cutting of the work week to four days and discontinuance of the 30 percent bonus begun during the war. Close to two thousand operatives joined the UTW and the mill owners promptly locked them out. Eventually, the Charlotte strikes ended in a partial victory for the union. Operatives agreed to the principle of the open shop in exchange for a reduced work week, free house rent for the strike period, the reinstatement of fired union workers, and the resumption of bonuses.[16]

The "success" of the strikes in Charlotte encouraged labor leaders to believe that such tactics might work against Cannon's mills. The drastic reduction of the bonuses and talk of further wage cuts disturbed Cannon's workers. Many believed that Cannon was reducing bonuses greater than was necessary and was taking advantage of them. Workers believed that Cannon did not respect the right to the higher wages that they had worked for so hard. Thus a breakdown in the workplace norms (the paternalistic compact) had taken place. The reciprocity and respect between management and labor that workers perceived were part of Cannon's type of paternalism had been broken by management. Their trust in and loyalty to James Cannon was now in question, so workers broke their part of the compact and turned to the union. In the summer of 1919, many operatives in Concord joined the union, and Cannon locked them out. Soon the unionization drive spread to Kannapolis, and there also the manufacturer locked the workers out of the mills. After three and a half months, the company and operatives ended the strike based on the Charlotte settlement.[17]

The 1919 strikes in the South enlarged the membership of the UTW. Though most of the strikes did not end as well as those in Charlotte, Concord, and Kannapolis, the UTW made tremendous inroads in organizing southern textile labor. In 1920, southern cotton mill workers comprised half the membership of all cotton mill workers in the UTW. Forty-three new locals and a total of fifty thousand union members had been added.[18]

Emboldened by its relative success, in spite of not being able to institute the forty-eight-hour work week throughout the southern textile industry, the UTW convened its annual convention in Baltimore on October 20, 1919. The guest speaker was Samuel Gompers, president of the American Federation of Labor. John Golden told Gompers, "I think one time years ago I said to you, 'Sam, if I can only live long enough, I will show you a real convention.' Here it is."[19] Delegates to the convention vowed to continue their fight for the forty-eight-hour work week. The battle lines were drawn, and the South would be the battleground. Timing would be the key to victory or defeat.

In late 1920, the textile industry entered an economic slump. The market was awash with textile goods because of canceled government contracts. As demand weakened, prices fell. Mills in New England and the South cut wages.[20] James Cannon reduced wages and cut operation to three days a week. He advised the president of the Buck Creek Cotton Mill to reduce the numbers of spindles and looms by half, lay off half the workers, and cut wages to prewar levels. He noted that many New England mills were closing indefinitely and that many more would go out of business by January 1921.[21] Sales figures for the flagship Cannon Manufacturing Company demonstrated the severity of the downturn. Between 1918 and 1921, towel sales rose, hitting a peak in April 1920 and then falling precipitously. April 1920 sales were $2,156,299, almost double the sales for April of the previous year. The weakness of the market, however, soon became evident. September 1920 sales fell more than $288,000 behind those of September 1919. Even worse, sales for October 1920 were about one-third of those of the previous October.[22] Cannon soon followed other manufacturers in reducing wages.

The opening salvo of the labor dispute of 1921 came when Golden appeared before the House Ways and Means Committee on January 31.

Golden responded to a letter from J. W. Cannon requesting a higher tariff on imported cotton products. The president of the United Textile Workers informed the committee that he had recently traveled throughout the South and was aware of the labor conditions in the region. He told the committee that Cannon had already reduced wages in his mills by 40 percent, cutting them 20 percent at first and then an additional 20 percent two weeks later. Golden requested that if the committee approved tariffs to protect the textile industry, it should also demand guarantees from the industry that wages would not be further reduced.[23]

In Kannapolis, a collective identity, in growing opposition to the mill village identity that James Cannon had attempted to create, was emerging among workers. Workers were now exploring the paternalistic boundaries in Kannapolis. They gathered in solidarity against the massive wage cuts enacted by the company and believed that collective action was needed since they were otherwise powerless to counter those cuts. More workers turned to the union, whose job was to convince workers that it was as powerful as management and could win. The union also was vital in reinforcing a collective identity among workers separate from the mill village identity.[24]

As the Kannapolis local became active in opposing continued wage cuts, the company responded by firing union operatives. On February 23, 1921, Kannapolis Local 1238 of the UTW presented a list of demands to Charles A. Cannon, the youngest son of J. W. Cannon and heir apparent to the Cannon empire. The letter demanded a 20 percent wage increase, an end to discrimination against union members, and a hearing for all union members fired since January 1 to determine if they were fired for "just cause."[25] The firm made no concessions to the local in spite of the February 28 deadline set by the union.

Tensions remained high at the mills from March to May. The local paper reported on two themes during this period—the strike was imminent and the mill owners were unconcerned. As mills made wage cuts of up to 40 percent, the pressure to strike became almost irresistible. On April 30, delegates from the surrounding locals met in Concord to discuss a general strike. Golden opposed a general strike in the South at this time. Several strikes in the North during 1920 had drained the UTW treasury, and Golden was concerned that the union did not have adequate funds to mount a successful general strike in the South. There were, however, contravening pressures for the UTW to support a general strike. If the 40 percent wage cut stood in the South, this would put pressure on the 22.5 percent wage cuts in New England, possibly encouraging New England mill owners to reduce wages further. In addition, if the union did not follow the will of its southern members by standing up to the mills, it would look weak and its membership might evaporate. At a Concord union meeting, members pushed for a strike and agreed not to demand UTW strike benefits. The UTW representatives promised to provide as much financial aid to the strikers as the union could when a strike was called.[26] The union continued to gage the support of the North Carolina locals for a general strike. In May, UTW vice president Thomas McMahon met with forty-five locals in Charlotte, a meeting that demonstrated support for a general strike.[27] McMahon called the strike for June 1.[28]

Conditions were not conducive for a successful general strike. Golden, president of the union for the past nineteen years, was seriously ill and his influence was now severely limited. He died on June 9.[29] Moreover, the union's strike funds were very low. The southern operatives could not depend on the four dollars a week benefit and therefore could not stay out of work for long. Their only hope was that the mill owners would settle quickly. And finally, a May 12 *Concord Times* article gave an ominous warning to the strikers. Citing an article in the *New York Journal of Commerce*, the local paper stated that a strike would not hurt the mills. In fact, an unnamed manufacturer noted that 90 percent of the southern mills had lost money in the last six months and were now operating for the benefit of the operatives. Closing the mills indefinitely would actually cut the owners' loses and please shareholders. With demand low and inventories high, a long strike would allow the cotton mills to dispose of inventories and save on labor costs. Manufacturers could withstand a long work stoppage while the operatives could not.

In spite of such ill omens, the walkout began on Wednesday, June 1 at 10:00 a.m. The local paper estimated that more than six thousand workers went on strike in Concord and Kannapolis.[30] Cannon responded by locking out his workers.

The union immediately began to help the strikers. It set up commissaries to distribute food and supplies, but it did not take long for the union's shortage of funds to become evident. The condition of the striking operatives came to the public attention by the end of the month. The local paper highlighted the terrible conditions and the shortage of necessities among the striking workers: "It is generally known that the strike resulted from cuts in wages that the workers thought were unjustified or, at least, which they were influenced to believe, were unnecessary." The last part of this statement referred to outsiders or the influence of the "northern" union. The article continued that during the good times of the world war, wages had increased sharply but had been cut during the current crisis merely to keep the mills from closing down indefinitely. Operatives received a 250 percent increase during the war, the paper figured, and with 50 to 75 percent reductions, they still had a net increase in wages from 75 to 100 percent over the prewar years. In addition, the cost of living had not increased faster than the increase in wages, and the welfare work of the mills further negated the rising cost of living. The mill operatives had experienced a real increase in wages over the last few years. Why then, the paper pondered, were the mills idle?[31]

The local paper questioned the reasons for the walkout. An article in the *Concord Times* of July 11 inquired why the operatives in Charlotte and Concord had gone on strike while workers in nearby Gastonia were still at work. In the striking cities, "it may be that the operatives are the more easily led astray by the arguments and oratory of the Northern agitators," while mills in Gaston County were known for "the fine spirit of co-operation existing between employer and employe [sic]." The message was clear. The union was an outside force of agitation and alien to the cooperative industrial spirit of the South.[32]

Charles Cannon, who had assumed control of the Cannon Group for his ailing father, closed the family mills to union members. Workers willing to break with the union, however, could return to work. Cannon was determined not to grant recognition to the union or to engage in collective bargaining. In addition, he fired and evicted from company housing some union operatives.[33]

While labor unrest erupted among Cannon's workers, mill hands at the Riverside and Dan River mills reacted differently to the downturn in the market and reduced profits. Under the structure of industrial democracy, the house (representing workers) voted in May 1921 for a 22.72 percent pay cut after a presentation by management on the financial condition of Riverside and Dan River. The house voted for a second cut later as the financial situation worsened.[34]

With the strike raging in Kannapolis, James William Cannon journeyed to the baths of Hot Springs, Arkansas, to recuperate. Early in his stay in Hot Springs, the elder Cannon wrote to his son, "I am beginning to feel a good effect from the baths already, and your Mother is looking like a sixteen-year-old girl."[35] The elder Cannon remained at the resort until mid-September.

While Cannon rejuvenated in the baths of Hot Springs, the conditions of the striking operatives in Concord and Kannapolis worsened. Newspapers carried stories of hungry operatives. The local paper recounted incidents of violence caused by desperation. One story chronicled a fight in a Charlotte store between an anti-union merchant and a despondent striker. In addition, journalists asked why the poor union operatives paid dues and received little tangible benefit. What happened to their dues? newspaper articles asked rhetorically.[36]

The city of Concord took measures to curb possible rioting. In their meeting in early August, the city aldermen passed an antipicketing law, the first such law in the state. The city attorney drew up the law at the request of the aldermen because there was "evidence that certain citizens in the city desire to go to work and earn an honest living and are afraid that they will not get the proper protection should an attempt be made to keep them from work by certain individuals."[37] Governor Cameron Morris did not support the city ordinance. Trying to appear impartial, he announced on August 15 that he did not recognize the authority of the city ordinance and that labor had a right to gather peacefully.

The general strike climaxed when the state militia arrived in Concord and Kannapolis, following the reopening of Locke Mill in Concord. Locke had been the first mill to go on strike, more than three months before the general strike. The Locke Mill strikers had received a dollar per week in strike benefits from the UTW until the general strike started, but once the general strike commenced, the union ended benefits and only provided help from the commissary. Discontent with the strike grew among the Locke operatives, and a delegation met with the mill manager and offered to return to work if they were provided protection.

On Thursday, August 11, the operatives met with Concord city officials to ask for protection and then returned to the mill. Hundreds of striking operatives from other mills gathered at the gates of Locke Mill when workers returned to work at 7:00 a.m. Law enforcement officials mingled with the crowd, which they characterized as well behaved.[38] The city officials, however, became concerned that local law enforcement might not keep order. The mayor of Concord, the city attorney, and several prominent mill owners met with the governor on Saturday and requested that he call the state militia to the city. Two companies of the state militia arrived in Concord on Monday morning, August 13, and took positions at the Locke Mill and Hartsell Mill, which also was slated to open that day. Troops moved to the other mills in Concord and Kannapolis as they prepared to open. Pickets disappeared at other mills as more troops arrived.[39]

The Cannons' opposition to the union went beyond winning the strike battle. They had their wills set on destroying the union local. James Cannon now believed that it was a mistake to have negotiated with the union in 1919. As management's determination not to negotiate became evident, a distinct "psychological climate" emerged among the workers. Workers realized that the battle was over the survival of the union local and the possibility of labor to challenge the paternalistic system in Kannapolis. But as the economic conditions of workers worsened and the union seemed ill matched against the power structure in Kannapolis, the back-to-work movement spread to the mill village. Mill operatives began to return to work the same week the troops appeared. By August 18, eight hundred workers had returned to work at the various Cannon plants. Writing from Hot Springs, James Cannon told his son Charles, "I think I approve of everything you have done, and I would try to hold down any rioting if possible, and by no means recognize a union."[40]

As the labor crisis continued, Governor Morrison announced that he would come to Concord. The elder Cannon asked Charles to meet with the manager of Locke Mill and others to try to convince the governor not to speak in Concord. Cannon was afraid that Morrison's appearance would boost the efforts of the union and force the mills to compromise. He informed Charles,

> I hope none of the mills will effect any compromise whatever. Just take back the help that want to work and are willing to work, and let the agitators go. I hope you will watch out carefully and confer with the others on how important it is to weed out certain operators that are always causing us trouble.[41]

The governor tried to be neutral in the dispute and spoke of the rights of both sides. He mentioned the right of contract and stated that the union had "a legal right to organize and to collectively bargain." His role as governor, he stated, was to ensure law and order, including the use of troops if necessary. The governor then admonished both sides to end the bitter dispute.[42] With no help from the governor, and little financial support from the union, hungry workers continued to drift back to the mills. By late August, the strike was broken, the union was in disarray, and the mills returned to full operation.

At the end of the year, Cannon's strength was spent. The effects of the baths of Hot Springs did not last, and Cannon died on December 19, 1921, of heart trouble after a two-week illness. He was buried in Oakwood Cemetery in Concord. Leadership of the Cannon textile empire passed to his youngest son, Charles Albert, who had ably guided the company through the general strike a few months earlier. James William had set a tone for leadership that Charles would diligently follow.[43]

At the time of his death, James W. Cannon had built a huge textile operation. The Cannon Group now included the Cannon Manufacturing Company, with plants in Concord and Kannapolis, North Carolina, and York, South Carolina; the Cabarrus Cotton Mills, with plants in Concord and Kannapolis; the Barringer Manufacturing Company in Rockwell, North Carolina; Franklin Cotton Mills, Hobarton Manufacturing Company, Norcott Mills Company and Gibson Manufacturing Company in Concord; Kesler Manufacturing Company in Salisbury, North Carolina; and Patterson Manufacturing Company in China Grove, North Carolina. These mills produced cotton towels, tire fabric, sheets, gray goods, cotton yards, dress goods, rayon fabrics, drapery fabrics, whipcords, madras fabrics, armor cloth, and supercarded cotton yards. In addition, Cannon had interests in other mills in Alabama, Georgia, and North Carolina. The commission house of Cannon Mills, Inc., marketed the products of the Cannon Group and those of many other southern mills in the United States and overseas. Through construction of new mills, acquisition of existing mills, and vertical integration, the textile empire of J. W. Cannon had become one of the largest manufacturers of towels in the world. After the death of the founder, the bonds of paternalistic management would continue and the company would resemble a modern corporation with the merger of its nine primary mills.[44]

Yet the strike of 1921 represented the most organized opposition of workers to the paternalism in Kannapolis. Was a working-class consciousness forming in the mill village? Did the organization and massive opposition of workers to Cannon management create a collective identity that would survive and challenge paternalism in the future? The answer to these questions was no.

A working-class consciousness along the lines of Karl Marx's definition was not forming in Kannapolis. Some elements of Marx's four aspects of class consciousness had appeared, but not all. The first aspect, the formation of a class identity, had emerged by 1921. Workers did feel separate and distinct from Cannon management and especially from James Cannon. They did feel a degree of alienation on the job with no input on the shop floor and little recourse for their grievances, however, this did not propel them to the other stages of working-class consciousness formation. Kannapolis workers were not in opposition to the capitalist system in general. They did not define themselves and society solely by class. And they did not conceive of and work for a future based on an egalitarian collective society.[45]

Yet something less structured had coalesced: a collective identity. This collective identity formed in relationship with management, recognized the differing status and power between workers and management, and bound laborers together in a common existence. It formed an opinion of and evaluated management based on the criteria of trust, legitimacy, reciprocity, and workplace justice. In addition, this collective identity began to understand the limits of workers' agency within the paternalistic structure of Kannapolis.[46]

The collective identity of mill workers of Kannapolis would survive the unrest of 1921 but would not seriously challenge Cannon's paternalism. Never again would the majority of workers organize and oppose management during the life of paternalism in Kannapolis. The limits of the system had been tested with harsh consequences. Staunch union supporters had been fired, evicted from mill housing, removed from the mill village, and blacklisted. The union had not proven to be as powerful as the textile firm. Charles Cannon had broken the union and had shaken confidence in organizing. The incident now passed into the collective memory of the mill village and became a part of the collective identity of the mill workers. While many workers may have ceased trusting the Cannons and may have chafed at the injustice they perceived in the mill village, few would venture into organizing again. Mill workers were powerless to oppose management without intervention from the government and the weakening of the power structure. Workers became very compliant not because they were content but because they were powerless.[47] Fear now became the motivating factor. The hope that arose in 1919 that workers could negotiate with management and exert a greater degree of agency was gone. Paternalism had not softened but had hardened under Charles Cannon, and workers became resigned to their fate.

CHAPTER 6

————●━➤◀✕▶◀●————

New Leadership, Market Decline, and Consolidation

James William Cannon selected his youngest son, Charles Albert Cannon, as heir to his textile empire. Charles was born in Concord, North Carolina, on November 29, 1892. He attended public school there and the Fishburne Military Academy in Virginia. After secondary school, Charles enrolled in Davidson College, an elite Presbyterian college in neighboring Mecklenburg County. Anxious to enter his father's business, however, he soon left Davidson. Charles Cannon began his career as a clerk and office boy at the Cannon Manufacturing Company in Concord. His first managerial position came in 1912 at age nineteen, when his father assigned him to the Barringer Manufacturing Company in Rockwell, North Carolina.[1] There the younger Cannon displayed the managerial skill and business savvy that earned his father's favor.

Evidently Charles was much like his father in character and disposition. The youngest Cannon son shared the same religious and work values as his father. Charles devoutly attended his father's First Presbyterian Church in Concord, where he served as a church elder until a disagreement in church policy led him to resign as elder and almost leave the church.[2] In addition, Charles followed his father's work ethic, which included maintaining "a rigid control of yourself, observing the rules laid down of strict attention to business, economy in handling the business and never having your integrity doubted [and] all times keeping a clear head."[3]

Furthermore, like his father, Charles kept meticulous records and had a knack for analyzing the cost effectiveness of a project or operation. He applied this analytical skill to both his personal life and his business. Once, when considering the cost of operating an automobile for personal use for five years, he developed a thorough cost analysis to ascertain the impact on his personal budget. This thorough analysis included the price of the automobile, interest, gas for five years at an average price per gallon, twenty-four tires, twenty-four inner tubes, a license, incidentals, repairs, insurance, and a chauffeur.[4]

The elder Cannon had ample opportunity to discover the business acumen of each of his six sons, for each worked at some point in the Cannon Group of family-controlled mills. Table 1 (page 66) discloses the management positions of Cannon family members in their various mills (approximately 1918). Of course, family control of the textile empire was most evident in the premier Cannon Manufacturing Company. From 1915 until 1918, only Cannons served as officers of the company. This only changed when James W. Cannon Jr. resigned as secretary and treasurer in December 1918 and a nonfamily member took the post. The family, however, remained in control through the time of the elder Cannon's death in December 1921 by controlling the office of president and one other office along with having four Cannons on the board of directors (the board usually contained seven members).[5] By 1921, Charles had become his father's choice to head the family businesses.[6]

James Cannon had decided to curtail some of his business activities before his health declined. From 1915 until 1920, he did not serve as an officer of the Cannon Manufacturing Company, though he did remain active as a director and was busy with the other mills in the Cannon Group. The elder Cannon became chairman of the board and Charles became president and treasurer of the Cannon Manufacturing Company in 1921. By the time James W. Cannon's health declined in midyear, his flagship company was in capable hands. Indeed, if anything, Charles's handling of the strike of 1921 proved to Cannon that his youngest son was up to the task of running his textile empire. Charles deserved much credit for breaking the union in Kannapolis and Concord and would prove every bit an enemy to unions as was his father.

James Cannon's will further demonstrated the faith he had in Charles. At the elder Cannon's death, Charles became the executor of the will along with David Blair, James's son-in-law. Blair's appointment as co-executor displayed Cannon's lack of confidence in the ability of any of his other sons to manage his estate. The will gave the household and all contents to his wife, Mary Ella, along with the insurance benefits. The terms of the will held the remaining amount of the estate, valued at more than three million dollars, in trust until December 1, 1940, when it would go to Mary Ella. If she died before that date, the estate would be divided into one hundred units as directed. The division of the assets displayed how James Cannon felt about his various children. To all four of his daughters he left ten units; to Martin, Eugene, and Junius Ross, five units; and to Charles, thirty-five units. To sons James W. Cannon Jr. and Joseph the elder, Cannon left nothing, but he did designate five units for Joseph's children. The executors managed the five units set aside for Eugene and J. Ross until December 1, 1940.[7] Even in death, James William Cannon displayed his favor for Charles.

The decade of the 1920s was not an ideal time to lead a textile firm. Long before the market collapse of 1929, the textile industry experienced a decade of market volatility. The market collapsed in the winter of 1920–21, recovered briefly until 1924, and then began a general decline until the stock market crash of 1929 and the Great Depression. The crux of the problem in the textile industry was overcapacity.[8]

Several indicators explained the condition of the textile market overall. One such indicator was the forty-five-year index of manufacturers' margin. The manufacturers' margin represented "the difference between the market price of one pound of some standard construction of gray cloth and the value, at the same or a corresponding time, of one pound of cotton."[9] Mill margins increased between 1915 and 1920. Starting at a point of approximately eleven cents per pound in 1915, manufacturers' margins peaked at approximately seventy cents per pound in 1920. In 1921, the manufacturers' margin fell to around eighteen cents per pound and then to approximately seventeen by 1929. By the end of the decade, many textile mills needed to have a mill margin of about twenty cents to cover costs. Several factors caused the decline in the manufacturers' margin and threatened the profitability of the industry. Increased competition and an emphasis on style weakened margins, but overcapacity was the most important factor.[10]

Another indication of the condition of the textile industry was net income after taxes. The net income after taxes for the industry, which in 1919 was $212 million, dipped to $28 million in 1921. It increased to $91 million by 1923 but fell to a deficit of $43 million in 1924. Industry income was still in the red in 1926 but recovered to $65 million in 1927. It decreased to $16 million in 1929. When the Great Depression hit the nation in late 1929, the textile industry was already reeling from many years of lower margins and profits.[11]

The main culprit of the decline of the textile industry in the 1920s was overcapacity. The textile industry grew greatly from 1870 to 1914, increasing from 956 to 1,287 mills.[12] During this period, the textile industry expanded to meet demand. By the time of World War I, however, further expansion was no longer necessary to keep up with consumer demand or even to meet the nation's war needs. One textile economist pointed out that "during the war . . . the needs of the country for cotton textiles was met, not by building new mills, but by operating existing mills day and night."[13] When the war ended, many southern mills continued to operate their night shifts. The use of night shifts actually increased to 43 percent of southern mills after 1924.[14] Mills continued the night shift to spread the fixed costs of production, including welfare costs, over a greater volume of products in an attempt to increase the profit margin.[15] Yet attempting to squeeze additional profit from production by night work only contributed to overcapacity in the market.

Nights shifts could create hardships for workers. Cannon Mills worker Glenn Kanipe and his wife Della both worked nights. As with so many of the Cannon Mills workers, Glenn had moved off of the farm and to Kannapolis to work in the mill. He believed that life in the mill village had distinct advantages over life on the farm. He rented a three-room house, which had both electricity and running water, from the company. Few farm homes of the period had these conveniences. Glenn met Della in the mill, married, and had a daughter named Katharine. Many married mill operatives worked opposite shifts to take care of children, yet this was not the case with the Kanipes. Both worked the night shift and took their daughter to Della's mother during the week, and the couple had her on the weekends. They paid Della's mother $7.50 every two weeks to care for Katharine.[16]

Besides night shifts, mills used scientific management, particularly after 1924, to squeeze more profit out of production. Scientific management in the textile industry focused on three goals: the elimination of wasted time, greater output at lower costs, and increased uniformity and quality of the product.[17] The Southern Textile Bulletin, a leading industry periodical, espoused the use of scientific management to improve efficiency:

> In these days of closer competition, and higher prices for labor and raw materials, many of our leading mills are taking measures to prevent unnecessary wastes. . . . Every process must be chiselled and carved into economic shape. The man who can prevent the most losses, and manufacture in the most economical manner, will be sure to outsell his less expert competitor, and bag a big share of the game.[18]

An important element of the efficiency movement in the mills was the introduction of new machinery to increase production and lower labor costs. During the 1920s and early 1930s, several new machines promised to improve production in various departments of the industry. The Barber-Colman Company introduced a new set of spooler and warpers that ran at higher speeds than older machinery, thereby reducing labor costs by almost half. To improve efficiency in the weave room, the Veeder-Root Company built weave room monitors to record the production of individual looms. An advertisement in 1929 called this device the "all-seeing eye in the weave room."[19]

Perhaps even more fundamental to the modernization of the textile industry were the improvements in the use of electrical power during this period. Mills moved away from the use of one large steam engine to power many machines and turned to the use of individual electric motors, such as those supplied by General Electric and Westinghouse, to power each machine. While this system of providing power entailed many new costs, the benefit was immediately apparent. No longer did the failure of a single engine halt production for many machines. Dan River Mills experienced a 20 percent reduction of unit costs in its weave room after implementing this change in power distribution. In addition, the Southern Power Company advocated the use of load meters to help in monitoring the production of individual machines.[20]

Scientific management had three effects on the operatives. First, mills let some workers go because machines replaced them. Laid-off workers often found jobs demanding less skill and pay than the ones they had earlier. Second, for those workers who remained, management increased their work load. Operatives complained about not being able to keep up with the machines and work speed assigned to them. In addition, workers went home extremely tired from their shift. Constant fatigue and frustration infected most textile villages. And third, the introduction of new machines reduced the needed skills of the work force. New machines took over the tasks of skilled workers, forcing skilled operatives into the ranks of the semiskilled. Historian Jacquelyn Hall noted that "hundreds of weavers . . . lost their jobs or were demoted to less-skilled and lower paid positions" once mill owners installed new textile machinery.[21]

Operatives opposed the changes of scientific management and despised efficiency experts. Worker control over their jobs and the speed of work was slipping away from them. For second-generation mill workers, the changes were hard enough to keep up with, but for operatives recently off the farm, it was almost impossible.[22] Workers sought ways to reassert their influence over the work environment, but the hard economic times and a large labor pool for mill owners to draw from stymied their efforts. Frustration led to a rise in labor militancy.

Foreign competition, especially from Japan, posed another problem for the textile industry during this period. American textile exports peaked in 1922 and then declined through the mid-1930s. Japanese competition was particularly severe in the markets of the Philippines and Latin America. In America's best textile market, the Philippines, U.S. imports fell from "67 percent of market in 1933 to 40 percent in 1934, while Japanese imports rose during the same period from 23 to 52 percent of the total."[23]

Besides threatening America's best overseas textile markets, Japanese textile imports to the United States also grew at an alarming rate. In cotton velveteens, the Japanese had secured about 21 percent of the American market by the mid-1930s. They also took advantage of gaps in the American tariff schedules, especially in bleached cloth, which was unprotected by tariffs. In this market, Japanese imports rose to 37 percent of the American market during the same period.[24]

To counter the problems plaguing American textiles, industry leaders sought recovery by increasing demand through price reduction and rationalization.[25] Utility fabrics, such as towels and sheets, were more sensitive to wear than price. Consumers replaced towels and sheets when they wore out. Sales did not increase demand, which were closely associated with population growth, but shifted the time of purchase. Innovative textile firms sought to increase demand for these products, beyond the increasing size of the population, by introducing style into the utility category and changing their use.[26]

The Cannon Manufacturing Company under Charles Cannon used advertising and marketing to bring fashion to towels. In 1924, Cannon offered towels that were still white but with colored borders. By 1927, home fashions for the bathroom incorporated sinks, bathtubs, and toilets in matching colors. Textile manufacturers made colorful rugs and bath mats to match the new color fixtures. Cannon began manufacturing color towels to match the new colors appearing in the modern bathroom. The firm became the leader in producing color towels and held the "first towel style show" in its New York office in 1929.[27]

Cannon also increased towel sales through making towels a display item. Display, in fact, became an important function of towels as bathroom decor now included towels for display only or for occasional use by guests. To increase the sale of display towels, manufacturers encouraged consumers to change bathroom towels to match their moods or to exhibit their creativity. The other road to recovery, rationalization, held more promise for recovery of the textile industry. Rationalization involved such things as horizontal integration, vertical integration, controls in selling, economies of large-scale merchandising, and diversification in marketing. For advocates of rationalization, mills with the greatest chance of succeeding in hard times were the ones that most closely implemented the various elements of rationalization.[28]

Horizontal integration, the merger of mills producing the same or similar products, had two advantages. It eliminated competition and could bring more profit to the firm. If the merged mills controlled enough of the market, they could raise their prices which encouraged smaller mills to follow suit and thus bring larger profits to all mills.[29]

Another means of cutting costs, vertical integration, entailed the controlling of all or nearly all of the processes involved in the production of a finished product. Manufacturers could reduce costs by controlling cotton buying, spinning, weaving, finishing, and sales through the company's own selling house. By this period, certain specialized areas of the textile industry were highly integrated, including mills producing blankets, towels, sheets, and bedspreads.[30]

Another method of rationalization was increasing the size of individual units or increasing the size of the mills. This was done partly to increase output and to spread the overhead costs over more units of production. In addition, there were financial benefits to larger size. Bigger mills could borrow money more easily than smaller mills. Also, larger mills obtained better interest rates and could market their securities more easily. Proven management usually marked the larger textile firms and they usually had a record of financial soundness.[31]

Diversification represented another means of rationalization. During this period, some mills, such as Cannon Mills and the Pepperell Manufacturing Company, expanded the range of their products. This diversification in marketing and manufacturing protected firms from losses when the market slackened for one particular product.[32] The larger and better capitalized organizations were usually the ones most able to take advantage of diversification in marketing.

Beyond individual mill efforts to promote stability, the momentum increased for industry-wide cooperation. The formation of the Cotton Textile Institute (CTI) in 1926 was an important step toward rationalizing the industry and attempting to work on the problems of the industry

TABLE 1
Officers of Various Cannon Family Mills, c. 1918

Mill	Cannon Family Member	Office
Cannon Manufacturing Co.	Martin Luther	President
	Charles Albert	Vice president
	James William	Secretary and treasurer
Cabarrus Cotton Mills	James William	President
	Junius Ross	Vice president
	Martin Luther	Secretary and treasurer
Kesler Manufacturing Co.	James William	President
	Joseph Franklin	Vice president
Barringer Manufacturing Co.	James William Jr.	President
	Charles Albert	Vice president
Tuscarora Cotton Mills	James Williams	President
Amazon Cotton Mills	Joseph Franklin	President
	James William	Vice president
Wiscassett Mills Co.	James William	President
	Joseph Franklin	Treasurer
Efird Manufacturing Co.	James William	President
Social Circle Cotton Mills	Martin Luther	President
	James William	Vice President
Gibson Manufacturing Co.	James William	President
Patterson Manufacturing Co.	James William	President
	Martin Luther	Vice president
Imperial Cotton Mills	James William	President
	James William Jr.	Vice president
	Martin Luther	Secretary and treasurer
Franklin Cotton Mills	James William	President
	Charles Albert	Vice president and secretary
	Eugene Thomas	Treasurer

Source: "Cannon Mills," n.d., Information Series, Box 1, Cannon Mills Collection.

cooperatively. The CTI, however, differed from previous organizations in its nature and scope. Earlier associations had been mostly dinner clubs and loose associations of textile mills. These textile dinner clubs dated from 1865, when the New England Cotton Manufacturers' Association appeared. Other associations included the Arkwright Club (1880), the Southern and Western Manufacturers' Association (1885), and the Southern Cotton Spinners' Association (1897). In 1906, the New England Cotton Manufacturers' Association became the National Association of Cotton Manufacturers, and the Southern Cotton Spinners' Association changed its name to the American Cotton Manufacturers Association in 1903. These two associations were the dominant textile organizations by the decade of the 1920s, and state associations assisted them. The CTI developed more income, members, and authority to coordinate the industry than any previous association.[33]

Established on October 20, 1926, the CTI became a nonprofit corporation whose members paid dues and voted on institute policies. Its bureaucratic structure consisted of a president, executive committee, and board of directors. The institute was a nonpolitical organization whose main purpose was to gain the support of mills to work cooperatively on the problems of the industry. Political concerns of the industry were left to the state associations.[34]

The CTI sought to stabilize the textile industry through a three-part strategy. First, an open-price plan encouraged members to share statistics on production, prices, unfilled orders, and inventory on hand. The institute believed that the sharing of information would allow its members to decide accurate production rates and would help end overcapacity in the industry.[35] The second part of the plan was to spread standardized cost-accounting methods throughout the textile industry. Accurate cost accounting, the CTI believed, would assist mills in knowing their exact costs of production and discourage them from unknowingly selling goods under cost. In addition, the shared information of the open-price plan would show members that other mills were not operating at lower costs and would discourage cut-throat price competition.[36] Part three involved research into new uses for textiles to increase demand. The institute created the New Uses Division to expand demand for American textile products at home and abroad.[37] Thus the three-part strategy went further and was more aggressive than activities of previous textile associations.

On October 16, 1929, at the Cotton Textile Institute's annual convention, the gap in plans and reality became evident. Stability in the industry, however, remained illusive. Overcapacity continued to be a persistent problem. In addition, despite a massive recruiting campaign, a third of the textile manufacturers had not joined the organization. Large firms such as Cannon Mills, Bibb Manufacturing Company in Georgia, and Avondale Mills in Alabama eventually joined the CTI.[38] The institute, however, did represent the greatest effort, to date, of the members of the industry collectively to deal with their common problems. Although it was not totally effective during this period, the CTI provided a means for common action and represented the best effort of the industry to deal with overcapacity.[39]

Evolution of CANNON & Device Trademark
as Evidenced by Registration Certificates

Reg. No. 100,501
Oct. 20, 1914

Reg. No. 111,711
Aug. 1, 1916

Reg. No. 147,948
Nov. 8, 1921

Reg. No. 200,629
July 7, 1925

Amendment to Reg. No. 147,948
June 20, 1961

Cannon trademarks. Courtesy of the Kannapolis History Associates.

While cooperating with the CTI, Charles Cannon worked diligently to keep his firm profitable. Cannon turned to advertising to increase brand loyalty and sales. Actually, James W. Cannon began using advertising as early as 1907 by signing a contract with the advertising agency of N. W. Ayer and Son,[40] one of the oldest and largest advertising agencies in the United States.[41] J. W. started the firm's first advertising campaign by advertising in trade journals in 1920.[42]

Cannon's advertisement prominently displayed the firm's trademark as part of its effort to increase brand loyalty. The trademark, a "Cannoneer," was a clever play on the Cannon Manufacturing Company name. Later, a "Napoleon Howitzer" became the trademark that associated Cannon quality and commitment to its products.[43]

Charles Cannon expanded the firm's use of advertising after his father's death in 1921. He realized that the firm needed to advertise to reach markets other than the hotels, hospitals, and steam ships that its trade advertising reached. The firm needed to inform the household consumer of the company's new product lines and get the Cannon name before the public. In response to these needs, Cannon initiated the firm's first consumer advertising in 1924 in mass circulation magazines and immediately became the leading advertiser in the industry.[44]

While the Cannon Manufacturing Company worked to win the loyalty of consumers, the firm also followed the trend toward consolidation. The industry witnessed a wave of mergers and consolidations. Indeed, between 1918 and 1936, forty-three mergers and consolidations occurred. Several different types of consolidations exemplified the trend. Some mills consolidated under the control of a holding company that owned the majority stock in several mills, and others merged through the outright purchase of another mill. In any case, some consolidations were horizontal merger while others were vertical combination.[45] Of the forty-three mergers in the industry, seventeen involved an exchange of securities and no outside capital. Many of these consolidations required no outside funding occurring with mills already controlled by the same interest. The Cannon Mills consolidation of 1928 was an example of this type of consolidation.[46]

On June 4, 1928, the board of directors for the nine mills of the Cannon Group unanimously voted for the consolidation of their mills into the new Cannon Mills Company. Approval by the stockholders followed on July 5.[47] The new Cannon Mills Company was incorporated in North Carolina on July 6, 1928, with its headquarters in Kannapolis.[48] The new company paid the secretary of state's office $44,273 in charter tax, the second largest payment in state history.[49] According to the *Concord Daily Tribune*, the merger made the new firm "the largest textile concern in the South in point of capital represented, since the $20,899,700 capital represented in the nine companies is greater than the capitalization of any single mill in the South."[50]

The merger occurred with the "exchange of one million shares of Cannon Mills Company no-par common stock for the stock of the constituent companies. A small amount of preferred stock of the constituent companies was exchanged for preferred stock of the new company and then immediately retired."[51] The trustees of J. W. Cannon's estate sold 187,378 shares held by the estate to the public through the National City Company of New York,[52] and the new company began selling stock on the New York Stock Exchange in September 1928.[53]

Charles A. Cannon became president of the new firm. A. Luther Brown, Alexander R. Howard, John J. Barnhard, Charles E. Stevenson, William J. Swink, A. W. Fisher, and F. W. Williams became vice presidents. Gilbert B. Lewis became treasurer with T. T. Smith as assistant treasurer. F. J. Haywood was secretary with T. T. Smith and J. J. Boyle as assistant secretaries. The board of directors consisted of John J. Barnhardt, A. Luther Brown, Charles A. Cannon, Marin L. Cannon, Mary E. Cannon, George W. Fraker, Alexander R. Howard, Gilbert B. Lewis, Joseph P. Ripley, Charles E. Stevenson, and William J. Swink.[54]

An official of Cannon Manufacturing Company stated that the main reason for the merger was economy of operation. The mills could operate more efficiently under one set of officers and one board of directors. In addition, the larger firm would have more clout on the financial markets and a greater ability to expand markets for it products.[55]

Consolidation required reorganization of the individual mills. Management renamed the individual mills as new entities of the new firm, though they continued to manufacture the same goods. Management redesignated the nine mills as illustrated in table 2. The creation of the Cannon Mills Company represented a further application of the vertical integration begun by the founder. It brought greater cost savings in production, which could make the firm more competitive. To analyze the cost benefits of this merger, one must consider the nature of the textile industry.

Typically, the textile industry consisted of atomistic mills involved in one aspect of the production of a finished good. Raw cotton was sold to spinning mills that spun the cotton into yarn. The yarn was then sold to a yarn merchant who sold it to a weaving mill. The weaving mill would weave the

TABLE 2

New Plant designations in the Cannon Mills Company

New Plant No.	*Company*	*Product*
Plant 1	Cannon Manufacturing Co. (Kannapolis)	Cotton towels
Plant 2	Cannon Manufacturing Co. (Concord)	Cotton towels
Plant 3	Cannon Manufacturing Co. (York, S.C.)	Cotton towels
Plant 4	Cabarrus Cotton Mills	Tire fabrics, sheets
Plant 5	Cabarrus Cotton Mills (Concord)	Tire fabrics, sheets
Plant 6	Gibson Manufacturing Co. and Hobarton Manufacturing Co.	Dress goods, rayon fabrics, drapery fabrics, whipcords, madras fabrics, colored goods
Plant 7	Kesler Manufacturing Co.	Sheets, gray goods
Plant 8	Patterson Manufacturing Co.	Sheeting, armor cloth, gray goods
Plant 9	Franklin Cotton Mills, Inc.	NA
Plant 10	Norcott Mills Co.	Super-carded cotton yarns
Plant 11	Barringer Manufacturing Co.	Cotton yarns

Source: Letter of new plant designations, Oct. 3, 1928, Treasurers' Office Series, Box 42, Cannon Mills Collection; Sales of Common Stock Announcement, July 10, 1928, Treasurers' Office Series, Box 42, Cannon Mills Collection . The three mills of the Cannon Manufacturing Company were under the same management as the two mills of Cabarrus Cotton Mills, so the number of mills in the consolidation were counted at nine instead of twelve. In addition, the Cannon family controlled six other mills not in the merger: Amazon Cotton Mills of Thomasville, N.C.; Wiscassett Mills, Albemarle, N.C.; Tuscarora Cotton Mills, Mount Pleasant, N.C.; Bloomfield Manufacturing, Statesville, N.C.; Social Circle Cotton Mills, Social Circle, Ga.; and Imperial Cotton Mills, Eatonton, Ga. Kennedy, *Profits and Losses*, 117

yarn into an unfinished cloth known as gray goods. Then the weaving mill would sell its gray goods to a finishing merchant, who sold it to a finishing firm. The finishing firm, usually a bleachery, would finish the gray cloth and sell it to a converter.[56] The converter completed the stylist touches (anticipating changes in fashion was an important job of the converter)[57] then sold the goods to a commission or selling house that resold it to retailers.[58] The price of articles purchased by consumers in retail shops reflected the costs of this complicated process.

The 1928 merger of the Cannon concerns rationalized the process and cut costs for the new company in various ways, especially in towel production. Cannon Mills operated both spinning and weaving plants and thus did not deal with yarn merchants and avoided paying their commission fees. Cannon Mills operated a bleachery, too, which eliminated the need of contracting a finishing merchant or outside bleachery. Since the cutting or stylistic finishing of towels was simple, the firm trained employees for this process, eliminating the need to do business with converters or the cutting trades. Lastly, Cannon's own commission house sold its products to retailers, avoiding the necessity of dealing with outside selling agents.[59]

As noted by textile economist Claude Murchison, this type of vertical integration was a helpful step toward survival and profitability in the textile market of the 1920s:

> Placing under a single control all of the processes which are necessary to the production and sale of a finished product means for the textile industry not only an inauguration of constructive features . . . but also the elimination of those destructive characteristics which prevail throughout the industry.[60]

While much of the textile industry suffered greatly during the decade of the 1920s, the Cannon Group and later the Cannon Mills Company fared well (see table 3). At a time when many firms lost money, Cannon consistently made a profit and paid dividends. During this period, the number of textile firms that lost money was alarming. Almost half of all mills were losing money by the end of the decade. The gravity of the situation is illustrated in table 4. In contrast to the losses of much of the industry, the Cannon Group/Mills remained profitable during the difficulties of the 1920s. Several factors made the firm profitable, including Charles Cannon's leadership, the production of specialized products, and the pursuit of cost cutting through vertical integration.

The consolidation of the Cannon Group marked a turning point in the relationship between the Cannon family and the new company. Power became more concentrated in the hands of Charles Cannon, while other family members lost influence. In fact, the trend had started before the

TABLE 3

Profits for the Cannon Group/Cannon Mills, 1921–1929

	Year	Net Operating Profit
Cannon Group	1921	NA
	1922	$4,094,547
	1923	$3,562,552
	1924	$2,542,995
	1925	$3,621,959
	1926	$4,540,641
	1927	$3,963,912
Cannon Group/Cannon Mills Co.	1928	$2,412,231
Cannon Mills Co.	1929	$3,462,877

Source: Sales of Common Stock Announcement, July 10, 1928, Treasurers' Office Series, Box 42, Cannon Mills Collection; *Moody's*, 1930, 295.

TABLE 4

Textile Mill Reports to the Internal Revenue Service, 1921–1929

Year	Number of Companies Filing Tax Returns	Number of Companies Reporting a Loss
1921	862	392
1922	782	190
1923	745	177
1924	976	634
1925	NA	NA
1926	1,061	541
1927	998	308
1928	1,005	501
1929	925	420

Source: Backman and Gainsbrugh, *Economics*, 212.

1928 merger. By 1927, only Martin Luther, Charles, and Joseph Franklin remained active in the family textile interests. Junius Ross, Eugene Thomas, and James W. Jr. no longer held management positions at any of the family mills, although they probably continued to own stock. Charles served as an officer of nearly all of the companies. Martin Luther Cannon served on the board of directors of at least three of the mills, while Joe Franklin severed as a director of one. One of J.W.'s daughters, Mrs. David Blair, served as president and director of Wiscassett Mills.

With the creation of Cannon Mills Company, Charles became president and Martin Luther served as a director. In addition, Mrs. J. W. Cannon briefly became a director, while Joseph Franklin no longer served as an officer. Although fewer Cannons were now directly involved in the operation of Cannon Mills than in the Cannon Group, the consolidation concentrated power in Charles's hands as president of the new firm. In addition, Charles had great influence over the nonfamily officers of Cannon Mills, who were longtime associates with Charles in the various family mills.

As Charles Cannon settled in as the president of the new Cannon Mills Company, labor unrest again hit the textile industry. Union activity, which had declined after the strikes of 1921, reappeared in 1929. Strikes broke out in Elizabethton, Tennessee, and Gastonia and Marion, North Carolina. The first of the big three strikes occurred in Elizabethton on March 12, 1929, at two German-owned rayon plants. More than three thousand operatives struck over the implementation of the "stretch-out" (that is, increasing the amount and speed of work required of the labor force) and wage reductions. The union provided inadequate relief for the strikers and their families and the strike ended on May 26. Under the terms of an agreement negotiated by the Department of Labor, the company agreed not to discriminate against union workers, but after the firm resumed full operation, it blacklisted union members.[61]

The defeat of the union in Elizabethton did not deter workers in Gastonia from walking out on strike. Absentee ownership was also involved in Gastonia, where a Rhode Island firm owned and operated the Loray Mill. Operatives struck on April 1, when the company fired five union members following a series of wage cuts. Instead of being organized by the AFL-affiliated UTW, the communist National Textile Workers Union (NTWU) organized the striking workers. At the request of the mill, the governor, O. Max Gardner, ordered five companies of the state militia to Gastonia. The situation quickly escalated to violence when most strikers violated a court injunction and police arrested them. Law enforcement personnel arrested more than a hundred operatives after a skirmish that resulted in the death of the police chief, O. F. Aderholt. The strike soon ended after pro-mill forces shot and killed striker Ella May Wiggins. A court convicted seven union members of Aderholt's murder, and the police were cleared of any wrongdoing. The affair destroyed the NTWU as an effective union in the South.[62]

The last major strike of the decade was in Marion, North Carolina. As with the two previous strikes, the mill involved, Marion Manufacturing Company, had an absentee owner. Management badly botched the introduction of a stretch-out plan that cost the firm forty thousand dollars in losses. Management required workers to work an additional twenty minutes a day to make up for the loss. The UTW sent an organizer from Elizabethton and informed the operatives that little financial assistance would come from the union. The workers struck anyway after the mill fired twenty-two operatives for union activity. A second Marion mill fired one hundred union activists and locked out the work force. The mills obtained an injunction against union pickets, and the governor sent in the state militia. Strikers and mill management came to a gentleman's agreement, setting a fifty-five-hour work week (at lower pay) and guaranteeing nondiscrimination against union members.

After the mills refused to rehire some union members, operatives struck again. When strikers refused to stop picketing the plants, Sheriff Oscar F. Adkins used tear gas to disperse the crowd. When an operative attacked the sheriff, deputies fired into the strikers, killing six and wounding eighteen. The governor ordered an inquiry into the incident handled by Judge W. F. Harding, who tried the sheriff and fourteen deputies for murder. A jury acquitted the law enforcement officers, and the strike ended when the mills evicted more union members from company housing. The Marion Baptist Church purged its rolls of strikers.[63] Except for less dramatic labor disputes in Pineville, Charlotte, Bessemer City, Draper, and Lexington, North Carolina, the Marion strike ended labor activity for the decade with another crushing defeat.[64]

While strikes took place in various parts of the state, workers in the Cannon Mills Company plants did not strike. There were several reasons for this. First, veteran Cannon workers remembered how decisively Charles Cannon had crushed the strike of 1921. Older workers retold the tale of that strike to younger operatives. The blacklisting and evictions of union members undoubtedly left a strong impression on the work force.

Another factor was the presence of Charles Cannon. The three large strikes had one common element: absentee ownership. German or northern concerns owned the mills at Elizabethton, Marion, and Gastonia. A family or paternalistic atmosphere did not exist at these mills as it did at Cannon. When management of these firms instituted the stretch-out and other efficiency measures that operatives believed threatened their working conditions and pay, the workers were less restrained by the bonds of southern paternalism. On the other hand, with Charles Cannon living in Concord, working in Kannapolis, and active in management of the company, Cannon Mills operatives were under the spell of a strong paternalistic ethos. The welfare work, loyalty banquets, and various other programs fostered the feeling of a company family. To oppose the company was to oppose Charles Cannon personally. While welfare work did not win the hearts of all Cannon workers, some undoubtedly remained loyal to "Uncle Charlie."[65]

Another reason workers did not strike against Cannon Mills is that the financial position of the company was more secure than that of many others in the industry. Cannon's textile empire experienced times of curtailment in production and short weeks, but it made a profit during the entire decade of the 1920s because of several reasons. Charles Cannon provided aggressive leadership. He pushed brand loyalty of Cannon products, especially towels, pioneered by his father. Charles accomplished a remarkable degree of brand loyalty by undertaking the industry's most extensive and aggressive advertising. Spending more on advertising than any other textile company during the period, the Cannon brand became more visible and established customer loyalty.

In addition, many of Cannon's products were specialty items that required special looms. These looms, especially for towels and tire fabric, were expensive and in limited supply. A mill producing other goods would think twice before shifting to these specialty products. Thus, the availability and cost of machinery limited Cannon's competition in specialty goods, especially towels.[66]

Although Charles had been successful managing the family mill interests, future success was not assured. Business historian Alfred D. Chandler Jr. noted two dangers when family companies grow into large national firms. Family control and management can delay or slow needed change, reorganization, and diversification. Family insiders often viewed young professionals, especially engineers, as outsiders to the company family and did not give full consideration to their suggestions. A further danger was that family remained involved in the daily operations of manufacturing and marketing long after the corporation had grown too large for such management to be efficient.[67]

Charles Cannon, however, did not realize the problems inherent with family control of the firm or of the weaknesses of the paternalistic management system. He had learned how to manage the paternalistic mill village from his father and would devote more energy to its maintenance. Indeed, Charles expanded the paternalism of Kannapolis far beyond what James had created.

CHAPTER 7

———————•◦⋈◦•———————

PATERNALISM EXPANDED:
Charles Cannon and Welfare Work

With Cannon Manufacturing Company under the leadership of Charles Cannon, the firm expanded its welfare work. Labor historian Stuart Brandes defined welfare work, or welfare capitalism, as "any service provided for the comfort or improvement of employees which was neither a necessity of the industry nor required by law."[1] Brandes believed that industrialists initiated welfare work for three reasons. First, altruism motivated some employers. Second, employers wished to get more control over their employees to make them better workers. If the programs begun by the employer made the workers more efficient and loyal, then welfare capitalism was an investment in personnel that resulted in a direct economic benefit for the employer. Third, employers used company programs to battle unions. They believed that by offering programs and fringe benefits advocated by unions, firms could blunt the attractiveness of unions and avoid unionization.[2]

James W. Cannon had laid the foundation of welfare work, or welfare capitalism, at the Cannon Manufacturing Company. Housing, education, and recreation, as mentioned earlier, received his attention. He was also interested in employee health. In 1917, the county health department began offering typhoid shots to the residents of Cabarrus County. The mill owner convinced the health department to offer the vaccinations to all Cannon employees in the county.[3] Charles continued and expanded the welfare work instituted by his father. In 1923 some mills of Concord, including the Cannon Manufacturing Company, employed a Metropolitan Life Insurance

TABLE 5

Mills' Contributions to Churches, 1928

Mills	Churches	Amount
Gibson and Hobarton Manufacturing Cos.	McGill St. Baptist Church	$50.00
	Kerr St. Methodist Church	$50.00
	Bayliss Memorial Presby.	$50.00
	Protestant Methodist	$50.00
	Calvary Lutheran Church	$50.00
Franklin Cotton Mills	Westford Methodist Church ($41.66 paid monthly to Rev. A. R. Bell through office payroll)	$500.00
	West Concord Baptist	$50.00
Norcott Mills Co.	West Concord Baptist	$50.00
Kesler Manufacturing Co.	Park Avenue Methodist	$100.00
Patterson Manufacturing Co.	China Grove Methodist	$100.00

Sources: G. B. Lewis to C. A. Cannon, letter titled "Welfare," Box 195, Gifts to Churches, etc., 1925–32, Charles A. Cannon Collection. This letter lists the mills as numbered plants, the new designations after the consolidation. Conversion to the older mills' names was made using a company memo converting the mills' names to the new plant designations. Cannon Mills Company, Treasurers' Office Series, Box 42, Cannon Mills Collection.

nurse. Besides seeing patients for illnesses, the Metropolitan nurse also conducted classes for mill operatives in health and hygiene. The Metropolitan nurse worked under the auspices of the county health department.[4]

Augmenting the work of the county and Metropolitan nurses, the county health department also employed a tuberculosis nurse. Charles Cannon understood that mill operatives were especially susceptible to tuberculosis because of the nature of mill work, indoor work with long shifts and limited circulation of fresh air. Cannon and his companies supported the work of the tuberculosis nurse by contributing to the Cabarrus County Tuberculosis Nurse Fund. The Cannon Manufacturing Company contributed three hundred dollars per year. Cannon served with the Cabarrus County Tuberculosis Association and routinely contributed three hundred dollars yearly during this period.[5]

The company took additional actions to promote the health of its employees. Replacing the work of the Metropolitan nurse, the firm created a medical department in 1928. As the company put more resources into its own medical staff, it ceased support for the Metropolitan nurse and became one of North Carolina's leaders in industrial medicine. Eventually, the medical department grew to a staff of fifty employees with three physicians.[6]

Charles Cannon did not confine welfare work to employee medical care. He continued his father's practice of supplementing pastors' salaries from mill coffers (see table 5). Reasons for supporting churches varied. Both J. W. and Charles Cannon were devoted church members. The Cannons may have believed that by giving to area churches, they were improving the spiritual life of the community and their workers. They believed that operatives who attended church regularly made better workers, as family stability, sobriety, and respect for civil leadership were usual messages of the churches and wholeheartedly supported by the industrialists.

Industrialists could also work through the churches to affect public issues to their advantage. One such issue in Concord was prohibition. Both the Odells in the Methodist community and the Cannons in the Presbyterian community worked through their churches to bring prohibition to Concord. Prohibition was a popular issue among industrialists because workers with drinking problems lowered productivity. In addition, the prohibition crusade gave the impression that the Cannons were progressive "entrepreneurs with a community vision."[7]

Paternalism and social control were also elements of church welfare work. While mill owners who gave to area churches seemed to be community benefactors, they also used churches as another means of social control. The term "social control" was first used by Edward A. Ross in 1901 to refer to the means by which one segment of society could exert control over another segment of society. Ross believed that forces beyond that of law and the police—such "instruments of control as public opinion, suggestion, personal ideal, social religion, art and social valuation"—helped maintain that control. Social control involved the use and regulation of education, work, leisure, and opinion to mold the lower class (working class) into the image of the dominant class (industrial class). Industrialists used churches as instruments of social control and to lend legitimacy to the status quo.[8]

Building on Ross's work, sociologist Liston Pope examined how the mill owners of Gastonia, North Carolina, used churches for maintaining the status quo. As in Concord and Kannapolis, mill owners in Gastonia built churches and subsidized pastors' salaries. Pope asserted that the churches in Gastonia were largely agents of the status quo. Never did they seriously question the power or economic structure of the mill town. Of course, many pastors acted out of economic self-interest, yet Pope was careful to note several reasons for supporting the status quo. Most churches experienced a rapid turnover in pastors, with a majority of pastors staying only three to five years. Having lived in the community a short time, most ministers realized they did not have the social capital to confront the prevailing social and economic structure. In addition, the ministers were overwhelmingly conservative, with little taste for the social gospel. Sermons focused on doctrine and spiritual life rather than the earthly concerns of the world. Most ministers believed that it was not their role to become directly involved in battling any evils of the economic structure and that they could best ameliorate economic woes by changing the hearts of the individuals through salvation.[9] Charles Cannon effectively used the churches of Kannapolis to quell labor unrest and to maintain the status quo, but the churches of the economically diverse town of Concord were less effective in that area.

Since mill churches maintained the status quo, they were bulwarks of community stability. Paternalism, or social control, operated best in stable, predictable environments. Welfare work helped maintain stability and provided "a response to the businessman's demand for a more systematic approach to labor problems."[10]

Charles Cannon also expanded the operation of the Kannapolis YMCA. The first YMCA was constructed in 1908 and enlarged in 1925. After the death of James Cannon, the YMCA was named for him. On December 20, 1937, the "Y" caught fire and a new YMCA was built and opened in 1940 to serve thirteen thousand members. The YMCA had a swimming pool, library, barber shop, reading room, gym, and the only theater in town until 1936. Many youth participated in organized sports, such as basketball, boxing, and baseball, at the Y. In addition, the Y offered a summer camp near Old Fort, North Carolina, and the textile company paid for transportation to Camp Elliot.[11] C. M. Deal Jr. spent much of his youth at the YMCA when not working. He often read in the reading room and later in life stated that the "YMCA saved me from destruction."[12]

The Cannons placed great importance on loyalty and used welfare work as a means to acquire and maintain worker loyalty. They held annual banquets for workers. Late in 1921, after Charles crushed the strike, the Cannon Manufacturing Company held a banquet for loom fixers, weave room second hands, and weave room overseers. An orchestra and quartet provided music and a speaker addressed the crowd on "Every Day Efficiency." The cuisine included oyster cocktail, chicken consommé, and North Carolina spring turkey. After a dessert of ice cream, waiters gave guests cigars and cigarettes. Clearly, for most of the 221 operatives who attended, this was the most formal affair they had ever experienced.[13]

The loyalty banquets also recognized workers who had been with Cannon Mills for their length of service, starting at twenty-five years. Aline Caudle attended one of these banquets:

> One day someone come around asking all the hands how long they had worked at Cannon Mills. Course nobody knew why such a question was being asked and some of the hands was afeared to tell how long they had worked. Well, I wasn't; when they asked me I said "thirty year" and was proud of it. Several days after that they sent for me to go to the office; "boys," I said to myself, ["]they're a-going to fire me now.["] When I went in the office Mr. there says "Miss [Caudle], you've worked for the Cannon Company for thirty year, ain't you?" and I said "Yes Sir, Mr., that's right." Then he said "We're a-having a big supper up at Kannapolis on Friday night for them that's worked twenty-five year or more for the company and here's your ticket.["] When the day come for the supper Rose Panell come down here to go with me because they was sending a car for us two. Hit was held up in Mary Ella Hall in Kannapolis. You went into a great big room, furnished jest as nice as you'd want, and they had a man who didn't do nothing but take your had and coat when you come in and hang 'em up fer you. I thought we would kill ourselves laughing and Rose kept a-wondering if we'd get the right coats and hats back. The other room where we was to eat looked as pretty as anything you ever saw. Such a sight of tables—and every one was covered all over and down at the sides with some of that white cloth that was finished down in the Bleachery; and there was flower pots set about on them. I didn't think they'd have much to eat for such a crowd, but the tables was covered. They had turkey and everything; hit was real good. Yes, they had speeches. Charles Cannon made a fine speech and give out the pins to us. He told about the way young'uns used to stand on the boxes to work—the way I done.[14]

These loyalty banquets continued through the 1970s.[15]

The paternalism that emerged in Kannapolis was multifaceted and complex. Sociologist Cynthia Anderson noted that Cannon "controlled the production process with vertical integration, and they controlled workers through workplace and community power structures. Owner power in the locality was reinforced by conditions of the labor market, the workers' economic dependence, and their lack of geographical mobility."[16] There were certainly benefits to living and working in Kannapolis. Mill houses were nicer than most farm homes. Life in the mill village was better for many than life on the farm. Why else would so many have moved from the farm to Kannapolis? A family atmosphere was prevalent in the village. Charles Cannon took care of his workers and their families. Kannapolis resident Paul Kearns reminisced that

> a benevolent paternalism set unrecorded standards and used company power to enforce them. We could leave our doors unlocked during the day and walk our street day or night without fear. We enjoyed the benefits of home maintenance, entertainment, maintenance of community infrastructure, advanced educational programs, and health care.[17]

Yet thinking back as an older man, Kearns wondered,

> Was it worth it? I understand and appreciate the wisdom and benevolence of company officials, and also regret that many workers spent their lives as subjects of the company. I wish workers had more pay, retirement funds, and representation in decision-making for the community. Things might have been better.[18]

The success of the Cannon Group's welfare work in securing the loyalty of its work force was mixed. Welfare work did please some operatives and gained from them a measure of loyalty, but for a large group of operatives, welfare work was not enough to secure their loyalty. The strike of 1921 highlighted the deep dissatisfaction among many workers.[19]

For some workers, welfare work represented an element of coercion. Especially in Kannapolis, the influence of the Cannon family and their companies seemed omnipresent. Indeed, the Cannon family, or its companies, owned the entire town and influenced practically everything that happened within it. From living in company housing, attending company supported churches, sending children to company schools, and participating in company recreational events, a worker could not be free of Cannon influence and control. This omnipresent nature of the family and company led to ambivalence among some operatives toward company welfare work. Despite continuing efforts by Charles Cannon and the Cannon Group with welfare work, some workers would continue to show their dissatisfaction and worked to unionize the mills.

CHAPTER 8

---❖◆❖---

THE GREAT DEPRESSION, THE NEW DEAL, AND CANNON MILLS

With the stock market crash of October 1929, a general and prolonged economic depression settled on the nation. The Great Depression brought worsening conditions for the textile industry. Demand for textile products dropped and more mills reported losses. Four hundred and twenty firms lost money in 1929; 686 did so in 1930. Total industry losses for the same period increased from $32,550,000 to $101,100,000.[1]

The textile industry tried desperately to ride out the Depression. Manufacturers' margins decreased from approximately 16 percent in 1930 to 8 percent in 1932.[2] Cotton mill dividends dropped from 4 percent in 1930 to almost 2 percent in 1932.[3] Worst of all were the profit statements. From 1930 to 1932, as illustrated by Bureau of Internal Revenue reports, most mills noted losses (see table 6).

In North Carolina, the Depression affected cotton mills that had already been ailing for a decade. Some continued to run two shifts, attempting to squeeze every bit of cost saving from production, while other mills ran short time or closed for periods. According to North Carolina textile historian Brent Glass, maximum wages dropped. Malnutrition and pellagra became acute in some mill villages, and the number of married women working in the mills increased, where work was available, to help make ends meet.[4]

Other industries in the state also felt the effects of the economic downturn, and state revenues fell as a result. North Carolina had $2.5 million in short-term bonds due with a group of New York banks but lacked the funds

TABLE 6
Textile Mill Income Reported to the Bureau
of Internal Revenue

Year	Firms Reporting No Net Income	Percentage of Total Firms
1930	686	76.4
1931	637	73.7
1932	628	75.31

Source: Backman and Gainsbrugh, Economics, 211.

to pay the obligation. Governor O. Max Gardner and a delegation from the state went to New York to ask for an extension, a request that the New York group turned down. The bankers were influenced by news of the default and scandals at banks in Asheville and the low rating of Buncombe County bonds. After meeting with the banking group, the governor happened to meet Charles Cannon, who was in New York City on business. Learning from the governor of the bond problem, Cannon said, "The principle [sic] bank you're dealing with just happens to be the Cannon Mills bank. Maybe I can help you. I'll stay up here tonight instead of going home as planned, meet you in the morning, and we'll go back to the bank together and see what we can do."[5]

The next day, the North Carolina delegation and Charles Cannon met with the New York bankers. Cannon asked that the state receive an extension on its notes, and the banks promptly refused. The businessman then reminded his company's bank that Cannon Mills had adequate funds on deposit to handle the state's obligation, and he threatened to assume the state's obligation if the banking group did not renew the notes. The banks immediately agreed to renew the bonds. For his help in this crisis, the governor and council of state awarded Charles Cannon a resolution of appreciation on February 1, 1932.[6]

Despite such terrible economic conditions in the state, Cannon Mills made a profit during those hard early years of the Depression. Profits for 1930 were almost half of what they were in 1929—$1,831,704—and from there they continued to flounder. They increased to $2,274,784 in 1931 but fell to a precarious $612,095 in 1932.[7] Doubtless, without the cost benefits of the vertical integration of 1928, Cannon Mills would have been in the red during this period. The decline in profits required a decrease in quarterly dividends from seventy cents per share in April 1929 to forty cents in June

1930.[8] Despite the industry-wide downturn, Cannon continued the tried-and-true formula that had worked so well in the 1920s: advertising its brand, modernization, and working with the trade associations to rationalize the industry.

The decline in sales and profits did prompt the company to cut its advertising budget. Expenditures for towel advertising fell from $321,640 in 1929 to $230,970 in 1930.[9] To validate its advertising expenditures, Cannon conducted a test of its brand name in 1930. Seven department stores participated in the survey by displaying unbranded and branded Cannon towels equally and pricing both the same. Saleswomen showed no partiality in assisting customers with the towels. The results of the survey revealed that customers preferred branded Cannon towels four to one over unbranded towels.[10]

For Charles Cannon, and other company officials, this survey demonstrated that their efforts to build brand name loyalty through advertising were successful and that advertising should continue even in the depths of the Depression. Advertising expenditures increased thirty-three thousand in 1931. Cannon Mills completed a second brand-name study in 1932; the customer preference test again pitted Cannon branded towels against unbranded towels, but this time Cannon towels were priced 10 percent above their rivals' price. Again, Cannon towels outsold competing unbranded towels. In this preference test the margin was 3.6 to 1 in favor of the Cannon brand.[11]

Advertising expenditures continued in the $220,000 to $250,000 range from 1932 through 1935.[12] The company remained committed to advertising the brand and worked closely with store linen departments. Their efforts evidently bore fruit because 1936 sales increased to $38,302,900 and profits rose to $5,587,600.[13] The advertising budget for towels grew between 1935 and 1941 as the sales of Cannon towels increased. Towel sales grew from $19,061,842 in 1935 to $35,721,980 in 1941.[14] Expenditures for towel advertising grew consistently from $245,665 in 1935 to $336,880 in 1941.[15]

While committed to advertising, Cannon Mills took other measures to maintain profitability. Not long after the company's board of directors cut the quarterly dividend in 1930, it also cut the salaries of the firm's officers. Charles Cannon's 1928 salary as president of the newly formed Cannon Mills Company had been forty thousand dollars, and twenty-four thousand from Cannon Mills, Inc. In 1931, the board reduced his salary as president of the firm to twenty-five thousand dollars, along with reductions for most officers. Another series of board-approved reductions occurred in 1933 after the low profits of 1932. Not until profits improved in 1933 and 1934 did the board institute a modest salary increase for the officers of Cannon Mills.[16]

Charles Cannon refused, however, to reduce expenditures on plant modernization. In fact, Cannon believed that a depressed market required the most modern machinery to improve efficiency of production and maximize profit, lessons he had learned from his father. Thus in 1933, after the company's worst year, the board of directors appropriated eighty-nine thousand dollars for new warping units and almost two million dollars to replace two hundred thousand old spindles.[17] Two years later, the company spent almost seven hundred thousand dollars on new machinery, an addition to Plant 4, and a new office for the shipping department.[18] In 1936, the textile manufacturer again purchased new equipment and made physical improvements in the plants. Equipment purchased included new spinning machinery, new equipment for the bleachery, two hundred new looms, and fifteen thousand new spindles. Physical improvements included an addition to the finishing department, an addition to the finishing goods warehouse, and additions to Plant 1, Mill 6.[19] The last series of Depression-era improvements came in 1939, when the board appropriated $1,013,500 for new equipment.[20] Evidently, the updating of the Cannon plants with new equipment helped keep the firm profitable because it was one of the few textile companies that did not lose money during the Depression.[21]

The third element of Cannon's plan for weathering the Depression was to work with trade associations and the federal government to rationalize the textile industry. Charles Cannon worked with the Cotton Textile Institute to limit production and stabilize the industry on the national level. On the state level, he served as first vice president of the Cotton Manufactures' Association of North Carolina, which lobbied for favorable state legislation.[22]

Some mill owners suggested that the industry should do more than limit the hours of production. Some CTI members wanted to combine a reduction of the work week with the elimination of night work for women and employment of minors. In 1931, President Herbert Hoover invited fifteen of the industry's most prominent manufacturers, including Charles Cannon, to the White House to discuss such a plan. Although the mill men could not agree on a proposal, the president encouraged the textile leaders to continue to work cooperatively on the industry's problems.[23]

Charles Cannon and five other manufacturers decided to go ahead with their own plan. This group announced that "the industry should voluntarily take steps to shorten the hours of employment in many localities which are now operating their mills long hours, that women and young people should be gradually eliminated from night work and night work in general discouraged." Furthermore, these six manufacturers advocated measures to implement these ideas.[24]

The CTI immediately supported the statement issued by the six manufacturers. Their recommendation, the institute believed, would help reduce overcapacity in the industry and serve as an important public relations tool. The humanitarian aspects of eliminating night work for women and minors would improve the industry's image and smooth relations with the federal government. If the CTI could convince its members to support the night work proposal, an idea that most members had denounced in the past, then the industry would present an improved and progressive image. The Hoover administration also favored the proposal.[25]

Building on the six manufacturers' proposal, CTI officers drew up a plan that became known as the "55-50 plan." This plan advocated that the industry limit the work week to fifty-five hours on day shifts and fifty hours on night shifts and eliminate overtime. Unfortunately, the proposal did not take into account the realities of northern mills. There were no night shifts there, and female employment was already prohibited by state law. In addition, state laws limited the maximum work week to forty-eight hours. Clearly the plan dealt was intended only for the most troubled sector of the industry, the South.[26]

After the CTI announced the 55-50 plan in February 1930, it immediately put pressure on members to accept the program and began working on adequate enforcement. It sent subscription forms to its members and urged compliance. Resembling a written contract, the subscription forms committed each mill to the guidelines of the 55-50 plan. Charles Cannon and his board of directors approved it on April 8, 1930.[27] Despite some industry holdouts, the institute reported in 1932 that 82 percent of the nation's mills were following the plan and 89 percent of the mills in the South were cooperating.[28]

As demand continued to fall and inventories grew, some industry leaders, including Charles Cannon, advocated a further reduction of operations. In September 1930, the CTI called for the elimination of night work for minors under eighteen years of age and for all women by March 1, 1931. Enforcement followed the pattern established by the 55-50 plan. The CTI sent subscription forms to the mills to ensure a written commitment to the night work program.[29] By 1932, the institute reported, 80 percent of the industry was sticking to the plan. The program did not eliminate night work entirely, only the participation of women and children, but eventually CTI members proposed the elimination of all night work.[30]

Many members of the CTI favored compulsion to make the nonconforming mills follow the institute's programs. With overwhelming support, the membership voted in October 1932 to change the CTI's bylaws to allow it to lobby Congress for appropriate legislation. Now the CTI had the power to influence national legislation in addition to regulating the industry.[31]

By the time Franklin D. Roosevelt was elected president in November 1932, many textile leaders were ready for closer cooperation with the federal government. The CTI had tried with only limited success to stabilize the industry, yet it had an impressive record as a trade association working with one of the nation's most atomized industries. With able leadership, it had cultivated a constructive relationship with the Hoover administration and had avoided antitrust action. Still, the CTI needed more. The industry needed self-regulation with the force of law and the Cotton Textile Institute was prepared to take the leadership role in working with the new administration toward such a goal.

In May a drafting committee appointed by Roosevelt hammered out a bill for industrial recovery. The resulting proposal included something for everyone. Businessmen got self-regulation through industrial codes and the suspension of antitrust laws. Labor received Section 7(a), which gave labor the right to bargain collectively and set minimum wages. Moreover, the bill set aside $3.3 billion for public works. Congress passed the bill and President Roosevelt signed the National Industrial Recovery Act (NIRA) into law on June 16, 1933.[32]

Even before the NIRA passed Congress, the CTI had begun to draft an industry code for cotton textiles. Hugh Johnson, who later became head of the National Recovery Administration (NRA), had asked the CTI to be prepared with a code for the cotton textile industry when the NIRA passed Congress. The Cotton Textile Industrial Committee (CTIC) met in Washington at the Mayflower Hotel to draft such an industry code.[33]

The CTIC's goals were the same as the CTI's: stabilization of the industry and an end to overcapacity. With the possibility of having the power of the federal government behind its code, the CTIC took a bold step to curtail overcapacity. It wrote into the code a production limitation of two forty-hour shifts. The 40-40 plan provided two benefits, the committee believed. First, it would engender praise from the administration and foster a deeper partnership with Roosevelt. Second, it would cut the production of textiles even more and hopefully end the plague of overproduction that had led to an industry awash in cheap products that depressed profits.

While others industries seemed hesitant to establish self-regulation with government oversight, especially the automobile industry, the textile industry became "a favorite son" of Roosevelt. Under the leadership of the Cotton Textile Institute, the industry had already endured a decade-long economic depression and was prepared to be the first to cooperate with the government under the NIRA. When the law passed, the industry was ready.[34]

Although a fine spirit of cooperation existed between the administration and the CTI, the trade association had some problems in drafting a code. The CTI found it difficult to accept Section 7(a) but acquiesced in the spirit of cooperation and in order to gain controls over production. The institute believed that the benefits of a strong industrial code would outweigh the drawbacks of Section 7(a).[35] After some haggling with the administration, the CTIC recommended a minimum wage of twelve dollars per week in the South and thirteen in the North.[36]

To balance out concessions to labor, the CTIC offered additional proposals to the code. The Cotton Textile Industry Committee requested logically that it become the Code Authority. The institute had more knowledge of the industry's problems than any other group and had competent personnel. As an extension of the Cotton Textile Institute, the CTIC inherited its experience and expertise.[37]

The president signed Code No. 1 on July 16, 1933. Now the CTI, through the Code Authority, had its best chance yet to rationalize the industry and bring the ruinous overcapacity under control. Hoover had been too timid to move toward industry self-regulation with government oversight, yet with FDR's help, the institute had what it wanted. As the first industry organized under NRA auspices, it would set the standard for others.[38]

Stabilization became the Code Authority's main priority. Members of the Code Authority consisted mostly of large textile manufacturers, a fact that garnered much criticism. Charles Cannon took his seat on the committee and served on the North Carolina board for the NRA. Now Cannon had the opportunity to stabilize the industry for North Carolina textile mills and for his Cannon Mills.[39]

The adoption of the industry codes fueled a speculative boom in the textile industry from July to December 1933. Anticipating higher prices due to higher wages, buyers placed abnormally large orders for textile products. The mill owners also contributed to the speculation. They produced more goods than ordered to sell at lower prices once full implementation of the codes raised prices. Mills hired additional operatives to meet the temporary demand. Lured by the promise of higher wages and a shorter workweek, southerners applied for textile jobs in large numbers. The CTI estimated that

between March and September 1933 the industry hired 145,515 new employees. NRA head Hugh Johnson praised the work of the Code Authority and
believed that recovery in the industry was under way.[40]

The road to recovery, however, would be long and rugged. The speculative bubble burst, and the textile market sputtered. When the industry
codes took effect, along with increased prices caused by the higher minimum
wage, demand for textiles dropped and the market was again awash in cheap
textiles. Furthermore, the code had increased manufacturers' costs substan-
tially. In fact, textile engineer Ralph Loper estimated in the fall of 1933 that
the cost of labor had risen for most southern mills by 70 percent.[41]

To compound the problem of rising costs, the Agricultural Adjustment
Act placed a processing tax on cotton used by textile mills.[42] Charles Cannon,
along with other leaders in the textile industry, believed that the processing
tax was a burden that the industry should not bear. To voice his opposition,
Cannon appeared before a U.S. House committee on agriculture considering
the processing tax for farm relief.[43] Later at a meeting at Plant 9 (Franklin
Mills) on January 1, 1935, the textile manufacturer explained the tax and
again voiced his opposition to it:

> I do not believe that it is a fair thing for the cotton mills to have to pay the
> processing tax when other branches of industry are escaping such a tax.
> The processing tax is only a tax paid by the cotton manufacturers to take
> care of the amount being paid by the Federal government for the cotton
> they are holding out of production by cutting their cotton acreage.[44]

Mills responded to the higher costs imposed by the NRA by further
rationalizing production. Since textile manufacturers had to pay higher
wages, they set high production targets for workers and fired those who
could not meet them. Firms also modernized their equipment to mitigate
the cost of higher wages, and workers had to operate more machines. Thus
the stretch-out of 1933 began. Some mills even cheated on the industry code.
These "Code chiselers" became a major concern for the Code Authority.[45]

By the winter of 1933–34, the Code Authority had not brought stability to the industry and it seemed about to lose control. Complaints about
the code piled up. Between August 12, 1933, and January 1, 1934, operatives lodged more than eighteen hundred complaints with the Cotton
Textile Industrial Relations Board (CTIRB). Mill owners and management
also expressed dissatisfaction. The Code Authority needed to act quickly.

It instituted, with NRA approval, a 25 percent curtailment of production beginning in December and lasting for ninety days. This action, the Code Authority believed, would liquidate inventories and end overcapacity. But the Code Authority paid little attention to the resulting reduction in workers' pay, which led to animosity between labor and the authority.[46]

Market conditions improved during the curtailment in late 1933. Inventories fell and prices for textiles rose. Nevertheless, the Depression had hurt buyers, and with higher prices demand fell again. This time the Code Authority imposed a curtailment for June through August 1934. Labor prepared for battle.[47] The Cotton Textile Industrial Relations Board received 3,290 complaints between August 8, 1933, and August 8, 1934.[48] The CTIRB, often called the Bruere Board after its chairman, Robert Bruere, forwarded labor complaints to the Code Authority, which sent investigators into the field. From its inception, labor accused the Bruere Board of a pro-management bias.[49]

States also had boards to investigate workers' complaints and code violations, reporting these to the Bruere Board. The head of the North Carolina board was economics professor Theodore Johnson, who labor alleged had been picked for the position by David Clark, editor of the *Southern Textile Bulletin*. Accused by the United Textile Workers of anti-union bias, the Bruere Board held a hearing to clear Johnson of the charges.[50]

Believing that the Bruere Board, state boards, and the Code Authority were unsympathetic, the UTW now pushed its own demands under the threat of a strike. The union demanded a twelve-dollar minimum wage a week, a thirty-hour work week, recognition of the union, abolition of the stretch-out, and reinstatement of fired union workers. On August 14, 1934, at a special convention held in New York City, the UTW set a general strike date for September 1. Already, operatives in some mills had walked off their jobs in wildcat strikes.[51]

On September 1, 1934, the general strike began. Soon flying squadrons, vehicles filled with strikers, fanned throughout the South. Within a few days, an estimated 450,000 operatives were on strike from Alabama to Maine.[52] *The Associated Press* reports for the first day put the number of strikers in North Carolina at 52,000. Even with the flying squadrons, some mills in the state remained untouched by the strikes. The number of strikers in the state increased as the strike continued. Yet more operatives stayed on the job than walked out. In all, 81,935 remained at work at 281 mills while 64,485 refused to work at 210 mills.[53]

Radio became an important medium for fostering labor unrest. It already was important in disseminating news, sports, and entertainment to mill workers, almost 70 percent of whom, it was estimated in 1934, owned radios.[54] Cabarrus and Rowan counties, the counties that Kannapolis straddled, were serviced by radio station WBT in nearby Charlotte. WBT, along with other stations in the Piedmont, played "hillbilly" music, which was popular with mill workers. Some of the musicians of this genre of music even came from the textile mills, and they often sang of the difficulties and frustrations of mill work. Songs such as "Weave Room Blues," "The Big Fat Boss and the Worker," "Cotton Mill Man," and "Cotton Mill Colic" became popular between 1929 and 1934. Sociologists Vincent Roscigno and William Danaher surveyed thirty-five songs popular with mill hands of the period and noted that twenty-six voiced complaints against paternalism and mill owners.[55]

The union took advantage of radio to further worker discontent. UTW vice president Francis Gorman made several radio appeals to textile workers encouraging them to join the union cause.[56] Radio became vital for the organizing effort. Mill music already had gone some way to breaking down the isolation of the mill villages and weakening loyalty to the individual mills. The job of the union was to further the work of forming a working-class consciousness by uniting the workers beyond the separate mill gates. Assisting the cause were President Roosevelt's fireside chats, which seemed to give legitimacy to the labor movement.[57] The culminate impact of Roosevelt's fireside chats, mill music, and union appeals were effective.

Four mills in Concord immediately closed because most of their workers struck. Half of the six hundred workers of Cannon Mills Concord Plant 6, the Gibson Manufacturing Company, walked out. Some operatives of Concord Plant 9, Franklin Cotton Mills, also left for the picket lines. The mills of Kannapolis, however, remained in full operation.[58]

Flying squadrons roamed throughout Cabarrus and the neighboring counties. Strike activity intensified, with pickets spreading to Cannon Mills Plant 10 (Norcott Mills).[59] At Cannon Mills in Kannapolis, however, few operatives walked off their jobs.[60] Charles Cannon virtually shut the mills off from the rest of the world, using the Kannapolis police and the county sheriff to block roads to the mills. Mill operative Jones Freeze described how the company dealt with flying squadrons:

> The funniest thing happened up at kannapolis [sic] when one of them squadrons went there. You know the mill owns the whole town. Well, the sheriff was on the lookout for these folks from out of town and every time

they started off the main street—hit's [sic] a State highway—the sheriff would say "This is private property, you can't come on it." So that squadron couldn't do a thing but go up and down main street till they got so wore out they jest give up and went back home.[61]

On September 5, North Carolina governor J. C. B. Ehringhaus mobilized the National Guard. When the governor of South Carolina also mobilized the Guard, fourteen thousand soldiers patrolled mill towns in the Carolinas. National Guard troops soon supplemented law enforcement in Kannapolis.[62]

Flying squadrons briefly picketed the Cannon plants in Kannapolis on September 10, 1934. Approximately three hundred strikers from nearby Salisbury and Mooresville picketed outside the plants while National Guardsmen, police, and special officers made sure that the nine thousand workers of Kannapolis had little trouble getting to their jobs. Law enforcement officers made it difficult for the strikers by keeping them off mill property and warning the picketers not to block city streets.[63]

The following day, flying squadrons again arrived in Kannapolis. More than five hundred picketers came to the city in another attempt to close the mills. The members of the flying squadrons parked at the west end of the city and marched toward the Cannon plants. Sheriff Ray Hoover intercepted the strikers and led them away from the mills.[64] Strikers from other cities again paraded in the mill town on September 13. But normal operation of the Cannon plants continued in spite of the presence of the flying squadrons in Kannapolis.[65]

Violence erupted on the picket lines in Concord the next day. More than three hundred strikers at Cannon's Plant 6 crossed the lines established by the National Guard near the plant entrance. While troops attempted to move the crowd away from the mill's gates, a scuffle broke out. One striker stabbed a guardsman in the back, and several police officers sustained injuries in the melee. The sheriff arrested four leaders of the riot.[66]

Even in Concord, the paternalistic bond remained strong among some workers. Jones Freeze, from the Franklin plant, held a strong affection for the Cannons:

I'll tell you hit's a pleasure to work for a company that treats you like the Cannons does. I've know'd all of 'em well. Many's the time back yonder that I hitched up Mr. J. W.'s buggy for him, drove him up town or down to the mill, and went to the Postoffice to get his mail. Charlie and Martin is the boys I know the best and they've turyn out the best. Why I consider Martin Cannon jest as good a friend as I've got in this world.[67]

Freeze and many other Concord workers refused to strike and turn their backs on the Cannons:

> Yes, me and a few others kept right on going to the mill all the time they was having the strike. It took nerve too to walk in that gate with all the crowd standin' there hollerin' at you. They'd call us all kinds of names, but I didn't say a word back to 'em—that was the best way to do. The mill wasn't running, but we got our pay fer going there.[68]

Even peer pressure could not break the paternalistic bond between the Cannons and some workers. These loyal operatives felt vindicated in their decision to remain loyal and go to work because they were paid even if the mill was not operating. Charles Cannon continued to reward loyalty. Paternalism was even stronger among mill workers in Kannapolis, where the Cannons owned everything.

While the strike intensified in Cabarrus County, the Roosevelt administration sought a way to end the general strike. President Roosevelt appointed John G. Winant to head a board to mediate the strike. Winant asked Code Authority members, including the ardently anti-union Charles Cannon, to meet with him at the Cosmos Club in Washington on September 7. Code members and manufacturers Charles Cannon, William D. Anderson, Thomas Marchant, and Benjamin Gossett flatly refused to meet or negotiate with union representatives. Cannon had no compelling reason to relent, since he had the situation in Kannapolis under control and his mills were operating normally. The meeting between the Winant board and the Code Authority ended with no agreement on the strike.[69]

Winant's board then held hearings to become acquainted with the issues of the strike. Thirteen of the leading mill men appeared before the board, including the president of Cannon Mills. Charles Cannon presented the "manufacturers' side of the controversy," while flying squadrons picketed near his corporate headquarters in Kannapolis.[70] On September 17, the board announced its findings. It recommended that a more neutral committee replace the Bruere Board and handle labor complaints without referring to the Code Authority. To determine if the industry could pay higher wages, the report suggested that the Federal Trade Commission investigate the industry. It further recommended the formation of a special committee to investigate the stretch-out. The board suggested no real changes in the code.[71]

The same day the Winant board made its recommendations, a new element in the textile strike against Cannon Mills appeared. Communist Party workers distributed leaflets to strikers in Concord. One leaflet attempted to unite workers against the manufacturer:

> Fellow workers of Concord: Every striker, every member of his family, every friend and sympathizer of the strike, should be on the picket lines early Monday morning to close every mill, do not allow a single scab to get into the mills. The eyes of the workers throughout the country are the Cannon Mills and the other mills in Concord. Closing the mills here 100 per cent will be a big step in winning the strike.[72]

Days later, police raided the home of a Concord man and seized more strike-related communist literature.[73] Support for the strike began to wane among some strikers with the involvement of communists in Concord.

Finally, on September 21, President Roosevelt requested that the UTW call off the strike. The union complied, and the strike ended the next day.[74] The UTW Executive Council announced, "It is our unanimous view . . . that the union has won an overwhelming victory, that we ought to terminate the strike as no longer necessary and that we now go forth in a triumphant campaign of organization."[75]

In Kannapolis, the union announcement rang hollow. For all intents and purposes Local 2265 was dead. The officials of the local believed they had received little support from the national organization. Writing to Francis Gorman, president of the UTW, the local's secretary expressed her frustration:

> Our local is gone and it dont [sic] seem there is any use to try now as they have lost faith in the union. We have had so many promises and nothing done I myself am almost ready to give up. . . . What is wrong[?] have the whole works sold out[?] . . . We as poor hungry people cannot live with[out] something to eat and something to wear and to keep us warm[.] How do you people in Washington think we can go on living on air and promises[.] What we need is help and if you cannot get that for us then say so and we will not depend on promises any longer . . . it looks like Cannon Mills are running the whole thing We want to know if they run the whole country it looks like it. . . . Please . . . do something that we may be able to still have faith in our Government.[76]

The final blow came when Cannon refused to rehire two hundred union members.[77] Again, organized labor had prepared insufficiently for war against Charles Cannon and had lost.

There were several reasons why the operatives at Cannon Mills in Kannapolis did not strike. Memories of how the company dealt with past strikes remained pervasive in the community. Cannon Mills had fired, evicted, and blacklisted workers who allied and struck with the union in 1921. For workers in Concord, this meant leaving company housing and finding a boardinghouse and another job in the diverse job market of the town. Yet for Kannapolis workers, being fired resulted in eviction from company housing and thus being thrown out of the mill village. Eviction doomed the worker to separation from friends and family. Most likely, the worker would have to move some distance from Kannapolis to find another textile job.[78]

The fears of the Kannapolis workers were justified as the textile firm punished Concord strikers. As mentioned above, more than two hundred were fired and evicted. In addition, management terminated the life insurance for those who were not fired. As Jones Freeze remembered, "There ain't but four or five of us [from his plant] has these anymore because they took the policies away from all hands that walked out during that big strike." Disloyalty to the firm and Charles Cannon had its price. Many workers in Concord later regretted their decision to cross Charles Cannon. Freeze noted that "plenty of 'em that walked out was sorry they had."[79] Charles Cannon's response to the strike in his Concord mills vindicated the attitudes of the residents of Kannapolis. If loyalty did not originate from love and respect, then it came from fear or a mixture of both.

The new Textile Labor Relations Board (TLRB) replaced the Bruere Board. In spite of the initial appearance of neutrality, labor gained little from the TLRB. Textile firms still refused to rehire union workers. Benjamin Squires, director of the TLRB, pursued cooperation with the Code Authority. In a December 1934 meeting with Charles Cannon, Squires relayed his conviction that "lasting peace is more likely to obtain by joint consent than by formal rulings." In this spirit, the TLRB and the Code Authority jointly investigated complaints.[80]

Manufacturers soon turned their attention to another crisis. A further slump racked the industry in the winter of 1934–35. By the spring of 1935, demand had withered for many textile products. The *New York Times* reported that for "nearly two months now demand had been at a practical standstill, prices have dipped steadily, and the pressure exerted on manufacturers has brought many to the breaking point." Only mills that had strong leadership and specialized products, such as Cannon Mills, made profits during this downturn.[81]

In typical New Deal fashion, the NRA formed a new board on February 25, 1935, to study the crisis in the textile industry.[82] The Textile Planning Committee had just gotten down to work when the U.S. Supreme Court struck down the National Industrial Recovery Act on May 27. After the demise of the Code Authority, textile industry leaders scrambled to repair the broken dike. They now feared a return to lower wages, longer working hours, and excess production. Unfortunately, the only foreseeable alternative was a return to the industry voluntarism that had proved a failure during the period before the NIRA.

In a June meeting of the American Cotton Manufacturers' Association (ACMA) in Charlotte, North Carolina, the trade group encouraged manufacturers voluntarily to maintain the code. With more than three hundred textile manufacturers present, ACMA officials, along with some larger manufacturers, encouraged the industry representatives to follow the guidelines of the old code. Evidently, no firm agreement resulted, since ACMA secretary-treasurer William McLaurine and industry leaders Donald Comer and William Anderson later wrote mills pleading for compliance.[83]

The CTI, under new president Claudius Murchison, also worked to uphold the old code. As under the NIRA, the institute sent pledge forms to mills committing them to follow the old code. Initial compliance reports seemed encouraging. Almost 90 percent of the industry operated under the old code, according to a CTI report released in the summer of 1935. This cooperation, however, did not last long.[84]

Although some parts of the code, such as the eight-hour shift, became the new industry practice, many mills ignored other elements of the old code. Some instituted around-the-clock production with three eight-hour shifts. Others gradually shifted away from the minimum wage. A 1935 AFL study claimed that over half the mills in Georgia, South Carolina, and North Carolina had departed from the code in various ways.[85]

In 1938, the federal government again attempted to aid the textile industry with the Fair Labor Standards Act (FLSA). Signed by the president on June 25, the FLSA set minimum wages, maximum working hours, and the minimum age for workers in manufacturing jobs. The FLSA set minimum wages at twenty-five cents per hour by October 1938, thirty cents by October 1939, and forty by October 1945. In addition, the FLSA set up industry committees under the new Wage and Hour Division of the Department of Labor, which was headed by Elmer Andrews. These industry committees harked back to the days of the code authorities under the NIRA. They could recommend changes in the federal minimum wage based upon their investigation of industry conditions.[86]

On September 13, 1938, Andrews chose Charles Cannon to serve as an industry member on Industry Committee Number One. As with the NIRA, the textile industry was the first industry to have a committee formed under the FLSA.[87] After six months studying the textile industry, Industry Committee Number One recommended a minimum wage of thirty-two and one-half cents. Cannon sided with a minority of committee members who called for only the thirty cents minimum mandated by law. During public hearings in Atlanta to consider the minimum wage increase, Cannon noted that the textile industry was still sick and asked the committee to consider the family wage of textile operatives and not just the individual wage. The manufacturer repeated statistics released by the Department of Labor showing that thirty-three thousand textile wages had been increased when the twenty-five cents an hour minimum became effective and that forty-two thousand more operatives would get a pay increase in October 1939. Cannon further accused Industry Committee Number One of not reviewing all the facts and argued that some members had made up their minds from the outset. He shocked those in attendance by saying that if the new minimum went into effect, Cannon Mills would have to turn two thousand employees out of work.[88]

In spite of Cannon's dire warnings, the new minimum wage went into effect on October 24, 1939.[89] The wage increase did not greatly affect the company's profits. Actually, sales and profits steadily increased after a dip in 1937 and 1938. Profits fell from the 1936 high of $5,587,632 to $3,252,292 the following year, while sales increased from $38,302,927 to $40,252,621. The recession of 1938 brought lower profits and sales to Cannon Mills, $2,842,169 and $37,572,191, respectively. Regardless of Cannon's predictions on the result of the minimum wage increase of 1938, profits increased from 1938 through 1941. Company profits increased and leveled off in range of $4 to $5 million, but sales rose to more than $65 million in 1941.[90]

While many textile mills suffered greatly during the Depression, Cannon Mills survived and prospered. The company was one of the few textile firms to record no losses during the economic turmoil. Indeed, Cannon Mills modernized its plants, developed new products, continued to advertise its brand, and remained financially stable. Charles Cannon, moreover, became a nationally recognized leader in the textile industry. Both the Hoover and Roosevelt administrations sought his advice, and the North Carolina manufacturer served on New Deal advisory boards and the board of the Federal Reserve Bank of Richmond. Cannon and his company emerged from the Depression poised to help the nation in the defense buildup and the war effort.

Furthermore, the paternalistic structure of Kannapolis survived and thrived. The only Cannon workers who became involved in the general strike of 1934 were those from the Concord mills, where the grip of paternalism was not as tight. The Concord strikers felt the wrath of Cannon management, as had the Kannapolis strikers of 1921. Kannapolis workers seemed to know what was in store for the Concord strikers, and they had less opportunity to organize living under more omnipresent management control.

Kannapolis seemed immune to the numerous factors that were at work to weaken industrial paternalism. Hillbilly, or mill, music had been popular for years and often vented the frustration of mill workers toward mill management and paternalism. This type of music was popular in Kannapolis, but it did not weaken the particular paternalism that had been established in the mill village. It did not abate the mill village identity and translate into a working-class consciousness that bound Kannapolis workers in a great labor cause with workers from other mills. Nor did the union's attempt to link their cause with the popular music. What is even more impressive is the strength of Cannon's paternalism in opposition to President Roosevelt's perceived support for labor. Instead of paternalism weakening at Cannon, the textile firm spent more on welfare work and expanded its control over workers in the mill village.

CHAPTER 9

———◆·▸×◂·◆———

Cannon Mills in World War II

World War II brought profitability to the textile industry. Even before the United States became directly involved in the fighting, the industry benefited from the conflict. American military preparedness and Lend-Lease solved the problem of overproduction more effectively than any New Deal policies had done.

Textile mill activity increased greatly between 1938 and 1940. Based on an index of 100 representing textile mill activity for 1923–25, textile manufacturing activity grew from 108 in 1938 to 132 in 1939 and 142 in 1940.[1] New government orders for all sorts of textile products fueled the boom. In October 1940, W. Ray Bell, president of the Association of Cotton-Textile Merchants of New York, noted that "since early May, the woven cloth markets have had their chief inspiration from the continuous and increasing demand of Federal purchasing agencies for supplies necessary in the preparations for National Defense."[2]

U.S. Army orders filled the largest share of the growing government purchases. By June 1940, military orders, mostly for the army, amounted to almost 2.5 million blankets, over 4.5 million sheets, 4 million huck towels, and more than 1 million terry towels.[3] U.S. government military appropriations continued to swell for the year 1941. Originally, Congress had set aside $102 million for textile supplies for the military for 1941, but it added $200,000 from an emergency supplement bill to supply eight hundred thousand new recruits.[4] To facilitate the logistics of the buildup and assist textile manufacturers, Maj. Gen. Edmund Gregory, head of the Quartermaster

Corps, announced that the army would alter requirements for some products, including sheets, to resemble commercial specifications more closely.[5]

Total income for cotton textile manufacturing firms grew tremendously from 1939 to 1941, rising from $37,270,000 in 1939 to $71,278,000 in 1940. By 1941, income had increased dramatically to $212,553,000.[6] The strong growth in income, however, did not necessarily translate into equally strong profits. Beginning in 1940, the excess profits tax took a larger share of manufacturers' income, rising from 2.3 percent of the industry's income in 1940 to almost 21 percent by 1941. Coming on top of the normal taxes paid by manufacturers, the excess profits taxes increased the tax burden of the industry to more than 43 percent of income in 1941.[7] Furthermore, the Office of Price Administration (OPA) limited textile manufacturing profits. Created in August 1941, the OPA set price controls in accordance with the General Maximum Price Regulation. The OPA used the base year of 1942 to set maximum prices, assuming that costs and labor would remain constant. Labor costs did not remain static, however, and the ratio of profits to sales fell. In short, the OPA attempted to control the price of textile goods while having no authority to control the rising cost of labor resulting from the labor shortage.[8]

Even so, Cannon Mills benefited from the defense build up. Sales and profits steadily increased after a brief dip during the recession in 1937 and 1938. Sales reached $38,302,930 in 1936 and increased to $40,252,620 in 1937. Profits, however, fell during the period from $5,587,630 to $3,252,290. With the recession deepening, both sales and profits fell in 1938 to $37,572,190 and $2,842,170, respectively. The end of the 1937–38 recession brought higher sales and profits for the textile manufacturer, with sales growing to $44,531,800 and profits to $4,354,980 in 1939. Despite Cannon's negative predictions on the result of the minimum wage increase of 1939, sales and profits increased for Cannon Mills from 1939 to 1940. Company sales rose by almost $3 million, with profits increasing more than $800,000 in 1940. In 1941, sales continued the pattern of growth, reaching $65,151,910, but profits dipped to $4,487,820.[9] In one month in 1941, the War Department placed orders for more than $1.5 million worth of towels and sheets from Cannon Mills.[10]

The trend of increased sales based on government contracts continued from 1942 to 1943. Sales grew during the two years from $78,944,230 in 1942 to $88,902,930 in 1943. Profits also increased from $11,970,720 to $14,070,980, respectively. The year 1943, however, was the best year for wartime sales and profits for the firm. In 1944, sales of Cannon products dipped to $83,444,080 and decreased again the following year to $79,385,790. Profits fell to a wartime low of $7,761,610 in 1944 but rose to $10,153,200 in 1945.[11]

In the war years, Cannon Mills continued to be the industry leader in advertising. The manufacturer spent three times as much on towel advertising as its nearest competitor, Martex. In sheet advertising, Cannon spent a little more than Pequot and more than twice as much as Pepperell. The advertising expenditures for this period, including for hosiery, totaled more than $1.5 million.[12]

Once the United States entered World War II, the government encouraged maximum production, although consumers experienced domestic shortages. An unprecedented infusion of federal funds flowed into the South. Total defense spending on war-related industries in the South eventually topped $4 billion.[13] New war plants paid high wages and caused nearly three million southerners to move away from home to seek better employment opportunities.[14] In addition, three million men of the region entered the military.[15] For southern textile manufacturers, this meant acute labor shortages.

Cotton mills ran three eight-hour shifts but often could not find a sufficient number of operatives. These labor shortages occurred despite federally mandated minimum wages and the availability of paid overtime. During the war, the total number of textile workers dropped by 167,000, declining from a 1943 peak of 1,330,000 to 1,173,000 in 1945.[16] The War Manpower Commission (WMC) tried to work with the textile industry to alleviate the labor shortages, advising cotton mills on means of recruiting workers and improving morale and training. WMC officials attended industry association meetings, where they often delivered keynote addresses. Eventually, the commission mandated the extension of the work week from forty hours to forty-eight and recommended the hiring of blacks as operatives. While usually open to WMC proposals, the southern textile industry resisted the suggestion of hiring blacks.[17]

Although he lost fifty-three hundred of his own workers to military service, Charles Cannon worked hard to retain existing workers and recruit new ones.[18] Cannon Mills made improvements and additions to downtown Kannapolis to complement the new YMCA completed in 1940. Along with the YMCA, the town's three theaters remained important recreational outlets for the workers. Near the end of the war, when the Gem Theater burned, the textile manufacturer quickly rebuilt it.[19]

Beyond improvements to Kannapolis, Cannon used other methods to retain workers and boost morale. Although he had opposed increasing the minimum wage in 1938, by 1941 he supported an increase to thirty-seven and a half cents per hour. As the war continued and the labor shortage worsened, Cannon again raised wages for his twenty thousand employees. In 1944, he received permission from the War Labor Board to increase wages another seven and a half cents per hour. By the end of the war, Cannon Mills was paying a minimum of fifty-five cents per hour, one of the highest rates in the industry.[20]

With an eye to future labor needs, the company also sought to stay in touch with its former operatives now in the armed forces. To accomplish this goal, the firm started a company paper, called the *Cannon News*, and distributed it freely to former workers in the armed services. In one edition, the manufacturer sought to ease any fear of unemployment among its servicemen returning to Kannapolis or Concord:

> We want all Cannon Mills Company employees to know that you will have a job here when you return. In so far as it is possible, you will be offered your same job and the same type of work. We realize this is going to be difficult to do and in some instances it may be impossible, but we assure you that you will have a job. Not only do we assure you a place in our organization, but we are also interested in helping you work out your personal problems in returning to civilian life.[21]

Cannon's promise to rehire returning veterans reflected the paternalistic nature of the firm. The textile manufacturer sought to take care of its workers, even those overseas serving the nation. In addition, the policy made good business sense during a tight labor market in the industry. Cannon spent less on training returning workers than new workers. Furthermore, veteran operatives had proven themselves with the firm while new workers represented an unknown quantity in that they might become good employees or they might not.

Of course, this policy limited the long-term employment of many new workers, especially women, in certain departments of the mills. With many Cannon men in the armed forces, the company hired women to take their place and opened up many jobs, such as weaving, traditionally available to men only. While "Rosie the Riveter" became a popular figure in heavy industry, "Wilma the Weaver" quietly did her job in the mills of Kannapolis.[22]

Company operatives vigorously supported the war effort. In 1942, Kannapolis led the state in the collection of scrap metal.[23] Cannon Mills and the Kannapolis American Legion constructed a replica of Mount Vernon at the town's park and affixed the names of armed forces personnel from Kannapolis on it.[24] Cannon employees answered the call of numerous war bond drives. More than 90 percent of the workers at the textile firm's Concord plants purchased war bonds and stamps through the payroll deduction plan.[25]

With the enthusiastic hard work of the operatives, wartime production at Cannon Mills soared. Not only did Cannon manufacture household textile goods for the military, but its products became components in combat-related materiel. A machine-gun belt manufacturer, for example, estimated that Cannon Mills yarn went into the manufacture of fifteen million machine-gun ammunition belts for the U.S. armed forces.[26]

While the company focused on maximum production and competed in a tight labor market, new concerns arose. The war caused an upheaval in Cannon's advertising office. Gordon E. Cole, head of the firm's advertising department, tried to understand the impact of the war on the firm's advertising. A staff member of Cole's New York office posed perhaps the most important concern of all. "Should a manufacturer's advertising be maintained," he asked, "when the stock of his product is greatly reduced in retail stores and, consequently, consumers may not be able to purchase what they want or as much as they want when they go into the store to buy?"[27] Cole answered this question in a strong affirmative. In his letter of March 5, 1942, to Charles Cannon, he analyzed the need to continue advertising during the war. To do otherwise, he argued, would be to risk the brand. He understood that advertising served purposes other than generating sales. One purpose of advertising, Cole wrote Cannon, was to maintain "the enthusiasm of purchasers after they have purchased a product."[28] The company advertising man demonstrated that he understood some of the less tangible characteristics of brands or "added values," which helped to differentiate products in the same market.[29] They were qualities that had built up over time and were important for brands to maintain leadership in the marketplace. Leading brands often asked premium prices because the consumer believed that the added values of the product were worth the higher price. Even in the midst of consumer shortages, Cole believed that the manufacturer needed to reinforce the past purchases of consumers to maintain brand loyalty.

Cole knew that the temptation of the manufacturer might be to cancel consumer advertising during the war. To an accountant, cutting the advertising budget might seem a splendid opportunity to save money in a slack business environment. But company advertising executives knew otherwise. The cessation of advertising would save money in the short term but would prove highly detrimental in the long term. They understood that brand leadership reputation required years to establish but could be quickly lost. Cole therefore argued that advertising should continue to keep the Cannon brand before the public, although the advertisements should be tailored to the current crisis. As Cole explained to Cannon, "Plants and machinery can be destroyed overnight and can be replaced within a reasonable length of time. Once a reputation is destroyed or a brand leadership is lost, it may never be regained, and if it is regained, it can only be done at tremendous cost and as the result of years of hard work."[30] Charles Cannon, persuaded by the weight of Cole's argument, agreed that consumer advertising should continue for the duration of the war. The firm concentrated on working with the advertising agency to gear Cannon's advertising campaigns to the protection of the brand and to maintain its market share.

While Cannon worked to meet wartime demand and keep the brand before the consumer, organized labor again prepared to bring the workers of Cannon Mills into their fold. Textile unionism had changed since the days of the 1934 general strike. In 1935 eight union presidents dissatisfied with the American Federation of Labor formed the Committee for Industrial Organization (CIO), later known as the Congress of Industrial Organizations.[31]

The United Textile Workers Union, a founding union of the CIO, found itself in a particularly difficult situation. Short on cash and discredited by its failure in the 1934 general strike, the union reached an agreement with the CIO in March 1937, creating a new organization, the Textile Workers' Organizing Committee (TWOC). John L. Lewis, president of the CIO, chose the officers of the TWOC, which took over the work of the UTWU in organizing textile workers. The TWOC assumed control of the old union's funds along with the authority to manage existing UTWU contracts and to grant new charters for locals.[32] In preparation to organize the South, the TWOC established headquarters in Roanoke, Virginia, and Atlanta, Georgia. The organization set up more than thirty offices throughout the South and spread union organizers throughout the region. With more than two million dollars in funds, contributed by various CIO unions, the TWOC hired 650 national organizers.[33]

Initially, the organizing campaign of 1937 went well, with sixty-four thousand workers joining the union. Twenty thousand operatives joined from North Carolina alone.[34] The union attempt to organize Cannon Mills, however, met with little success, and the firm dismissed thirty-one workers for union activities. In response, the TWOC filed a complaint on the workers behalf with the National Labor Relations Board. In June 1938, Cannon Mills settled with the dismissed operatives for three thousand dollars.[35]

Three things, however, doomed the drive in the South. First, the TWOC allocated too few of its resources to organizing the region. Of the 650 organizers, the union only assigned 112 to the South, with a mere 30–50 to cover the region from North Carolina to Texas.[36] This reflected the union's decision to concentrate on the dues-paying North. Second, most textile manufacturers in the South refused to negotiate with the union. By the end of the campaign, union contracts covered only 21,000 southern operatives and only 450 operatives in North Carolina.[37] Finally, the recession of 1937–38 led many mills to cut costs, including labor costs. Cone Mills in Greensboro cut wages 12.5 percent in the summer of 1938.[38]

The work of the TWOC ended in 1939 at the May convention in Philadelphia, when the TWOC and the United Textile Workers Union merged to form the Textile Workers Union of America (TWUA-CIO). The TWUA claimed a membership of 424,000, but the southern textile industry remained largely non-union. Only 20 percent of the region's operatives belonged to the new union, with a mere 5 percent of the South's spindles under union contracts.[39]

Organizing the South became the immediate goal of the TWUA. The union initiated another organizing drive in 1940, but with fewer resources than were available in the 1937 effort.[40] Still, union representatives had hopes of success. Allen Haywood, CIO director of organization, stated, "I know we can organize the South in spite of the obstacles we have to face. We've done it in other sections. With hard work and cooperation, we can do it anywhere we try."[41]

As with the campaign of 1937, the results of the 1940 drive proved meager. The only important victory in North Carolina involved the Marshall Field Company (Fieldcrest), which operated five mills employing three thousand workers.[42] Cannon Mills' twenty-four thousand workers remained untouched by the union drives. Throughout the South, the TWUA could only boast of twenty-three contracts covering seventeen thousand operatives. The union filed twenty-five complaints with the Nation Labor Relations Board against manufacturers for unfair labor practices, few of which resulted in success for the workers.[43]

The union did achieve some measure of success against Cannon Mills during World War II. Workers at the firm's Amazon mill in Thomasville, North Carolina, voted in favor of the union on February 28, 1944, and attempted to get a contract from management with the help of the National War Labor Board (NWLB).[44] Getting a union contract, however, did not guarantee that the mill would follow it. As labor historian Paul Richards noted, "Management hostility [at Amazon] was so intense the NWLB contract remained virtually unobserved."[45]

The organization of Amazon hardly represented a union breakthrough with Cannon Mills. Though technically unionized, the absence of an effective contract at Amazon meant that management did not recognize the union as the bargaining agent for the workers. In addition, with two plants and eleven mills in Kannapolis, five plants and six mills in Concord, and other plants in surrounding towns, Cannon could shut down one unionized mill and shift production to another. To unionize Cannon Mills effectively, all of its plants would have to be organized at once.[46] This level of organizing would be costly and require the commitment of a large force.

In 1943, the Textile Workers Union of America began planning for such a campaign. To lay the foundation for a future organizing drive against Cannon Mills, the TWUA conducted a survey of Kannapolis and Cannon Mills. This survey included information on the company, the officers of the firm, the plants and their products, and a 1940 census report on Cabarrus County.[47]

The second step toward a union drive against Cannon Mills involved finding a location for a union hall. From Greensboro, North Carolina, TWUA representative J. D. Pedigo worked with sympathetic Concord attorney Bernard Cruse to find a suitable building. The search concentrated in Concord since finding property for a union hall in the company town of Kannapolis had been impossible. Even in Concord, Cruse had difficulty finding property. By October the search had narrowed to a building under absentee ownership and managed by the local law firm of Hartsell and Hartsell. Cruse made discrete inquiries about the property and told Pedigo that "you must remember that Hartsell is one of the Cannon Mill[s] attorneys, and if you told him what you wanted to do with the building, you could never rent it or buy it at any price."[48]

If negotiations for the targeted property fell through, Cruse believed that prospects for another property would be bleak because Charles Cannon's influence pervaded the entire county. Cruse noted that the local state senator, two state house members, the county prosecutor, the county judge, the county Democratic party chairman, and the entire county bar association, except Cruse and one other attorney, all had Cannon connections. Therefore, "one must be awful careful who he talkes [sic] to and when to talk" in finding property for the union.[49] Eventually, the union acquired space for a meeting hall in the Concord Hotel.

While the war brought increased profits to Cannon Mills and laid the groundwork for future labor activity, it had a personal impact on Charles Cannon as well. To the great joy of Charles Cannon, the J. A. Jones Construction Company of Brunswick, Georgia, built the Liberty ship SS James W. Cannon, which Mrs. Charles Cannon christened in July 1944. Charles personally stocked the library on the ship that bore his father's name.[50]

Unfortunately, the war brought a personal sacrifice to the Cannon family. Charles Cannon joined thousands of other American fathers in losing a son in the war. The young Charles A. Cannon Jr. served as a pilot in the Second Weather Reconnaissance Squadron stationed in Burma. Leaving his base at Myitkyina on March 10, 1945, his airplane failed to arrive at its destination of Chengtu, China. The War Department declared 2nd Lt. Charles Cannon Jr. killed in action on March 15, 1946.[51] Decades later, Charles Cannon established a scholarship fund in his son's name. In memory of the young Cannon who had left Duke University to enter military service in

Charles Albert Cannon Jr., 1943. Courtesy of the Kannapolis History Associates.

1944, this scholarship fund helped the children of Cannon Mills employees attend college.[52]

As the war ended and Cannon mourned the loss of his son, the textile industry and Cannon Mills entered the postwar market. The firm faced several postwar issues. Cannon Mills had to honor its pledge to employ all returning Cannon veterans and accomplish this feat as efficiently as possible. Production had to shift to consumer production with the expectation of high consumer demand. The textile industry still operated under wartime government regulations, and unions were becoming more active. How Cannon responded to these issues would determine the prosperity of the firm in the postwar market.

CHAPTER 10

———◆◆)◆(◆◆———

CANNON MILLS AND POSTWAR AMERICA:
Market Maturity and the Loss of Brand Loyalty

Charles Cannon entered the postwar years with guarded optimism about the business climate. Sales had increased from $44,532,000 in 1939 to $79,386,000 in 1945, with net profits growing from $4,355,000 to $10,153,000.[1] At the start of the war, the textile manufacturer had controlled 70 percent of the towel market in the United States and had built strong brand recognition and loyalty. In addition, Cannon's sheet and hosiery divisions had also achieved strong sales.

The postwar company continued to reflect the influence of the Cannon family. By this time, the board of directors, ten in all, consisted of four Cannons.[2] Besides Charles Cannon, his brothers Eugene Thomas and Martin Luther served on the board. Charles's son, William C. Cannon, also served, having been appointed on September 1, 1939.[3] In 1946, William became a vice president of the company.[4]

Kannapolis continued to reflect the influence of the Cannon family. Demonstrating Mrs. Charles Cannon's interest in colonial architecture and antiques, Charles rebuilt Kannapolis in the Williamsburg style. The renovations included a shopping center—an innovation for the time—and other new buildings in the business district. The firm remodeled older buildings to ensure that the Williamsburg theme remained uniform throughout.[5]

Charles Cannon had two immediate postwar concerns. First, he wanted to terminate the Office of Price Administration's regulation of the industry. Many months after the end of World War II, the OPA continued to regulate much of the American economy. The business sector generally opposed the continued existence of the government agency. As president of the American Cotton Manufacturing Association, Cannon worked to end the government agency.[6] Appearing before a Senate agriculture subcommittee twice in early 1946, Cannon blasted the OPA for depressing production through price controls. He outlined the ACMA's opposition to the maximum average price plan and accused the agency of incompetence in dealing with the textile industry. In addition, Cannon accused the OPA of being "arrogant, high-handed and short-sighted," claiming that its policies resulted in shortages of textile goods that led to a black market.[7]

Charles Cannon believed that OPA price controls were unnecessary. While economists expected a slight jump in prices with the end of price controls, Cannon believed it would not lead to rampant inflation.[8]

> If an increase would inevitably follow the lifting of price controls, it would be just as inevitable later as now as long as OPA continues price-squeezing policies which discourage production and perpetuate scarcities. If eventually we must go through a transition period, why not now? Whether the danger of more inflation is great or small, we cannot afford the luxury of permanent government control and we will be much better off to stand the change now than later.[9]

Speaking for the textile industry, Cannon asked for and received a 5 percent price increase to stimulate production, cover higher labor costs, and update equipment.[10]

The other immediate postwar objective for Cannon Mills entailed keeping its promise to resettle its returning war veterans. Even before the war ended, Cannon Mills created a new Personnel Department for veterans coming back to Concord and Kannapolis. In February 1944, Charles Cannon created the Servicemen's Personnel Department with Capt. J. Harry Cannon, a veteran, as its head. Captain Cannon, unrelated to the Cannon family of Concord, had taught at Kannapolis High School as a vocational teacher and had served in the armed forces in North Africa.[11] The new veterans' personnel office, in Room 213 of the Professional Building in Kannapolis, had all the files of Cannon workers who had left the firm to serve in the military.[12] The Servicemen's Personnel Department worked to find a job for each veteran and to provide assistance in securing benefits from the Veterans Administration.[13]

Veterans filled out two forms at Cannon, the application for employment and the "Veteran's Service Record." After filling out the forms, a personnel officer reacquainted the applicant with the company's policies and went over the veteran's service record in detail to ascertain what job would best fit his skills and needs. If the veteran expressed a desire to work at his old job, the company attempted to place him there. All returning veterans also received physical examinations to ensure that they had the strength for their chosen jobs. If the doctor believed the applicant was unsuited for his prospective job, the department recommended another position.[14]

At regular intervals the Servicemen's Personnel Department assessed the progress of "reconverting" the veteran to civilian life. After one week,

A GI house in 1947. Courtesy of the Kannapolis History Associates.

A neighborhood of GI houses in Kannapolis, 1947. Courtesy of the Kannapolis History Associates.

three weeks, and six weeks the department analyzed how well the veteran was adjusting, his work performance, and his job satisfaction. With the recommendation of his supervisor, the department could move the veteran to another job until one seemed to "fit" the employee, or a veteran could request a job transfer.[15] Eventually, the Servicemen's Personnel Department helped to resettle thirty-five hundred veterans who returned to work for the textile firm.[16]

In addition, the textile manufacturer built more housing to help resettle returning veterans. The company "purchased fifty prefabricated houses at a cost of $60,000" with an option for fifty more.[17] The section of Kannapolis where Cannon Mills built the new houses became known as "GI Town," and it remained in place for half a century.[18]

Cannon's long-term goal was to maintain its huge market share in towels during the postwar years. The textile firm sought to continue its dominance of the towel market through effective advertising and new product development. Cannon Mills had advertised heavily during the war years in an attempt to keep its brand before the public and thus position itself to take advantage of postwar pent-up consumer demand.

The expected textile boom emerged in 1946. Measured by the "poundage of all fibers consumed," 1946 textile activity stood at only 8 percent below the record year of 1942.[19] Textile mill earnings hit an all-time high. Firms largely reinvested profits, purchasing new textile equipment at record levels to replace equipment worn out by wartime production.[20]

Cannon Mills also benefitted from the postwar boom. In 1946 the company had its most profitable year ever. Sales of Cannon products dramatically increased from $79,386,000 in 1945 to $113,955,000 in 1946. Profits grew even faster, more than tripling during that same period, rising from $10,153,000 to $32,517,000. Even more impressive, the earnings per share of stock grew more than fivefold.[21]

Workers at Cannon Mills also benefited from the firm's prosperity. Already among the highest paid textile workers in the South, Cannon's operatives received two minimum wage increases in 1946. By July, the minimum wage had increased from fifty-five cents an hour in 1945 to seventy-three cents.[22] Cannon workers, however, still lagged behind the national average wage of almost seventy-nine cents per hour for cotton textile workers.[23] In late December 1946, the board of directors moved to eliminate that disparity by approving a 4 percent bonus wage to be paid in installments over the next eight months.[24]

Despite the rosy economic climate, some industry experts warned of the return of "normal market competition."[25] In October 1946, Cotton Textile

Institute president Claudius Murchinson told industry leaders at the twentieth anniversary meeting of the trade association that stiffening competition would return with the end of government controls: "In the past we have been told what to produce and to get it out irrespective of what it was. From now on production will be determined by the choices of the consumer. Prices will revert to their honorable function of determining what should be produced and how much."[26] In addition, some economists predicted a recession in the future. Economist Stacy May warned of a downturn in textiles because existing consumer spending could not be sustained. Once pent-up demand became satisfied, demand would weaken.[27]

To take advantage of pent-up demand for household textiles, Cannon Mills concentrated its efforts on marketing, advertising, and product development. The textile manufacturer moved to maintain its 70 percent share in the towel market and increase its sales of hosiery and sheets. Advertisements announced that retailers once again had Cannon products available for consumers.[28] Product development and marketing, dormant during the war years, slowly geared up for the consumer market. In 1946, Cannon again marketed its hosiery "Handy Pack," which had first been introduced in 1938.[29]

The textile industry experienced another good year in 1947. While mill activity lagged behind the previous year's levels, profits topped those of 1946.[30] *Textile World's* mill index fell slightly from 187 in 1946 to 182 in 1947.[31] Purchases of new equipment, meanwhile, rose 39 percent over the previous year.[32] For Cannon Mills, 1947 marked the beginning of a general decline in profitability for the postwar years. Although sales increased in 1947 to more than $158 million, almost $44 million more than in 1946, net profits fell $7 million to $25 million.[33] Even so, 1947 remained the second most profitable year in the history of the company. The board of directors approved a one dollar per share quarterly dividend, and workers again received a 4 percent bonus.[34]

Cannon's declining profitability reflected the saturation of the postwar household textile market and the intensification of price competition. Economists and the trade journals predicted an imminent recession in the industry. Pent-up demand for durable goods, mostly automobiles, had not been satisfied because of strikes and labor unrest. Most consumer spending, therefore, had gone toward "soft" goods, including textiles. Economists expected that once durable goods became readily available, the demand for soft goods would decline.[35]

The industry experienced an increased emphasis on cost cutting to provide a competitive edge in the postwar market. The textile industry, however, had little control over the price of cotton, up 220 percent from the prewar levels, and wages had doubled since 1941.[36] Government regulation and the labor shortage pushed wages higher. In the postwar period, this labor shortage continued because of competition from higher-paying industries. To protect profit margins in the atmosphere of renewed competition, and in the light of a predicted economic downturn, textile firms now needed to cut costs per unit of production, which entailed modernizing mill machinery. Obsolete, worn-out wartime equipment needed to be replaced as quickly as possible. Otherwise, textile mills would find it difficult to compete on price in the competitive postwar market.[37]

Charles Cannon and the board of directors realized that Cannon Mills needed to modernize its plants, replace worn-out wartime equipment, and cut costs in order to remain competitive. The impetus for modernization became more acute when the textile manufacturer's share of the towel market fell to 45 percent by 1947.[38] The board issued 4.4 million shares of stock to raise capital for modernization. In order to maintain the hold of the Cannon family and its friends on the firm, three-fourths of the shares issued consisted of "Class B common stock of a par value of $25.00 each without voting rights."[39] Modernization of the plants and Kannapolis soon followed.[40]

The textile market slumped in 1948. While the index of textile mill activity rose from 182 in 1947 to 185, evidence of the end of the postwar boom appeared.[41] Mill margins, based on average weekly earnings, fell by almost $30 million in the course of 1948.[42] Towel output peaked in the first quarter of the year and fell throughout the rest of 1948.[43]

Some evidence of the industry-wide decline appeared at Cannon Mills, but the firm generated better profits than did the rest of the industry. Net profits from sales in 1948 totaled almost $44 million, a gain of $19 million over 1947. Yet net sales declined slightly from almost $158 million in 1947 to almost $154 million in 1948.[44] The large net profit to net sales reflected an unusual financial situation for the year at Cannon Mills. The company's Annual Report to Stockholders for 1948 stated that

> a substantial portion of the cotton inventories maintained on the last-in, first-out basis was liquidated, and since the valuation of such inventories was considerably lower than current replacement costs, the net income for the year is materially higher than it would have been had sales been wholly from current purchases of cotton at prevailing 1948 price levels.[45]

Thus profits for 1948 represented an aberration. The company would not achieve a net operating profit level of more than $40 million again until 1965.[46]

Both stockholders and workers benefited from Cannon's most profitable year to date. Employees received another, by now almost standard, 4 percent bonus. The company paid stockholders a seventy-five cents per share quarterly dividend.[47]

Cannon Mills responded to its loss of market share with the largest one-year increase in its advertising budget in the company's history. The towel advertising budget grew to $962,000, an increase of $211,200 over the previous year.[48] Sheet advertising increased from $403,500 to $523,800.[49] Hosiery advertising and promotion fell slightly from 1947 levels by $1,300 to $121,900.[50] In all, including consumer education space, Cannon Mills' advertising budget increased to $1,669,900 from the previous year's total of $1,369,300.[51]

The textile market continued to decline in 1949. The *Textile World* mill activity index fell from 180 in 1948 to 154 in 1949.[52] The production of cotton broad woven goods, which included towels, dropped 10 percent from the previous year.[53] The output of towels continued its general decline since the first quarter of 1948.[54] Purchases of new textile equipment fell.[55]

Charles Cannon hoped that advertising would help pull Cannon Mills out of the slump. He increased the advertising budget $4,390 over the 1948 level, but without apparent success.[56] Sales and profits fell dramatically in 1949 for Cannon Mills. The saturated household textile market continued to put pressure on Cannon's sales and profits. Sales for 1949 dropped to $135 million, a loss of $19 million from the previous year, and profits fell by $30 million.[57]

World events, however, turned the market around. The invasion of South Korea by its northern neighbor on June 25, 1950, changed the nature of the textile market. War in Korea greatly increased demand for textile goods in the second half of the year. Fearing shortages and rationing as in World War II, consumers stocked up on consumer goods, including textiles. Furthermore, growing military orders greatly pushed up demand for textiles, causing prices to rise. By September, production of cotton textiles had risen by 15 percent, while prices had increased by 25 percent over May's figures.[58]

Cannon shared in this unanticipated bounty. Sales of Cannon products reached a record high in 1950, increasing by $37 million over 1949 sales, to $172,400,000.[59] The year should have brought record profits for the firm but did not do so. Profits fell by $2.6 million from the previous year. Because of two years of declining profits, the board of directors reduced the bonus paid in addition to workers' wages from the now usual 4 percent to 2 percent.[60]

Two factors in particular account for Cannon Mills' lower profits on higher sales. First, the upturn in sales in the later part of the year did not make up for the lower profits of the first half. In other words, the higher prices of the last two quarters did not make up for the intense price competition of the first two quarters. Furthermore, towel production and demand did not rise as much as some sectors of the textile industry, such as print cloth.[61] Second, the textile firm's cost structure decreased its profitability. During the postwar period, Cannon's cost of production increased. From 1946 to 1950, the textile manufacturer's cost of production rose from 70 percent of sales to 90 percent.[62] Clearly, Charles Cannon and the board of directors had not been aggressive enough in cutting the cost per unit of production. The high cost per unit of production also hurt Cannon's market share. To generate a profit, the textile firm had to sell towels at higher prices than many manufacturers. Cannon Mills had not competed well in the market for lower priced towels.[63]

In an attempt to adjust to changing market conditions, the firm altered its advertising in 1950. The preeminence of mass-circulation magazines as a medium for the company's advertising declined to some extent. While towel advertising in mass-circulation magazines accounted for the bulk of the firm's advertising budget (at $919,600 for consumer magazines and $77,000 for trade magazines) Cannon initiated a slight shift toward newspaper promotion in 1950.[64] The new advertising outlet, Charles Cannon believed, would assist the manufacturer in reaching local markets and in coordinating the firm's advertising with that of local merchants. Newspaper advertising would become an increasingly important avenue for Cannon's advertising in the future. In the midst of a buyer's market in household textiles, characterized by price-conscious customers, greater emphasis on point-of-sale promotions became increasingly important.

The mature, or saturated, household textile market also pushed Cannon to advertise on the price theme in its magazine advertisements. While style remained an important theme, price became increasingly important. The entire 1950 advertising campaign remained simple, emphasizing style at low prices. No hidden messages appeared within these advertisements. The overt message was clear: Cannon offered quality, stylish towels at low prices. Low price became the crux of Cannon's message.[65]

Because of lower profits, Cannon Mills increased its modernization efforts. The company built a new office building in Kannapolis, made improvements to the plants, and built a new boiler plant to produce heat for the mills in Kannapolis and many downtown buildings. In addition, the firm completed expansion of its bleachery plant.[66]

In spite of the firm's attempt to modernize its operations after World War II, Cannon Mills had lost its dominant position in the towel market.

Several reasons explain this decline. First, Cannon Mills remained complacent after the war. It did not invest in new equipment to replace its war-worn
equipment as quickly as it should have, which adversely affected its cost
per unit of production. The higher costs of production cut into profits and
forced the company to sell its products at relatively higher prices at the very
moment the market warranted lower prices after pent-up wartime demand
had been satisfied. The outbreak of the Korean War spurred modernization
at Cannon Mills, but with the Korean conflict and mobilization, industry
experts warned of a new labor shortage. Again the textile industry would
compete with high-paying war industries for workers.

In other areas, also, Cannon Mills became complacent. Product innovation fell to a low ebb in the postwar years. Cannon Mills had been far more
prolific in the development and marketing of new textile products in the late
1930s than in the late 1940s. The company introduced few new products in
the postwar period. Furthermore, Cannon missed opportunities in advertising. While maintaining a high brand visibility with its consumer magazine
advertising during World War II, Cannon initially ignored both the class
market and the rural market. Executives at Cannon Mills believed that
the style magazines had served their purpose when towels became stylish
staples and abandoned the style magazines. Cannon's withdrawal from the
classy magazines, however, left an advertising void that other manufacturers of high-end towels filled. Martex, for example, gained market share at
Cannon's expense.

In addition, the textile manufacturer ignored the rural market until 1947.
In spite of pressure from Ayer to add the rural and small-town market to
its advertising coverage in 1945 and 1946, Cannon refused to do so until
1947. This market became increasingly important because of rising income
resulting from World War II. Cannon's high prices also hindered its competitiveness in the rural market.

The firm's marketing, in addition, suffered in the postwar period.
Cannon Mills allowed its relationship with department stores to deteriorate.
In the 1930s, Cannon had developed an active relationship with department stores. The firm had remained attentive to department store display
of its towels and active in the training of saleswomen on how to sell Cannon
towels. Cannon Mills had even distributed booklets to saleswomen inform-
ing them of the qualities of Cannon towels and how to sell them. By the
late 1940s, the textile manufacturer was giving less attention to department
stores. Other towel brands found more prominent display space than did
Cannon's, as department stores pushed cheaper towels.

Consequently, Cannon's market share and profits suffered. The textile manufacturer's brand loyalty weakened under the intense price competition of the postwar years. In many ways Cannon Mills remained the same company it had been before the war. Although it issued more than four million shares of stock to capitalize its modernization program, control of the firm remained with Charles Cannon and his board of directors. The stock issuance of 1947 did not diffuse power since nonvoting stock made up three-fourths of the stock issued. Charles Cannon, the Cannon family, friends, and members of the board of directors purchased the bulk of the voting shares of stock.

Yet Cannon Mills encountered another problem in the postwar years. A new union, the Congress of Industrial Organizations, organized a major drive to unionize the South and especially the southern textile industry. As the premier textile firm in the South, Cannon Mills became the prime target for the CIO's organizing effort. Again management would battle vigorously to keep Cannon Mills unorganized.

CHAPTER 11

———————— ◆▸)◂◂◆ ————————

CANNON MILLS AND OPERATION DIXIE

In the summer of 1946, the Congress of Industrial Organizations launched its ambitious drive to unionize the South. The CIO modeled Operation Dixie, as the southern campaign became known, on the organizing pattern it had employed successfully in the North. This strategy concentrated efforts on the main industry in an area and targeted the premier or bellwether company of that industry. Organizing the bellwether firm first, organizers believed, would reduce opposition to unionization in the rest of the industry. Thus the hard work would be finished early in a quick drive that minimized expense. Operation Dixie, therefore, needed to focus on the South's key industry, the textile industry, and concentrate its resources in the main textile state of North Carolina. As the bellwether company in the textile industry, Cannon Mills became the target of the CIO organizing campaign.[1]

CIO president Philip Murray chose Van A. Bittner to lead Operation Dixie. George Baldanzi became the deputy director and set up headquarters for the campaign in Atlanta. Baldanzi, in turn, appointed state directors, including William Smith for North Carolina.[2]

The southern drive began optimistically with what seemed impressive resources. Close to one million dollars funded the efforts of 250 workers in the southern organizing drive.[3] North Carolina received 57 of those organizers, the largest number assigned to any of the twelve southern states. From its Charlotte headquarters, the leadership of the North Carolina campaign included a director, a public relations director, and two secretaries. The remaining workers were divided into four regions, each headed by an area director. Cannon Mills fell into the Southern Area, headquartered in the Independence Building in Charlotte and led by Draper Woods. The Southern Area's main focus became Cannon Mills in Concord and Kannapolis, with a secondary drive two counties to the west in the combed yarn industry of Gastonia. Experienced organizer Dean Culver directed the drive against Cannon from his office in Concord. Ten organizers usually worked in the Concord-Kannapolis area, but at times the regional director temporarily assigned Culver's workers to help in Gastonia.[4]

State director Smith highlighted the importance of organizing Cannon Mills as part of the CIO southern strategy:

> Of all the campaigns under progress, we consider the campaigns in the Cannon chain and in the combed yarn industry of Gaston County our major projects. . . . It has long been a recognized fact in the industry that the pattern set by the union mills is always duplicated by the Cannon Chain. The Cannon interests are the employer of the largest single group of textile workers in the industry, and we feel that it is important that these workers assume their natural position of union leadership, thereby furthering the progress towards better wages and working conditions. We have our largest concentration of workers in this situation.[5]

Dean Culver seemed a wise choice to organize the Cannon Mills for the CIO-affiliated Textile Workers Union of America. Born in Iowa, Culver had come to North Carolina in 1936, worked at the Alcoa Aluminum plant in the company town of Badin, thirty miles from Kannapolis, and organized the plant for the CIO. Having lived in North Carolina for ten years and having successfully battled one paternalistic firm, Culver seemed the ideal candidate to tackle Cannon Mills.[6] Yet nothing in his past had fully prepared this thirty-two-year-old labor activist for his confrontation with Charles Cannon.

In June the Cannon Mills organizers began their work. They could not find space for a proper union hall in Cannon-controlled Kannapolis, so they secured a hall in the Ritz building in Concord. The CIO had five distinct objectives for June. First, organizers had to familiarize themselves with the area. As none of the new union staff in Concord came from Concord or Kannapolis, they had to learn the layout of the town of Kannapolis and the Cannon plants.[7]

Second, organizers had to contact workers who had signed union cards during the minor 1944 drive, when workers at the Thomasville Amazon Mill had organized and tried to convince them to sign new union cards. Workers who signed up under the Operation Dixie drive paid a one-dollar initiation fee, while World War II veterans signed without paying the fee. Not surprisingly, this policy caused some confusion among the union supporters at Cannon Mills. Some questioned why they had to re-sign union cards and pay a dollar. To head off any bad feelings, state director Smith instructed organizers to waive the initiation fee for workers who had previously signed a union card.[8] Although this policy smoothed relations with previous union supporters, it did not help raise funds for the campaign. Along with contacting past union supporters, the organizers also contacted veterans, whom the union believed would be less susceptible to the power of Cannon's paternalism. These Cannon veterans had seen more of the world than most workers in Kannapolis and, the CIO thought, would be more open-minded to the message of the union.[9]

Some veterans who returned to Kannapolis did indeed believe that Cannon's wages remained substandard. Marvin Searborough noted that while in the army he had made "$190.00 a month plus food, shelter, clothing and medical and dental care for myself," but after returning to Cannon Mills he made "approximately $120.60 a month which has to cover my own living costs as well as those of my family." He believed it would "take a union to get our wages even up to what we were making in the Army, let alone up to Northern standards." He did not belong to the union yet, but he stated he would "sign the first union card I see."[10] The union hoped to tap into such sentiments, and organizers believed that a large veteran membership would have the added benefit of countering charges of communist domination in the union. The CIO, therefore, concentrated efforts on the GI Town section of Kannapolis."[11]

Union activists also attempted to organize women in the Cannon work force. Culver deployed the women on his staff to contact the women of the company town. The Concord staff, however, quickly learned how difficult gaining the support of Kannapolis women would be. Organizers Marcelle Malamas and Nancy Blaine worked among the Cannon women. Malamas initially reported that the "majority [of the women] are inclined to sit on the fence."[12] Later, however, fear became more pervasive than indifference among the women in the mill village. Reporting two weeks later, Malamas said that the "women are plenty scared."[13] Insecurity seemed to be the source of their fear. Charles Cannon and his company provided stable employment and affordable housing. Involvement with the union meant opposing "Uncle Charlie" and a possible loss of employment and eviction from company housing.[14]

The final objective for June was to find space for a union hall in Kannapolis. While meeting in Concord had its advantages, most notably a degree of freedom from Charles Cannon's scrutiny and influence, organizers worried that distance prevented some Kannapolis workers from attending meetings. Organizers searched in vain for space in Kannapolis.[15] In their search, the Concord CIO staff quickly encountered their main obstacle, the power and prestige of Charles Cannon. The degree of control that existed in Kannapolis made people afraid to oppose the Cannon family, the "dominant fundamental group."[16] Everyone knew how Uncle Charlie felt about unions. Workers remained fearful that their union involvement would be reported to management by other employees, and many of them believed management employed spies throughout the mills to report on workers who became union members.[17] Even taking union literature at the mill gates could be dangerous because management might be watching. In addition, Cannon workers were afraid the union might abandon them as no union had ever stayed long in Kannapolis. The risk of signing union cards only to have the union leave was too great for most workers. Organizer Malamas found that workers "are [a] little wary of [the] union's intention to come in and really do [the] job this time."[18] Activist L. L. Sheperd believed that Cannon workers "want a union, but they are afraid that we are not going to stay in Kannapolis and for that reason want to wait."[19]

In spite of repeated assurances from the CIO that organizers would stay in Cabarrus County until they organized Cannon Mills, few workers believed it. Memories of how Charles Cannon had crushed the United Textiles Workers' strike of 1921 lingered in the mill village. Although Cannon workers did not participate in the 1934 general strike, its failure remained vivid in Kannapolis. Unfulfilled union promises had left bitter feelings among many workers. In addition, the allegations of communist involvement in labor unions and congressional investigations did not help the CIO cause in Kannapolis.

Organizers who transferred into the Concord staff after working in other areas of the state became amazed at the level and intensity of fear among Cannon Mills workers. Fred Wingard found the degree of fear greater among Cannon employees than among the workers of the Firestone plant he had tried to organize in Gaston County.[20] Paul Faucette, who had transferred from Winston-Salem, noticed on his second day in Kannapolis "considerable fear from the workers."[21]

Recent incidents at Cannon Mills also perpetuated fear. Zeb James Plott, a first-shift worker in Cannon's Plant 2 in the number 1 weave room, reported being sent home from work for discussing the union. While at work, Plott had discussed the benefits of the union with fellow worker Bond Dry. Immediately, Dry went to his boss and reported on Plott. The assistant overseer angrily accused Plott of work deficiencies and sent the worker home for the rest of the day and all of the next. Plott defended his work performance unsuccessfully and believed that his union views had caused his punishment.[22] News of such episodes spread throughout Cannon's plants and dampened enthusiasm for the union among workers. Not only did management's reaction cause fear, but workers also worried that other employees might report one's organizing activities causing distrust to spread among the workers.

Nevertheless, a few Cannon workers vented their discontentment. Some complained that Cannon denied employment to some returning veterans. Organizer Malamas visited one family with three veterans whom the company had refused to hire.[23] Other workers believed favoritism governed one's advancement within the firm. In late June, an overseer in a sewing room in one Cannon plant confided to an organizer his disgust with the company's favoritism in promotion. As a secret way to strike back at the firm, he made sketches of several Cannon plants to assist the union in distributing its literature.[24] Still other workers saw through the veil of paternalism in Kannapolis and resented the control Cannon had over their lives. In a report on the town's YMCA, organizer Nancy Blaine stated that the Y had been "undoubtedly conceived and built and with a view toward keeping the workers 'contented' so that they would not feel the need of [union] organization. There are certainly workers who resent the paternalism of this gesture."[25] The union's success would hinge largely on how effectively it could fan the fires of discontent.

By July it had become apparent to the organizers that if they could not calm workers' fears, their plan to organize Cannon Mills would die. The path to organizing the huge textile firm had been clearly set out by the state director.[26] First, organizers would make initial contacts and sign up as many as possible. Then each organizer would form small committees of his recruits. These committees essentially would assume the burden of organizing the plants. Committees would meet weekly, sign up new members, and collect initiation fees. Organizers would attend committee meetings and serve as liaisons with the local director. If organizers could form enough committees in each plant, the union would grow quickly as workers recruited other workers. Fear would dissipate as the drive gained momentum. Yet if union organizers could not form enough active committees, the drive would inevitably die.

The union organizers now concentrated on forming active in-plant committees, but they enjoyed little success. Union workers formed few committees. Despite the lack of progress, the Concord CIO staff tried to remain optimistic. At times, organizers expressed the hope that the "fear . . . is slowly subsiding" and that their work would "pay off soon."[27] More typically, however, union activists felt much less optimistic and frustration increased. Inactivity soon became a common complaint among the organizers. One reported that the Cannon workers would not "take the lead," that many veterans who signed union cards remained inactive, and that workers seemed "reluctant to take [an] active part in the union."[28]

Frustration with the organizing effort became evident at a July meeting of the Concord staff attended by William Smith, the state director. Organizers' reports "were lousy," Smith said. The Concord CIO staff, looking for encouragement and direction, received only "instructive criticism." The director questioned the organizers' creativity in the drive and wondered aloud why the union workers had made no positive suggestions.[29] The Concord staff evidently believed that Smith did not understand the obstacles to organizing Cannon Mills, while Smith did not understand the lack of progress in the drive.

Dean Culver attempted to enlighten the director by reporting in greater detail on the problems facing his staff in organizing Cannon's workers. Culver outlined the psychology and conditions of the workers to his superior. Employees at Cannon Mills had comparatively high wages and light workloads, he said. Jobs remained more secure at Cannon than in most textile companies, the firm offered housing at "below cost," and Kannapolis seemed "neat, clean, and comfortable." Further, the family wage provided a high standard of living compared with most southern textile mills. Literacy among workers remained high, and they experienced little isolation from the outside world. Besides reading the newspaper, most mill families listened to the radio and owned a car. Indeed, widespread car ownership allowed Kannapolis workers to leave the village for vacations in other parts of the state, especially the mountains and beaches.[30]

In addition, there existed what Culver termed the "Cannon myth." In certain ways the people of the community identified with Charles Cannon. The textile manufacturer had been born and raised in Cabarrus County and had worked all of his life in the company. Cannon remained highly visible in the village and cultivated the belief that a personal connection existed between the textile magnate and his employees. Workers attributed their prosperity to Cannon, and many of them viewed the mill owner as a benefactor to the community.[31] On the surface, the mill community reflected a love for its Charles Cannon: "Everybody loved him. He was their daddy. The father, the grandfather, the great-grandfather, all lived here. And everybody looked to Uncle Charlie Cannon. He was a Santy Claus."[32]

Charles Cannon's power, influence, and control in Kannapolis existed on different levels. First, there was the obvious demonstration of power and control that engendered dread of opposing Cannon. Few people publicly criticized Charles Cannon or his company for fear of his wrath. The textile manufacturer's power even muted criticism from politicians since they owed "their jobs to the grace of Mr. Cannon."[33]

Perhaps the softer aspects of Cannon's paternalism, however, remained more powerful. The mill owner had delivered material prosperity to his workers and in return Cannon demanded hard work, the surrender of control in the workplace and community, and loyalty. Supporting a union would represent a violation of the unwritten contract between Cannon and his workers. Finally, if a sense of obligation did not keep workers in line, then force would. Open union support would bring "Mr. Cannon's displeasure and lead to absolute ruin."[34]

To counter such a hostile anti-union environment, Culver suggested several tactics. First, he proposed to continue to identify and exploit the elements of discontent in Kannapolis. Workers who had suffered from favoritism and veterans not yet fully reintegrated into the Cannon mentality would be prime targets. Second, he argued that the union should not attack the Cannon myth directly because this would probably alienate workers. Instead, he wanted to use the myth to the union's advantage. If Cannon were such a great person and employer, the union could agree that "we expect a much higher degree of success in labor relations . . . than we would in a lesser man." And third, Culver needed to educate workers about the union. He advocated using radio spots, direct mailings, and continued leaflet distribution to raise awareness of the union's benefits to workers, even if the campaign would be long and costly.[35]

By the end of July, few workers had joined committees. Culver reported to area director Wood that the Concord staff had formed twenty-two committees. Yet attendance remained low. Workers failed to go to five of the scheduled committee meetings and another six meetings proved to be disappointments.[36] Wood informed state director Smith that "some of the staff members are having it a little tough in forming committees" but assured him that "the staff in Concord is making every effort to carry out the instructions in forming these committees."[37] At the end of the month, union membership stood at approximately 245 out of Cannon's work force of 24,000.[38]

Financial problems also compounded the Concord staff's difficulties. News of Operation Dixie's financial problems reached Concord in early August. Culver received the news in a reply to his request to the state director for twenty-six thousand leaflets and ten thousand envelopes.[39] Smith denied

the request, noting that "the Atlanta office has called me asking us to dras-
tically cut out expenses."[40] He revealed the he had gone into personal debt
attempting to keep the state organization financially solvent.[41] Culver immediately became concerned that he would have fewer resources to organize the
huge Cannon plants and contacted Smith again:

> If the expense situation becomes too tight for us to do a reasonable job of
> development in these situations that are being started, would you be will-
> ing to take a couple of days and go with me, and perhaps one or two other
> members of the staff, into some of our more cooperative locals in this state
> and see if we can obtain donations of several hundred dollars for you to use
> in the development of the Cannon situation?[42]

The local organizing leader also notified the state director that he
needed more staff to organize Cannon Mills.[43]

A few days later, Culver became entangled in a legal conflict with the
city of Concord. City police arrested him and organizer Paul Faucette for
using a loudspeaker at the gates of Plant 2 in violation of a city ordinance.
The Concord police court convicted the two union men. The union's legal
counsel, Concord attorney Bernard Cruse, and Birmingham attorney
Jerome Cooper immediately appealed the convictions. The court released
the organizers on a fifty-dollar bond.[44] Magistrate's court heard the case
on appeal and upheld the convictions, charging both organizers a fine and
court costs.[45] Eventually, the case made its way to Superior Court, where the
city dropped the charges based on the "informal opinion announced from
the bench by Superior Judge J. H. Clement that the ordinance of Concord
forbidding [the] use of loudspeakers violate[d] the Constitution of the United
States."[46]

Legal problems did not stop the Concord union staff in its organizing
work, but progress remained slow. Ominously, Culver reported that Cannon
workers had no real reason to unionize. "The workers have no pressing reason to join the Union and we must give them some, some issue in their behalf
that they see as practicle [sic]," he stated.[47] Kannapolis's prosperity hurt the
organizing effort. The U.S. Bureau of Labor Statistics issued a report in
April 1946 that revealed that Cannon workers made the highest average wage
of any textile workers in the South. At an average of eighty-five cents per
hour, Cannon Mills workers earned more than textile workers in the reporting areas of South Carolina, Georgia, and Alabama. In addition, textile

wages in the Concord-Kannapolis area had risen more than nine cents an hour since January.[48]

CIO organizers now began to understand the full measure of their task in organizing Cannon Mills. They not only had to battle the leading textile firm in the South in the largest company town in the nation but also had to convince the prosperous workers that they needed the union. But high relative wages dampened workers' interest. One Cannon worker voiced the opinion of many: "I know that when there is a time for better pay, Cannon is always ready to start better pay first. . . . I make more money now in nine and a half hours than I made in 120 hours when I first came here. So you can see why I don't want a union."[49]

Furthermore, rising wages reinforced the notion of Cannon as a caring, fatherly employer. Many Cannon workers attributed their prosperity to Charles Cannon. Labor historian Timothy Minchin noted that many workers believed that higher wages were a "product of Charles Cannon's personal benevolence rather than economic conditions."[50] In a sense, Uncle Charlie had delivered on his part of the paternalistic pact. He had brought the highest level of material prosperity that Cannon workers had ever known. Therefore, for many workers, the choice between the union's promises and Uncle Charlie's actions represented no choice. The union might never deliver on its promises, but Charles Cannon had already delivered.

By the beginning of September, Culver's situation was extremely difficult. He had to battle workers' fears and the positive perceptions of Charles Cannon's paternalism and convince a largely disinterested work force that it needed the union. In addition, Culver had fewer organizers than he wanted, with little hope of receiving more. Compounding the problem, he had to nurse his dwindling resources by switching from nicely printed leaflets to cheap mimeographed pamphlets. The Concord staff also needed to reduce their travel expenses to Kannapolis.

In mid-September, Culver made an in-depth analysis of the "Cannon problem." He noted that Charles Cannon had developed several techniques that effectively thwarted union advances. First, Cannon "pursued a policy of developing Cannon families in which two, or more, members of the family are employed," resulting in "a high family income on relatively low wages." Second, the textile baron had built local pride among the workers of Kannapolis along with effective political and social controls. Third, Cannon did not allow conditions at surrounding mills to cause discontent among his workers. The manufacturer matched all wage increases of nearby union mills, provided stable employment, and provided "clean and comfortable Mills [sic] in which to work." Cannon workers had a sense that they had "a superior deal" over other textile workers. And fourth, Charles Cannon knew how to control his female work force.[51]

According to Culver, Cannon understood how women thought and how to satisfy their social needs. Kannapolis represented a departure from the typical drab mill village. The Cannon company town had broad streets, unusual architecture for a mill village, and even looked "cute." Moreover, the town's many women's clubs and organizations drew women outside the home and involved them in community life. This carefully crafted environment, or "show town," provided women "an effective background" in which to "feel important." Women felt "proud to live in Kannapolis."[52]

With such apparent satisfaction among the women in Kannapolis, Culver suggested that the organizing effort not attack the paternalistic nature of the mill town directly but emphasize to the women what they did not have because of the family wage system. Organizers should focus on the car or vacation families could have if the firm became unionized, tell the women how the labor movement provided them another outlet for public involvement that would constructively influence the community, and stress the need for high enough wages that "only one member of the family would need to work." Yet Culver cautioned that organizers needed to avoid the impression that the union would deny work to family members (that is, women) who wanted a job.[53] He sensed that many men did not become involved because of the indifference or hostility of their wives to the organizing drive and believed, therefore, that influencing the Cannon women would greatly assist the unionization of the firm.

To jumpstart the floundering organizing movement in Cabarrus County and display its commitment to organizing Cannon Mills, the CIO Organizing Committee leadership went to Concord and held an open meeting.[54] Speakers for the September 21 meeting at the Hotel Concord included Van A. Bittner, national director of the southern organizing drive, George Baldanzi, executive vice president of the Textile Workers Union of America, and state director William Smith. To ensure that the union leaders did not "speak to a group of empty chairs," area director Draper Wood instructed union members from nearby locals to attend.[55] Two hundred people showed up. Many of those present were union members from Erwin Mills, Thomasville, and Winston-Salem. Baldanzi pledged that the CIO would remain in the South until workers in every textile mill had a union vote.[56]

At the meeting, union leaders assailed the local press, which stirred up a spirited response. Baldanzi commented that "when you want the truth, come to the CIO, for you'll never get it from the Kannapolis paper." He accused the *Daily Independent* of being the mouthpiece of Charles Cannon and refusing to report objectively on the organizing drive. After the rally, Thomas Wingate, editor of the *Daily Independent*, responded by charging the union with dishonesty. Contrary to the union's publicity, the meeting had not been open to all because the labor leaders had not taken questions from the audience. Further, Wingate equated the union drive with an invasion of Cabarrus County and asked if it would "not be better to have more home town boys working for you?" Accusing the CIO of violating southern racial taboos, Wingate also alleged that the union treated blacks members as equal to whites. Specifically, he wanted to know if "white workers could be forced to work under a Negro overseer" and if whites and blacks would be forced to use the same restrooms.[57]

Wingate voiced concerns of both mill management and white workers at Cannon Mills. Even though only 2.1 percent of the workers in the textile industry were black in 1940, the rise of the civil rights movement after World War II could change race relations and the textile industry.[58] Furthermore, a combination of labor and the emerging civil rights movement was a threat to the segregated mill village, and this was taking place only fifty-five miles away in Winston-Salem, North Carolina. The black tobacco workers of R. J. Reynolds had formed Local 22 of the Food, Tobacco, Agricultural, and Allied Workers of America and unionized the tobacco manufacturer. In addition, Local 22 worked with the National Association for the Advancement of Colored People (NAACP) to get a black minster elected to the Winston-Salem Board of Aldermen. The combining of labor and civil rights activities in Winston-Salem between 1943 and 1950 foretold the direction of growing civil rights movement toward political and economic equality.[59] As a newspaper editor, Wingate would have been aware of the activities in Winston-Salem and perhaps wondered if the Textile Workers Union of America planned to work with the association in organizing Cannon Mills.

Baldanzi responded at length to most of Wingate's inquiries. The TWUA executive informed Wingate that "over 75 per cent of the CIO drive leaders and organizers are Southerners." In response to the race issue, Baldanzi informed the newspaper editor that "it is not the CIO's purpose, as you imply, to force a change in the long established mores of a large section of our people. Custom and law determine the cultural pattern." Union opponents, Baldanzi responded, used such questions "to stir up racial prejudice in a desperate attempt to defeat the efforts of textile workers to organize." While not giving a timetable, the union official expressed confidence that the drive would succeed and "Cannon Mills will be organized."[60]

The Concord Tribune also attacked the union drive, publishing an editorial in early October comparing the union with the Nazi Party:

> If the southern textile worker is as intelligent as he is said to be, he will take a good look at the CIO before he joins. He will observe them as they flop along in their martial goose-step. He will think twice before he becomes initiated into that order, for once he joins it won't do much good to think. . . . May the southern textile workers wake up before they find themselves doing the goose-step through Dixie.[61]

Such analogies had an impact on some textile workers in the postwar South. The author found a way to slur the CIO and instill fear of the union among textile workers.

While opposition from the pro-Cannon local press intensified, the CIO faced a media counterattack from the textile industry throughout the nation. Charles Cannon was the leading proponent of a massive public relations campaign through the Textile Committee on Public Relations (TCPR) to counter negative views of the cotton textile industry. Formed in 1946 under the leadership of Martel Mills president G. Ellsworth Huggins, with Charles Cannon's involvement from its inception, the committee became the industry's mouthpiece.[62] The TCPR distributed information on the importance of the textile industry to the nation's economy and sought to acquaint the public with "the progress which the industry is making in research, training, modernization, job opportunities and good working and living conditions in the industry."[63] Financing for the committee came from mill subscriptions.

To distribute positive news on the industry, the committee established the Textile Information Service (TIS), which sought to use a positive message to battle the negative publicity issued by the CIO and the TWUA. Editorials and more overt jabs at the union came in the Textile Information Service's *Textile Neighbor*, a "magazine-type 'house organ' for industry employees."[64]

At the death of Ellsworth Huggins in 1951, Charles Cannon became the chairman of the Textile Committee on Public Relations and J. Harry Cannon of Cannon Mills became its secretary. Cannon Mills contributed heavily to the work of the TCPR, giving more than any other mill from mid-1950 to mid-1951.[65] The annual budget for the committee was approximately one hundred thousand dollars. By May 1951, the TIS had issued 810 news items to twenty-five hundred newspapers, sponsored exhibits with a total attendance of two million people, built the circulation of the *Textile Neighbor* to ten thousand, and sent speakers to many clubs. Wire services looked to the Textile Information Service for authoritative information on the industry and frequently printed releases from the TIS without attributing their source.[66]

The Cannon drive continued in spite of the textile industry's media blitz. By early October 1946, Culver, evidently believing his sacking to be imminent, felt compelled to reiterate to his superior the reasons for his staff's continued lack of success. He noted that Cannon Mills had conducted a whisper campaign with the workers and that the local newspapers had smeared the truth about the organizing drive. Culver defended his staff members, stating that they had worked hard, followed orders, and done their best with the resources available. Without additional resources, the Concord organizer warned that the union drive would be a hard and long process.[67] "My in-ability [sic] to produce more movement since July 3 is due to my physical inability to reach enough people to produce more movement with the number of organizers at my disposal and the tools of propaganda that I have had," he declared.[68]

In spite of the many obstacles to organizing Cannon Mills, Culver assured his superiors that some movement had taken place. The Concord CIO staff reported signing 29 new union members since mid-September, adding to the previous membership of 503.[69] Culver, in fact, remained optimistic about the Cannon drive. Given enough time and resources success would come, but Culver needed both.

In response to the negative press in Cabarrus County, the CIO Organizing Committee began broadcasting a series of radio programs in the area. The fifteen-minute radio programs aired at 5:15 p.m. on thirteen Saturdays on Charlotte radio station WBT beginning on October 19.[70] The organizers attempted to get radio time on the local Concord radio station, WEGO, without success.[71] Listeners to the CIO radio programs received an education on the history of the CIO, information highlighting the story of veterans involved in the local drive, and a discussion of the successful drives in other areas of the state.[72] Organizers hoped that even though workers might be afraid to take union literature at plant gates, they would listen to the union message in the privacy of their homes. The radio spots, union leaders believed, would serve as an effective counter to the biased reporting in the local newspapers.

The new radio broadcasts did not turn the situation in Kannapolis around, however, and Dean Culver lost his position as head of the Concord CIO staff. On October 23, 1946, Smith replaced Culver with Joel Leighton. A New Englander, Leighton had worked to organize the Marshall Field plants in North Carolina and the Dan River Mills in Virginia. Culver remained on the Concord staff as an organizer until November, when Smith reassigned him to Asheville, North Carolina, to head the organizing effort at the American Enka Company, a rayon plant.[73]

Leighton began his work in Concord optimistically.[74] He immediately moved to invigorate the floundering plant committees. While convincing Cannon workers to serve on committees continued to be a problem, Leighton was even more disturbed at the inactivity of workers who had already consented to join committees. Attendance at committee meetings was disappointing. Leighton sought to weed out the inactive members and to form viable committees. The new Concord labor leader confirmed Culver's opinion that the organizing staff had been working hard to build attendance at the committee meetings.[75]

While Joel Leighton remained optimistic about the Cannon situation, by the end of October 1946 Operation Dixie had yielded few results in the North Carolina textile industry. Only nine National Labor Relations Board elections had been held in the state, and the union had lost six of these. The three newly organized textile mills combined employed fewer than five hundred workers. Elections had still not been held at the larger textile companies, but Baldanzi stated confidently that the drive would continue "until the South is organized." Moreover, the labor leader said that the organizers would be in the South permanently.[76]

As CIO and TWUA leaders promised to persevere, Cannon Mills proudly touted the loyalty of its employees. More than seventeen hundred workers attended two huge banquets held on two successive nights to recognize longtime Cannon workers. The highlight of the banquets was the awarding of service pins by Charles Cannon. As a gesture of egalitarianism, fifty-five-year Cannon employee Jonas I. Freeze pinned Charles Cannon with a thirty-five-year service pin.[77] The pinning of the mill owner by an employee reinforced the idea among workers that the powerful and wealthy Charles Cannon remained, at heart, one of them, a product of Kannapolis and its mills. In contrast, the union organizers represented outsiders who had come to the mill village to tell the workers how to live their lives.

National news stories also helped to alienate workers from the local organizers. News reports of possible communist infiltration of the CIO did not help the organizing effort in Kannapolis. Paralleling the Truman administration's purge of communists and subversives from the federal government, the House Committee on Un-American Activities investigated communist influence in Hollywood and in the unions. Committee member J. Parnell Thomas (R-N.J.) explained that the committee aimed to "spotlight the sorry spectacle of having outright Communists controlling and dominating some of the most vital unions in American labor, unions (that) are now being used as Moscow pawns for ambitious and unscruplous [sic] Communist leaders."[78] The congressional investigation of the unions tainted the organizing efforts of the Concord CIO staff.

Bad publicity aside, Leighton also had more immediate financial concerns. Operation Dixie had put the CIO heavily into debt. The union's Southern Organizing Committee had estimated that the drive would cost $1 million, but at the prevailing rate of expenditure, it would cost $1.8 million. The CIO, however, had raised only $768,800, and by October it owed $438,000 and had only $87,000 on hand.[79] Soon the Concord drive experienced another round of cost cutting that further diminished its effectiveness. In late November, state director William Smith issued a directive to cut expenses more drastically. He explained that "the CIO Southern Organizing drive must go on and in order for it to continue efficiently, we must cut expenses to the bone."[80] Areas targeted for cuts included transportation, printing, and mimeograph paper. The Concord staff was especially hard hit by the cut in travel reimbursements. Local organizers needed generous transportation budgets to travel to Kannapolis from the Concord office and to cover the sprawling mill complexes. In addition, the reduction in printed material hurt the staff's ability to get the union message out to the workers and to battle the biased reporting of the local press. Slowly, the local organizing effort began to die because of lack of financial nourishment.

By the end of the 1946, the local union organizers had little to show for their seven-month effort to organize Cannon Mills. The Concord CIO staff had formed few active plant committees. Only 561 Cannon workers had signed union cards, less than 3 percent of the 24,000 work force.[81] Already the drive was a financial drain on the coffers of the CIO.

Leighton and the Concord organizers continued to search without success for an issue to motivate the Cannon workers. Cannon Mills effectively defused the wage issue by matching wage increases in union mills in the South. In February, the management of Dan River and Marshall Field mills announced an agreement with their unions for a 10 percent wage increase, which Cannon Mills promptly matched.[82]

In April 1947, the Concord staff initiated weekly labor rallies at the union hall to try to energize the drive.[83] Organizers distributed mimeographed leaflets advertising the first rally to the workers of Cannon Mills' Plant 2, Plant 5, and Plant 9.[84] Although Leighton pushed for high attendance, he privately admitted to a friend at the TWUA headquarters in New York that he would be happy if fifty workers showed up.[85] The first two weekly rallies

had little appreciable impact on the mood of the workers. Attendance continued to be disappointing, but the Concord CIO staff persisted and publicized
them as successes.[86] The organizers also decided to begin a contest to boost
attendance. Starting on May 24, they began giving away a union-made gift
at each rally to the worker who turned in the most signed membership cards
for the week.[87] Even so, the rallies attracted few workers.

By June, the financial condition of the CIO drive in North Carolina had
become acute. No longer did the Concord staff have CIO letterhead statio-
nery. In addition, the state organization began to transfer and terminate some
organizers throughout the state, including those in Concord. After expend-
ing tremendous effort in organizing Cannon Mills with few results, the
state organization decided "to retrench for a while in the Cannon Drive."[88]
Although the Concord staff continued to organize plant committees and to
hold the weekly labor rallies, Leighton closed the union hall during part of
the day. By July, the union hall remained opened only two hours and fifteen
minutes each weekday.[89] Overall, the staff reductions seriously limited the
organizers' effectiveness and further slowed the momentum of the drive.

The final blow to the union effort came in August when the Concord
CIO staff lost its union hall. Joel Leighton received a letter from the landlord
requesting that they vacate the building by September 15, 1947.[90] Leighton
knew it would be difficult to find another building suitable for a union hall
in Concord and there was no chance of finding one in Kannapolis. The landlord did agree to allow the organizers to use the office part of the union hall
through October, but by that time attendance at the weekly labor rallies had
fallen to four workers.[91]

The loss of the union hall effectively ended the union drive against
Cannon Mills. Leighton and some staff members attempted to maintain
some presence in Concord and Kannapolis and tried to use private homes to
keep the few remaining committees active. Yet without a union hall to direct
the drive and hold rallies, any remaining chance of organizing Cannon's
mills in Concord and Kannapolis ended.

A further blow to the CIO came with the strike at the Cannon Amazon
plant in Thomasville, North Carolina. As mentioned in an earlier chapter, the
Amazon plant had become unionized on February 28, 1944. Representatives
of the Textile Workers Union of America Local 633 negotiated unsuccessfully with the management of the Amazon plant on several issues, including
continuance of the union dues check-off system, additional vacation time
for workers with five or more years of seniority, a wage increase, and the
addition of health and life insurance for workers. Management agreed to a
10 percent wage increase but balked on the other issues. On March 1, 1947,

the local voted to strike against the plant.[92] The seventeen-month conflict killed Local 633.[93] Management saw the strike as the opportunity to destroy the only organized work force under Cannon control and therefore did not budge from its original position. When the strike ended, the Textile Workers Union of America Local 633 was effectively dead, drained of its funds and having lost most of its membership.[94] The 1947 organizing drive at Cannon yielded meager results. Only 192 workers joined the union that year, bringing total membership to 753 for 1946 and 1947, or slightly over 3 percent of the Cannon Mills work force.[95] The following year, a much diminished organizing campaign recruited only 66 new members.[96]

Operation Dixie had ended in Kannapolis but continued on the national level until 1953. The financial condition of the southern drive improved in 1948 when the CIO increased union dues and sent most of the new income to Operation Dixie. Internal strife, however, hurt the drive's effectiveness. Van Bittner died in 1949 and George Baldanzi replaced him as the national director of Operation Dixie. Conflict soon broke out between Emil Rieve, head of the Textile Workers Union of America, and Baldanzi, with each accusing the other of ineffectiveness in the southern drive.[97] In addition, a 1951 strike at the TWUA's largest unionized plants in the South detracted from the organizing effort. The strike, which included Marshall Field, Dan River, Erwin, and the Cone mills, cost the union more than $1.2 million and ended with the union's defeat.[98] Defections of some locals to the American Federation of Labor also weakened the movement. After the debacle of the 1951 strike, workers at Dan River overwhelming voted to join the AFL-affiliated United Textile Workers.[99] Operation Dixie officially ended when Philip Murray, head of the CIO, died in 1952 and Walter Reuther became the new leader. In 1953, Reuther abolished the Southern Organizing Committee and left organizing to the individual unions.[100]

In sum, the CIO failed to organize Cannon Mills for several reasons. First, the CIO organizers did not overcome the powerful paternalistic social structure of Kannapolis. Nothing had prepared the union organizers to face the control that Charles Cannon had in Kannapolis. For a town of fifty thousand, Cannon had almost unimaginable power and control over people's lives. As labor historian Barbara Griffith noted, Charles Cannon "was firmly in control of the town's economic, political, and social climate. Almost every street, every home, even the fire stations and grocery stores were owned by Cannon. The mayor, the police chief, and the ministers were all part of the Cannon 'family,' as were, of course, the workers."[101]

Relatively high wages constituted another obstacle to organizing Cannon Mills.[102] High wages resulted from the changing postwar economy, which in the textile industry was characterized by increased competition and a continued labor shortage. Once pent-up consumer demand had been satisfied, the market was flooded with household textile products. This condition resulted in consumer demand based on price. With rising production costs, especially labor, the margin per unit of production shrunk greatly. To maintain profits, textile firms had to produce great quantities of goods to spread the higher production costs over more units of production. Cost savings came with investment in modern machinery and greater efficiencies in the flow of production.[103] With an industry loss of 110,000 textile workers since the war, Cannon had to pay higher wages to retain his labor force and ensure a degree of work-force stability to compete effectively in the textile industry.[104] Without paying higher wages, Cannon Mills risked losing employees to union mills or to newer and high-paying industries that had moved into the region during World War II. A substantial loss of trained workers would have led to a loss in production, higher costs associated with training new workers, and reduced profits.

As a part of his welfare capitalism, Cannon's determination to match union pay increases eliminated the union's main issue against the non-union firm.[105] Cannon Mills proved that it had perfected the art of welfare capitalism by providing "for the comfort or improvement of employees which was neither a necessity of the industry nor required by law."[106] Firms used welfare capitalism, or industrial paternalism, as unions called it, to increase worker loyalty, ensure a stable work force, and fight against unions.[107] As labor historian Stuart Brandes noted, companies used welfare capitalism as a defensive mechanism to battle unions. According to Brandes, welfare capitalism peaked in the 1920s and then died off because of the Great Depression and its replacement by government programs and regulation.[108] But long after most firms had abandoned welfare capitalism, Cannon Mills used it effectively to thwart union organization.[109]

In addition, higher wages brought the mill workers of Kannapolis into the consumer culture. The higher wages paid by Cannon Mills allowed its workers to enjoy consumption and leisure along with the rest of Americans and thereby pacified the work force. As historian Daniel Rodgers argued, the move from the preindustrial self-employed worker to the industrial mass-production wage earner lowered job satisfaction and caused workers to seek fulfillment in leisure and consumption.[110] The postwar wages made it possible for Cannon's workers to enjoy life outside work, unlike previous generations of Cannon employees. As CIO organizer Culver noted in a letter to his superior, Cannon workers "own radios and many automobiles. . . . They have travelled and visited around considerable [sic]."[111] Prosperity in

Kannapolis bolstered the Cannon myth. Many Cannon workers remained convinced that Cannon had brought the good life to them. Instead of crediting the wage increases of the 1940s to the changing economy, workers of Kannapolis credited Charles Cannon. The condition of mill workers seemed better than at any time in the past. For many Cannon workers, prosperity offset the lack of control they had at work or in the mill village. In effect, relatively high wages had pacified Cannon's work force and the union found no way to agitate the worker into union membership.

Race was also a factor in the union's defeat. The *Daily Independent* effectively questioned the union's stance on maintaining the racial status quo in Kannapolis. Racial attitudes were entrenched among whites in the mill village. Few whites believed that blacks were equal to whites and shared the attitude of Jones Freeze on the laziness of black men. Freeze, a supervisor of black men unloading cotton, said that "the worst part of it [his job] is bossing the Niggers that handle it. You have to talk to 'em like you're a-goin' to kill 'em or they lay down on you and not do a lick of work."[112] Whites believed that black men were suited for the hard physical jobs at the mills but needed close supervision, while black women were best employed as domestics. Many white mill workers, such as Dolph Parsons, who employed a "settled negro woman," employed blacks as domestics.[113] Mill management believed that production jobs and supervisory positions should remain the domain of whites and that blacks should do the menial labor. Undoubtedly, many white workers believed that a union victory would jeopardize this racial status quo.

In the end, the CIO's organizing effort in Kannapolis failed because it did not commit enough resources to crack Cannon's paternalism. CIO and Operation Dixie leaders did not understand how much control Charles Cannon had over his workers. Once Dean Culver recognized the degree of Cannon's control in Kannapolis, he knew a successful organizing campaign would "be expensive" and "somewhat lengthy."[114] Success in the face of the Cannon myth required a long-term commitment to the Cannon drive and a permanent presence in Cabarrus County. Although the CIO publicly stated its commitment to organizing Cannon Mills in hopes of opening the other non-union textile chains, the union spread its resources throughout the South and in different industries. In North Carolina, the CIO attempted to organize furniture and tobacco workers as well as textile workers. Eventually, the unfocused drive proved too costly and the union withdrew. The next concerted union drive against Cannon Mills did not take place until the 1970s.

CHAPTER 12

———————◆┼◀┼◀◆———————

THE DANGER OF LARGER FORCES:
War, Imports, and Government Policies

As Operation Dixie came to an end, the textile industry turned its attention to a more pressing issue: providing textile products for America's war effort in Korea. The textile industry had been working with the government to prepare for such a conflict for some time. A plan to "convert [the industry] to large scale war production immediately," in the light of growing Cold War tensions, had been in place for more than three years before the Korean War. Industry leader Charles Cannon, past president of the Quartermaster Association, believed that the plan would draw upon the experiences of World War II to avoid bottlenecks and other production and distribution problems.[1] The textile industry quickly moved to meet the nation's military requirements.

The Korean War helped pull the industry out of the slump of 1949. Mill activity in 1950 outpaced the war years of 1941–45.[2] In addition, purchases of new textile equipment hit a record high.[3] The record setting pace of 1950, however, did not carry over into the following year. Market conditions turned against textile mills in 1951 as demand for textile products fell in spite of the war. According to figures issued jointly by the Securities and Exchange Commission and the Federal Trade Commission, the textile industry suffered the greatest decline of twenty-two major manufacturing industries during the second and third quarters of the year.[4] Mills responded by laying off workers and temporarily shutting down.[5] Fully half of all textile mills were shut down in late 1951.[6]

Industry spokesmen blamed the downturn on several factors. First, the industry's modernization effort following World War II had been highly successful. With fewer textile mills and workers than during the wartime period, the industry had met consumer demand and more than twenty billion dollars in military orders during 1950 and 1951 "without visible strain."[7] A press release from the Textile Information Service summed up the problem as "a very real underestimation of its [the textile industry's] productive power, coupled with an exaggerated estimate of military requirements."[8] Second, cotton prices hit an all-time high of more than forty-five cents per pound in March 1951.[9] Mill margins fell as costs for raw material increased, wages remained high, and demand fell as mills filled government orders quickly. And third, mill owners blamed government wartime economic programs for the downturn.

Textile leaders reserved their harshest criticism for the Office of Price Stabilization (OPS). Established in January 1951, the OPS "established and administered price regulations" with the help of various "industry advisory committees."[10] The office set up wage and price controls over raw cotton and textile production to combat inflation. Textile trade associations, however, accused the government agency of contributing to the downturn of 1951. The president of the American Cotton Manufacturers Institute (AMCI), Charles Hertwig, accused the OPS of vacillating in setting price controls on cotton textiles: "Starting with the voluntary 'hold the line' freeze of December 1 [1950], followed by the wage-price freeze of January and the general order for all manufacturers on April 25, a series of actions of a temporary nature by OPS had done nothing more than to throw the industry into a state of confused indecision."[11] ACMI press releases accused the OPS of canceling a directive the day it was to go into effect and replacing it with another that required a team of industry lawyers to unravel its meaning.[12] Julian Robertson, president of the North Carolina Cotton Manufacturers Association, expressed the belief that OPS policies and other government wartime business regulations were unnecessary since the industry had met consumer and military demand with capacity to spare.[13]

Charles Cannon also chafed under government wartime regulations. He became concerned over the price of cotton, government price supports for cotton, and the difficulty of textile firms in following wartime regulations. Known as "Mr. Cotton" by his colleagues, Cannon was renowned for his knowledge of cotton and cotton policy. The textile manufacturer believed that "of the factors affecting cotton, the two principal ones are weather and politics. Of the two, the weather is more predictable."[14] As a result of his reputation, Cannon served on various trade association committees that dealt with cotton policy matters, including the Council Advisory Committee of the National Cotton Council, a trade association of producers, shippers, ginners, and manufacturers. At the outbreak of war, Cannon also became a member of the council's Cotton Mobilization Committee. He served, in addition, as chairman of the Cotton Committee for the North Carolina Cotton Manufacturers' Association.[15]

While an outspoken opponent of the Office of Price Administration in the previous war, Cannon remained low key in public criticism of the Office of Price Stabilization during the Korean crisis. As chairman of the Textile Committee on Public Relations, Cannon instead used the Textile Information Service to disseminate criticism of the OPS to the news media. He proofed articles for the *Textile Neighbor*, a publication that presented the industry's view of government regulations to textile workers.[16] In addition, Cannon widely publicized negative commentaries on the OPS through TCPR news releases. Under such business criticism, and under a new Republican administration, the OPS was abolished on April 30, 1953, almost three months before the Korean conflict ended.

As the rest of the textile industry weathered the downturn in 1951, Cannon Mills experienced increased sales and profits. Sales increased $16 million over 1950 with profits advancing at the same rate.[17] After the bad year of 1950, the rest of the decade experienced a period of slow but stable growth. Sales from 1951 to 1959 ranged from a low of $180,180,000 in 1954 to a high of $207,096,000 in 1959. Profits, however, grew at a slower rate, ranging from the decade high of $27,953,000 in 1951 to a low of $17,735,000 in 1952. The decade ended with profits of $20,941,000 in 1959.[18]

Plant modernization continued during the 1950s. Cannon Mills installed air conditioning in several of its plants in 1951, followed by the latest textile machinery. In 1955, Plant 8 in China Grove, North Carolina, received the Draper XP2 looms. These machines did not work to Cannon's specifications, so Cannon engineers modified them for maximum performance. Plant 10 became the testing center for the new Draper Shuttleless Looms in 1959. Engineers for the Draper Company and Cannon Mills perfected the new looms while testing these at the Cannon facility. Cannon Mills, consequently, became the first textile manufacturer to operate the new looms.[19]

Besides modernizing its own plants, Cannon Mills also expanded through acquisition and mergers. In 1955, the textile firm gained operating control of Brown Manufacturing Company of Concord. Cannon further consolidated its operations in South Carolina in 1957 with the absorption of Central Mills as Plant 12, an investment in which the Kannapolis firm had bought a controlling interest in 1943.[20] To facilitate the purchase of new equipment, plant improvements, and expansion, the board of directors steadily increased the operating capital of the firm. The board had set working capital at $33,776,000 in 1949, and by 1959, working capital had increased to $50 million.[21]

During the 1950s, the board of directors went through changes that would have a profound impact on the future of the firm. In 1952, Charles Cannon's older brother and long-time Cannon board member, Martin Luther Cannon, died. The passing of Martin consolidated Charles's control of the firm. Since Charles and Martin often disagreed, the younger Cannon had made sure that his brother had a limited role in the firm. Martin had felt so outmaneuvered by his brother that he had moved to Charlotte and busied himself in other business activities.[22] After Martin's death, George Batte Jr., Charles Cannon's longtime friend and personal secretary, took Martin's place on the board.[23] Now the only two Cannons on the board were Charles and his son, William. Charles Cannon, however, retained control as the board consisted of his close friends and associates. Don Holt became a member of the board in 1953 because of his excellent work in turning around the faltering Plant 6.[24] In 1959, the last major change came when the board created the positions of the chairman of the board and assistant chairman of the board. Charles Cannon became chairman and remained president of the firm, while William Cannon became the assistant chairman.[25]

Charles Cannon was willing to allow some fresh faces on the board, such as Don Holt. At sixty-six years of age, however, Cannon continued to run the firm on his terms. Charles still had the power to reward whom he wanted to reward, and at the time his son had the manufacturer's favor. Nothing would wrench the firm from Charles Cannon's control but death.

While Cannon Mills' business remained stable during the 1950s, Charles Cannon became concerned with the threat to the textile industry from Japanese imports. In 1948, the Japanese textile industry posed no danger to American producers. World War II had devastated the proud Japanese textile industry, once the world's second largest producer of wool textiles and the largest producer of rayon filament. Of the prewar inventory of 12 million spindles, Japan had only 2.6 million in operation in 1948. Cotton yarn production declined by approximately 86 percent from 1937 to 1947, while the production of cotton cloth had fallen by 94 percent during the same period. The Textile Division of the Economic and Scientific Section, under the authority of the supreme commander of allied powers in Japan, worked to rebuild the nation's textile industry and to set early postwar production targets. American economic experts recognized the need for Japan to develop a viable export base for textiles to pay for imported raw cotton and to bring much needed income into the country. The challenge for the Japanese textile industry involved balancing production for internal consumption with exports needed to raise revenues to rebuild the nation and make it self-sufficient.[26]

By 1951, Japan had made such tremendous advances in rebuilding its textile industry that it began to worry American textile executives. Claudius Murchison, economist for the American Cotton Manufacturers Institute, warned of the threat from Japanese imports.[27] Japanese textile firms had added more than a million spindles to their capacity since the allied supreme commander removed restrictions on the industry before the outbreak of hostilities in Korea. Japan had already become the second largest exporter of textiles in the world. American textile leaders became concerned that because of the low wages paid to Japanese textile workers, American textiles would not be able to compete with cheap Japanese imports.[28] American producers now faced the prospect of losing domestic market share to Japanese textile imports, which were growing exponentially. Charles Cannon and the Textile Committee of Public Relations sounded the warning.

Compounding the import situation, some of President Dwight D. Eisenhower's foreign policy initiatives clashed with the interests of the textile manufacturers. Rebuilding Japan as a regional economic power and keeping her an American ally became one of the main foreign policy goals of the new president. The administration's stance on Japan soon brought it into conflict with the American textile industry. In 1954 the administration announced that it would support Japan's admission to the General Agreement on Tariffs and Trade, extend most-favored-nation trading status to Japan, and reduce textile tariffs.

At public hearings, the ACMI expressed its opposition to reductions on textile tariffs.[29] Textile officials believed that the president, and especially the State Department, were willing to sacrifice the American textile industry to rebuild Japan and keep it out of the communist sphere. The textile industry was the largest manufacturing sector in Japan and the only one that could export in sufficient quantities to earn foreign exchange. No other industry in the American economy faced the same level of competition from Japanese imports. Heavy industry, such as automobiles and steel, had no competition from Japanese imports. The State Department realized that Japan's main prewar textile markets, China and India, had been closed and therefore Japan needed to export to the United States. Increasingly, textile industry leaders felt expendable, and the editor of the *Textile World* accused the Eisenhower administration of capitulating in a textile Munich pact to appease Japan.[30]

The administration's trade bill of 1955 further expressed the administration's goals in foreign trade. This bill eventually became law, but not without concerted opposition from more than twenty-five textile trade associations. Under the new law, the president gained greater authority to cut tariffs. The textile industry did not have enough influence to kill the bill, but it did succeed in getting the more objectionable elements eliminated.[31]

Preferring industry agreements to legislative import controls, the administration encouraged the Japanese and American textile industries to work out an agreement on Japanese imports. The precedent for voluntary quotas had been set in 1937, when Japanese textile executives, in consultation with officials of the Cotton Textile Institute, had agreed to limit exports of textile goods to the United States.[32] Japanese textile officials sent a special trade delegation to the United States in 1955 to confer with American textile executives. Japanese and American textile leaders attempted to reach a mutually beneficial limitation on Japanese imports. All seemed amicable until the Japanese announced their proposed voluntary import limits for 1956. Believing the limits to be too high, American textile officials petitioned Ezra Taft Benson, the secretary of agriculture, to impose import quotas under Section 22 of the Agricultural Adjustment Act, which allowed the president to impose import quotas or fees if "these imports render or tend to render ineffective, or materially interfere with, U.S. agricultural programs." With advice from the secretary of agriculture, the president could recommend that the Tariff Commission investigate the situation. Upon a recommendation from the commission, the president could impose import relief.[33] Benson, however, did not act.

The administration tried to reassure textile executives that it had no intention of destroying the American textile industry. In a letter to Donald Comer, chairman of the Board of Avondale Mills, Sherman Adams, the assistant to President Eisenhower, stated that the administration had no intention of pursuing foreign policy objectives "to the detriment of any American industry—and that of course includes our textile industry."[34] Textile manufacturers remained skeptical.

Charles Cannon did not believe such reassurances. Japanese imports had already captured 65 percent of the velveteen market, 58 percent of the damask market, and half the gingham business by 1956. In addition, the Japanese exported twenty million towels and twelve million sheets and pillowcases to the United States.[35] The administration gave the textile industry no relief from this flood of cheap imports. Cannon believed that the government's policies would "liquidate the industry" and advised executives to spend all of the money in the ACMI since the future remained so uncertain. Further, Cannon demonstrated his concern by advising the officers of the ACMI to learn Japanese "because I am afraid they will be our bosses."[36]

Cannon made sure that the industry's view on the Japanese import issue received wide dissemination in Kannapolis. The *Daily Independent* ran stories on the damaging effect of Japanese textiles. A story that appeared in the May 20, 1956, issue of the paper garnered praise from the American Cotton Manufacturers Institute. Robert Jackson of the ACMI complimented Cannon:

> I have just had an opportunity to read the May 20 issue of The Daily Independent. You folks did a real job in handling the subject effectively and thoroughly. This is the type of agitation that serves a mighty good purpose here in Washington, and you can be sure the clippings eventually find their way to these agencies in the Government.[37]

Beyond import policies, the administration's response to cotton surpluses further concerned textile manufacturers. Government involvement in storing commodities had begun with the first Agricultural Adjustment Act (AAA) of the New Deal. The act created the Commodity Credit Corporation (CCC), which provided storage loans to farmers who could sell their crops to the government or redeem the loan later and sell on the market. Although the Supreme Court struck down the first AAA, the CCC survived as part of the second Agricultural Adjustment Act, which passed in 1938.[38] In 1942, because of the agricultural act, the CCC began to receive large quantities of commodities for storage. At the end of 1952, the stocks of cotton had grown to 5.6 million bales.[39]

Secretary Benson, believing that the huge stocks of commodities depressed prices, further hurting farmers, became concerned with the accumulation of agricultural surpluses. The administration, therefore, supported the Agricultural Trade Development and Assistance Act (PL 480) of 1954 for dealing with the stockpiles. PL 480 authorized the sale of surplus commodities to "friendly" nations in foreign currency and limited an annual loss of up to $700 million to the CCC. The law provided for the development of foreign markets by using the foreign currency acquired from commodity sales.[40]

In spite of the administration's hopes, PL 480 did not solve the surplus problem. In 1955, surpluses continued to grow. Storage costs now ran at a million dollars a day as cotton stocks climbed one million bales above the

1954 level. Overseas market development and sales promotion under PL 480 had not measurably increased demand for American commodities.[41] In addition, price supports overpriced many American commodities on the world market, and Secretary Benson refused to sell CCC stocks below the level of domestic price supports.[42]

Benson came under intense pressure, however, to sell cotton at lower prices on the world market. Fifty-six senators and 129 representatives sent letters to Benson asking the CCC to sell its stockpile of cotton at world market prices.[43] But both Secretary of State John Foster Dulles and Secretary of Commerce Sinclair Weeks objected to "dumping" American commodities on the world market. Weeks believed that the sale of cheaper American rice would hurt Cuba's rice industry, and Dulles objected since cheaper American cotton could jeopardize Egypt's cotton industry.[44] Yet under intense pressure from southern congressmen, and believing that taking a loss on the sale of surplus commodities would be better than endless storage, the administration supported the Agricultural Act of 1956. Under the authority of the act, the U.S. government began to subsidize the exportation of cotton to bring it in line with world prices. Paying the difference between the higher support price and the world market price, the administration believed this program would increase demand of American cotton on the world market. At first, the subsidy ran at six and a half cents per pound, but later it increased to eight and a half cents per pound.[45]

The two-price cotton system aggravated the cotton textile import situation. Foreign manufacturers paid a lower price than domestic textile manufacturers for American cotton. American mill executives became outraged that foreign cotton mills could undercut domestic textiles with cheaper American-grown cotton. Already the foreign mills had a wage advantage on the domestic producers, but now they could use the price advantage of American cotton against the American mills. Charles Cannon and the ACMI vowed to end the two-price cotton system.

Although the administration continued to receive pressure from the textile industry, Eisenhower did not want to place quotas on Japan. The Eisenhower administration began government-to-government negotiations to limit Japanese imports, since no agreement had resulted from meetings of industry officials of the two nations. After negotiations, in January 1957, government representatives announced a five-year limitation on Japanese textiles imported to the United States.[46]

The five-year voluntary limitations did not appease American textile officials. American manufactures continued to apply pressure on the administration for import relief. The textile industry now stepped up agitation in Congress for legislative action. Charles Cannon added his considerable influence to the lobbying effort. He appeared before the House Committee on Agriculture in June 1957 and outlined the gloomy realities facing the textile industry and cotton growers. While worldwide cotton consumption had increased dramatically, he stated, American cotton exports had fallen. Cotton acreage in the United States had dropped from twenty-eight million acres in 1951 to approximately fourteen million in 1957. Government agricultural programs had priced American cotton out of the world market.

In addition, the demand for cotton had lessened because of the increased consumption of man-made fibers, which had grown 52 percent since 1946. Consumer demand for textile products had expanded slowly. As consumer spending increased 28 percent from 1948 to 1957, demand for textile products grew only 4 percent. Cannon believed that the government should help cotton farmers by reducing price supports and allowing greater acreage allotments. Thus demand for cheaper American cotton would increase on the world market and possibly slow the demand for man-made fibers. Lower cotton costs would enable American textile manufacturers to cut the costs of production and compete more readily against textile imports. The industry still needed relief from cheap imports, however, to make a complete program for the cotton and the textile industries.[47]

Because of his understanding of government support programs for cotton, Charles Cannon became the chairman of the ACMI's Special Cotton Policy Committee (SCPC), formed in 1957. For Cannon, the nation's cotton policy had to address the interests of both growers and manufacturers. Agricultural cotton policy needed to provide a decent living for cotton farmers and yet provide enough cotton at reasonable prices to enable American textile mills to compete with textile imports. The committee succinctly identified the problems of the current price supports for cotton. First, the method of maintaining a minimum price for cotton through the reduction of acreage had broken down. Increasing yields per acre had decreased the efficiency of this policy. Second, high price supports had overpriced American cotton on the world market, resulting in decreasing exports of the fiber and mounting domestic surpluses. Third, the higher cost of cotton resulted in greater demand for man-made fibers. And fourth, the flood of cheap imported textiles took markets away from American textile firms, thus lowering the domestic demand for cotton even more.[48]

After identifying the problems with the current price support programs, the committee drew up a list of "fundamental principles" for a healthy long-term cotton program, including an increase in cotton acreage allotments, a one-price cotton system, and a reduction in cost of the cotton support system.[49] The committee knew that opposition existed against some of its proposed reforms.

Cotton farmers remained reluctant to support agricultural reform. A 1953 survey showed that more than 90 percent of cotton farmers supported high price supports.[50] Farm income had fallen from $15.1 billion in 1952 to $11.6 billion in 1956, and price supports for cotton had already fallen 12 percent from 1952 to 1957 under Benson's flexible parity system.[51] Naturally, farmers were wary of any reforms that might further reduce their income.

The Special Cotton Policy Committee's call for reforming the costly cotton agricultural support system reflected the ideas of Secretary of Agriculture Benson. He advocated reductions in the government subsidies to agriculture and believed a greater free-market approach would benefit farmers in the long term.[52] Benson and the entire administration, however, seemed little concerned about the plight of the textile industry.

With inaction by the administration, the textile industry appealed to Congress for assistance. In 1958, the Senate assigned the Committee on Interstate and Foreign Commerce the task of conducting "a full and complete study of all factors affecting commerce and production in the textile industry of the United States." To gather information on the problems of the textile industry, the committee created the Subcommittee on the Domestic Textile Industry, chaired by Senator John Pastore of Rhode Island.[53] The Pastore committee, as the subcommittee became known, collected data from various executive departments that illustrated the growth in Japanese textile imports under the administration's framework of voluntary import restrictions. In 1957, Japanese textile imports totaled 235 million square yards. The Japanese had requested an increase of the voluntary quotas to 247.2 million square yards in 1959. Of the proposed 1959 total, 33 million square yards represented household textile products, including pillowcases and dish towels.[54] Henry Kearns, the assistant secretary of commerce, wrote the committee expressing the administration's opinion that the voluntary limits on Japanese textiles "would not be unduly damaging to the United States cotton textile industry."[55]

In September 1958, the Pastore committee opened hearings in Charlotte, North Carolina, the heart of the textile industry and the headquarters of the ACMI. Industry leader Charles Cannon, testifying before the committee on September 30, 1958, expressed his frustration with the administration, whose lack of "understanding of the problems of the textile industry, coupled with the great influence exercised by the Department of State under the guise of foreign relations" remained the main problems

for the industry. Compounding the situation was the unsympathetic attitudes of the Department of Agriculture and Department of Labor.[56] Cannon
reminded the committee of the safeguards of the Agricultural Adjustment
Act. He explained that Section 22 provided a means to protect American
farmers from competition from imported cotton and argued that the government should use it to protect textile manufacturers. If government
converted imported textiles into their bales of cotton equivalents, Cannon
suggested, then the administration would realize that the current rate of
textile imports surpassed the thirty-eight-thousand bale limit previously set
under Section 22. Already the textile industry had a disadvantage in competing with foreign textile producers because of the low wages they paid,
and the two-price cotton system compounded the problem by allowing foreign competitors to purchase American cotton from thirty to forty dollars
a bale less than American manufacturers. Establishing import quotas under
Section 22, Cannon explained, would help to alleviate the harmful effects of
cheap textile imports. The secretary of agriculture, the manufacturer noted,
had refused to open a Section 22 investigation.[57]

Cannon elaborated on how the textile industry had suffered under the
current administration. The industry now had two million spindles less than
in 1955, and consumption of cotton by American mills had fallen by more
than one million bales annually. Furthermore, this reduction had resulted
in the loss of more than two hundred thousand textile jobs. The number of
spindles for the entire industry now numbered twenty-one million, fewer
than during World War II. Cannon believed that the industry could not
match the levels of production achieved during the war and that this represented a threat to national security. While American textile production had
fallen, Cannon noted, production in the communist world had risen since
the Korean War.[58]

To remedy the problems in the industry, Cannon and the Special Cotton
Policy Committee of the ACMI suggested solutions. First, he asked for protection under Section 22 of the AAA from "imports of cotton goods from
low-wage countries which deprive American farmers of domestic markets
and American workers of jobs." Second, the administration needed to allow
an adequate acreage allotment of cotton production moved through "normal trade channels at competitive prices" on both the world and domestic
market.[59] The industry only wanted the modification or elimination of
government programs that made the American textile industry uncom-
petitive. Cannon made it clear that the industry did not want "the Federal
Government to embark upon any program to try to do for the mills what

they have tried to do for agriculture. We are in bad enough shape as a result of the programs to save the cotton farmer and if anything the cotton farmers are worse off than we are."[60]

With its investigations complete, the Pastore committee submitted its report to the Senate on February 4, 1959. The committee concluded that the textile industry had not shared in the economic growth enjoyed by the rest of American industry and that Congress and the administration needed to take action to avoid a greater decline in the light of national security concerns. Committee recommendations resembled those advocated by Cannon: A further decline in textile capacity resulting from cheap imports should be checked through establishing import quotas and either the two-price cotton system should be eliminated or import tariffs should be increased to offset the difference in domestic cotton costs and world market prices.[61]

Confident that the Pastore committee had accurately assessed the deteriorating situation of the textile industry, trade associations again worked for Section 22 protection. The National Cotton Council, with support from the ACMI, petitioned Secretary Benson for a Section 22 investigation on June 29, 1959.[62] Supporting its call for an investigation on textile imports, the council argued that cheap imports had damaged domestic cotton manufacturers. Textile imports for 1958 totaled the equivalent of 286,630 bales of cotton. The bale equivalent of textile imports had risen more than seven times since 1949, resulting in the loss of markets by American textile mills. Shrinking markets for American textile products resulted in reduced demand for American cotton by domestic mills. In addition, while the United States had supplied half to the world's cotton in the past, it now only supplied one-seventh. Cotton production had grown dramatically outside the United States. The council concluded that "in view of the fact that imports are damaging the cotton farmer's market, it follows inevitably that the government's cotton program is being 'materially interfered with.'" The answer to helping American cotton producers involved increasing the domestic demand for cotton by improving the competitiveness of domestic textile mills through the imposition of import quotas.[63]

Bowing to industry pressure, Secretary Benson requested that President Eisenhower authorize a Section 22 investigation. Both the Department of State and Department of Commerce opposed an investigation, but President Eisenhower relented and authorized on in November 1959.[64] The president, however, limited the scope of the Tariff Commission to "whether a fee on imported cotton textiles, equal to the amount of the subsidy is necessary in order to prevent cotton textile imports from interfering with programs of the Department of Agriculture," thereby ruling out quotas.[65]

While the Tariff Commission held hearings, Charles Cannon continued to press the industry's case with the administration. Writing to the president's assistant, fellow North Carolinian Wilton B. Persons, Cannon linked the health of the domestic cotton farmer to the health of the domestic textile industry. Foreign textile imports threatened the future of both, he argued. In addition, Cannon repeated that such a disastrous level of imports had the potential to weaken the domestic industry to the extent that it probably could not meet future wartime demand.[66] Persons assured Cannon that the administration remained concerned over the "welfare of the domestic textile industry" but communicated no support for tariffs.[67]

Continuing to receive little support from the president, Cannon also made his concerns known to the vice president, Richard M. Nixon. The textile manufacturer called Charles McWhorter, legislative assistant to the vice president, on March 1, 1960, to discuss his feelings about the Section 22 investigation.[68] In subsequent correspondence, Cannon discussed the chance that Nixon had of carrying North Carolina in the upcoming presidential election. Nixon should connect himself with the interests of the textile industry, Cannon suggested, increasing his popularity in the state.[69] McWhorter encouraged the mill man to keep the vice president's office informed about the textile industry.[70]

Direct pressure on the administration by Cannon, however, did not influence the decision of the Tariff Commission. In June 1960, the commission voted four to two not to take any action on textile import restrictions.[71] The president accepted the recommendation of the commission in August.[72] Charles Cannon and the textile industry now turned their attention to the election and getting help from the next administration.

The import issue contained a cruel touch of irony. Southern textile manufacturers complained about imported textiles undercutting domestic prices based on lower wages paid overseas, yet the southern textile industry had prospered because of the wage differential between the North and South. The center of textile manufacturing had shifted to the South because of a business atmosphere built upon the dual footings of low wages and little union activity. Now southern manufactures felt threatened by cheap, imported Japanese textiles produced on lower wages than paid in the South.

While Cannon Mills had not suffered materially from Japanese imports during the decade, Charles Cannon feared for the future of the household textile market. Competition from low-wage imports could increase greatly as international trade expanded. In addition, the government had created a couple of disadvantages for American textile firms. Because American textile manufacturers had to pay the minimum wage, domestic mill wages had a floor that many foreign competitors could easily undercut. Additionally, the American minimum wage continued to increase. While textile manufacturers did not advocate the elimination of the minimum wage, they believed that the government should not establish policies that would further hamper the competitiveness of the domestic industry.

Yet that is exactly what the government had done with the two-price cotton system. Charles Cannon remained determined to end it. He hoped that the future administration would be more sympathetic to the plight of the industry than the Eisenhower administration had been. The fate of his firm might depend on it.

PART III

The Decline of Cannon Mills and Paternalism

CHAPTER 13

———————◆◆◆◆◆———————

CANNON MILLS IN THE 1960S:
The Paternalistic Firm in a Modern World

Textile manufacturers entered the new decade with apprehension. Domestic textile manufacturers still wanted relief from foreign textile imports. Cheap imports from Hong Kong, in addition to Japan, now worried industry leaders. In January 1960, the United States and Hong Kong failed to agree on voluntary import quotas, but the Eisenhower administration refused to impose limitations.[1]

The two-price cotton system compounded the import issue. Domestic mills paid forty dollars a bale more than foreign producers for American cotton. In addition, Section 22 of the Agricultural Adjustment Act required domestic mills to purchase all but approximately one day's worth of cotton from American farmers. Domestic manufacturers, led by Charles Cannon, vowed to end the two-price cotton system and hoped for more sympathy from the new Democratic administration.

Industry leaders believed the impact of rising textile imports and the two-price cotton system caused the weakness of the textile industry in the late 1950s. The failure of 161 textile mills in 1958 and 1959 was particularly disconcerting. Moreover, the failure rate had increased in the latter part of 1959 over the previous year, and the stock prices of the largest mills had fallen an average of 20 percent from mid-1959 to January 1960. Cannon Mills was no exception, and its stock fell 10.7 percent during the same period.[2]

While battling imports and the two-price cotton system, Charles Cannon also battled a threat to his control of the firm. In 1960, the New York Stock Exchange (NYSE) demanded that Cannon Mills' twenty-five-dollar par nonvoting (class B) stock be converted into voting stock and that the firm provide certain proxy information. The NYSE was concerned that the 3.3 million (B) shares authorized in 1947 had no voting rights and that Cannon Mills might not have solicited proxies of all of the non-attending voting shares for shareholders' meetings. Cannon believed the NYSE had no right to request the information and refused to provide it.[3]

Charles Cannon's control of the publicly traded company rested on two elements. First, he controlled the board of directors by only appointing friends and associates who shared his vision of the company and deferred to him. Forbes noted that "nary an outsider sits on Cannon's board."[4] Second, Cannon controlled the voting stock of the voting stockholders. He owned 163,155 shares of the 1,037,189 shares of common stock (15.73%) and 75,271 shares of the class B stock, of which 992,627 remained outstanding.[5] In total the Cannon family, including in-laws, controlled 40 percent of the voting stock, and the board of directors owned an undetermined amount.[6] Shareholders' meetings routinely rubber stamped the recommendations of the board of directors. Allowing the class B stockholders to vote would have weakened Cannon's control of the modern-looking yet paternalistic firm.

Not surprisingly, Cannon received the stockholders' support for his refusal to comply with the NYSE requests. At the thirty-second annual stockholders meeting of April 12, 1960, stockholders voted to terminate trading on the NYSE. Board members also endorsed the move to a new stock exchange.[7] In 1962, the NYSE delisted Cannon Mills, which had been a member since 1927 and the first southern textile company to be traded on the "big board."[8]

In addition to not tolerating objectionable requests from the NYSE, Charles Cannon would not tolerate board members who disagreed with him. In 1962, Cannon dismissed his son, William C. Cannon, from the board of directors. The rumor mill in Kannapolis stated that the father and son had had a disagreement and that William had been "disobedient." A strict Presbyterian teetotaler, any kind of "disobedience was never Mr. Charlie's cup of tea."[9] As part of the board reshuffle, Don Holt became president of Cannon Mills and heir apparent to Charles Cannon, who remained chairman of the board.[10]

Despite the delisting of Cannon Mills and the shakeup on the board of directors, the textile firm increased sales of its products between 1960 and 1964. Sales rose from $202,939,000 in 1960 to $270,524,000 in 1964 at an average rate of $17 million. Profits, however, grew at a much slower pace, increasing only $9 million from 1960 to 1964. The slower growth of profits in proportion to sales probably reflected the higher costs of cotton under the two-price system.[11]

To accommodate the increasing sales of Cannon products, the firm built a new distribution center. In 1963, Cannon Mills began operation of its modern, computer-controlled distribution center at Plant 1 in Kannapolis. At one million square feet, the new distribution facility, the firm claimed, was the largest in the world. The size, complexity, and cost of the new facility led Charles Cannon to jokingly call the new center "Holt's folly" after Don Holt, who headed the project.[12] The textile company, however, announced that it would delay other capital improvements until the new administration took action to control textile imports.[13]

The Kennedy administration quickly demonstrated that it would be more sympathetic than its predecessor toward the domestic textile industry. President John F. Kennedy appointed former North Carolina governor Luther Hodges as secretary of commerce. Before becoming governor, Hodges had worked as vice president for Marshall Field, handling the firm's textile division, Fieldcrest Mills, Inc. The new secretary of commerce was not a protectionist, however, and did not believe that all of the domestic textile industry's problems stemmed from textile imports. Kennedy and Hodges immediately began to work on a plan to help the industry while following a free trade approach.[14] The president appointed Hodges to chair the President's Cabinet Textile Advisory Committee to study the problems of the industry and to suggest solutions.[15]

While pleased that Hodges had been included in the new administration, Cannon nonetheless became concerned with some of the secretary's public statements. In an April 1961 Meet the Press television interview, Hodges noted that Japan and West Germany had reached a degree of productivity that surpassed the United States in some fields and that United States' exports were "priced out of the market" in soft goods and electronics. American industry, Hodges stated, needed to work toward better efficiency.[16] Cannon believed that the secretary had accused the industry of inefficiency and "feather bedding," so he wrote to Hodges in defense of the industry.[17] The secretary of commerce responded that his comments may not have been clear in the UPI report of the broadcast and sent Cannon a copy of the transcript. Hodges did not intend to question the character of people who worked in the industry and reminded Cannon that he had been a textile executive and could "still hold my own at a loom."[18] In subsequent correspondence, the secretary assured Cannon that he would do what he could to assist the industry:

> I am very much aware of the problems besetting the industry and you
> may rest assured that as Chairman of the President's Textile Advisory
> Committee I will do everything possible to effectuate some relief. It is one
> of our largest industries and I believe that unless we take some action that
> will cure some of the ills of the industry that it will not survive.[19]

After attaining the secretary's pledge to help the industry, Cannon
pressed the matter of imports and two-price cotton with him. Cannon suggested that PL 480 hurt domestic manufacturers by selling excess American
cotton on the world market at market prices, thus allowing foreign textile
manufacturers to reap the benefits of cheap labor and cheap American cotton. Domestic textile mills, on the other hand, had to purchase American
cotton at the higher domestic price maintained by price supports. Cannon
estimated that the net effect of this was the loss of ninety-five thousand
American textile jobs.[20] Hodges replied that the committee would review the
manufacturer's concerns.[21]

Cannon and the industry did not have to wait long before the administration addressed their problems. On May 2, 1961, President Kennedy issued
a seven-point plan to assist the textile industry based on the findings of his
committee. He promised aid to the industry while avoiding import quotas.
The president directed the Department of Commerce to expand its research
to find new uses for textiles and new markets. He instructed the Treasury
Department to study the feasibility of increasing the depreciation allowance
on textile equipment. Kennedy ordered the Small Business Administration
to assist the industry with equipment financing and the Department of
Agriculture to create a plan to eliminate the two-price cotton system. The
government would seek constructive voluntary import quotas from the
major textile-producing nations. In addition, the president promised that
the administration would duly consider petitions for relief filed under the
Reciprocal Trade Act of 1934. Lastly, the government would provide unspec-
ified aid to mills injured by foreign imports.[22]

Generally, industry leaders reacted positively to Kennedy's seven-point
plan.[23] It seemed that the new administration, only in office a few months,
had already proposed more to assist the textile industry than Eisenhower
had in eight years. The problems of the industry, however, could not be
solved overnight.

In July, the State Department sponsored a meeting in Geneva to reach
an international agreement on textiles. Sixteen nations agreed to the Short-
Term Arrangement on Cotton Textile Trade, based largely on American

proposals. The agreement limited exports for one year based to 1960 levels, established an international group to study the world textile trade in the long term, and lowered textile trade import restrictions imposed by Western Europe. Textile executives, who believed that the one-year ceiling remained too high, did not fully support the Geneva plan.[24]

Imports from Japan continued to bother the industry leaders. In the fall of 1961, the United States signed a bilateral agreement with Japan to limit Japanese textile imports for 1962. The agreement allowed an 8 percent increase in imports over 1961 levels. Neither the Japanese nor the domestic textile manufacturers were happy with the arrangement. Japanese officials had sought a 30 percent increase but settled on the lesser increase, hoping for larger increases in the future. American textile executives, on the other hand, believed that the voluntary limits remained too high.[25] As it became obvious to the domestic textile manufacturers that the administration's import agreements and voluntary quotas would not bring about favorable results, industry leaders lobbied Congress for import restrictions. Domestic manufacturers hoped for better results from the rest of the administration's program.

The administration took some favorable steps in October and November. On October 11, President Kennedy announced an accelerated depreciation schedule for textile equipment. For 80 percent of textile equipment, the new depreciation plan cut the average useful life from twenty-five to fifteen years.[26] Kennedy alluded to the benefits of the new schedule:

> The industry is experiencing a major technological breakthrough in which advancing techniques engender further advances and make even recently developed equipment economically outdated before it is physically worn out. The pressure for the adoption of technological innovations is accentuated by competition of foreign producers who, in most cases, enjoy the advantages of very liberal depreciation allowances as well as low wage costs.[27]

The textile industry responded favorably to the new depreciation plan. Both W. J. Erwin, president of Dan River Mills, and J. Craig Smith, president of Avondale Mills, were encouraged by the administration's action.[28] The American Cotton Manufacturers Institute also called the move encouraging.[29] Industry leaders, however, wanted to see movement on the rest of the seven-point plan and continued to press for import controls.[30]

Charles Cannon also continued to be concerned about textile imports. Cannon often corresponded with the secretary of commerce regarding imports, at times requesting import information. Sometimes Cannon found the information issued by the Commerce Department confusing and asked for clarification.[31] Secretary Hodges supplied as much data as he could. If his agency did not have the facts requested, Hodges referred the question to the appropriate agency.[32] Consequently, the mill owner corresponded with the Bureau of the Census, the Department of Commerce Field Services in Atlanta, and Field Services in Greensboro, North Carolina.[33] Cannon, along with the rest of the industry, continued to pressure the administration for import relief.

Bowing to industry pressure, the Kennedy administration authorized a Section 22 investigation on November 21, 1961, concerning imported cotton products. Kennedy limited the scope of the investigation by the Tariff Commission to whether a tariff should be added equal to the export subsidy on raw cotton. Both the ACMI and the Cotton Council recommended such a remedy. On September 6, 1962, however, the commission decided that imported textiles did not interfere with the domestic cotton program and took no additional action.[34]

While the Tariff Commission conducted the Section 22 investigation, the textile industry continued to lobby for import restrictions. Charles Cannon wrote every member of Congress from North and South Carolina about the Trade Act of 1962. The act, Cannon wrote, should eliminate the two-price cotton system and provide quotas on textile imports. He included a resolution passed by the ACMI that recommended import quotas set at the average of the 1955–59 period and a remedy for the two-price system. Cannon believed that the act would "be the battle of the century in so far as employment in North and South Carolina is concerned."[35] Many members of the Carolina delegations expressed support for the industry, including Senator Strom Thurmond of South Carolina.[36]

In addition, Cannon received support from powerful Senate Judiciary Committee member Sam Ervin Jr., who also seemed troubled by the situation of the textile industry in North Carolina. In addition, the senator was disturbed by what "our foreign policymakers think our trade policies should be." After a December letter from Cannon, Ervin called on the administration to sell no additional cotton under Public Law 480.[37]

Cannon also lobbied important congressmen outside the North and South Carolina delegations, including delegations from other southern textile states. Representative Carl Vinson of Georgia, chairman of the Armed Services Committee, assured Cannon of his support. Vinson told Cannon that "you can count on me to do everything I possibly can to see that this great industry is protected."[38] Despite such support, Congress did not place quotas on imports.

The administration hoped that a long-term agreement on imports would provide some relief for the domestic textile industry. In February 1962, the General Agreement on Tariffs and Trade (GATT) finalized the Long-Term Arrangement for Cotton Textile Trade (LTA). The LTA set guidelines on the export of cotton products for five years. Japan continued to ship cotton goods to the United States in excess of the Short-Term and Long-Term agreements, however, due to less than vigilant oversight by the administration.[39]

Unhappy with the results of international textile import limitations, the ACMI's Special Cotton Policy Committee called for the administration to impose unilateral import quotas.[40] Highlighting the problems caused by imports, the body issued a study on the state of the domestic cotton textile industry in early 1960. The report reflected the ideas of its chairman, Charles Cannon, who wrote the draft. The picture on the cover page clearly illustrated the central idea of the report, showing a scale with "Two Million American Jobs" on one side and "Unrestricted Textile Imports" on the other. From 1947 to 1961, the domestic textile industry lost 34 percent of its employees and 32 percent of its spindles, the study stated.[41] Additionally, profits had fallen, the amount of American cotton consumed by domestic mills had fallen, and cotton textile imports now exceeded exports.[42] Cannon and the SCPC placed the blame for the problems of the industry on the government's implementation of PL 480, the two-price cotton system, and the administration's failure to impose unilateral import quotas. The study recommended that the government collect an equalization fee on imported textiles to eliminate the two-price cotton advantage of foreign producers and halt PL 480 sales of cotton. It also insisted that nations drop discriminatory restrictions on the importation of American textiles and establish reasonable import quotas.[43]

Charles Cannon made sure that the industry's fight for import quotas and elimination of the two-price cotton system received coverage in Kannapolis. The *Daily Independent* printed the entire testimony of the town's benefactor before a House subcommittee on agriculture in late 1962. Cannon presented the standard industry argument:

> As a nation, we have been pursuing policies which penalize our textile industry and which work against the interest of our farmers. We have been favoring our foreign competitors by making cotton available to them on more favorable terms than it is made available to domestic mills. Primarily,

as a result of this policy, we have a shrinking textile industry, the domestic use of cotton is declining, the number of cotton spindles is being constantly reduced, and the incentive for investment in new plants and equipment is weakened.[44]

To broaden the appeal of his message, Cannon testified that the elimination of the two-price cotton system would save consumers money. The reduction in the cost of cotton would lower the production cost of domestic textiles and producers would pass the savings, estimated at more than $600 million, along to the consumers.[45] Lower prices for domestic textiles would increase domestic consumption, help cotton farmers by increasing demand for cotton, and allow domestic textile mills to compete more effectively with imports.

Although Cannon worked for stricter import quotas for textile goods as a leader in industry trade associations, his own firm had little competition from imports. As late as 1978, imported sheets accounted for less than 1 percent of the sheets sold in the United States and imported towels totaled less than 6 percent of the domestic market.[46] Working as a member of the Cotton Council and the SCPC, Cannon represented the interests of the entire industry. He wanted a healthy textile industry in the United States and fought anything that would weaken the industry, such as cheap textile imports. Furthermore, Cannon must have realized that his support for stricter import restrictions could serve the firm in the future if foreign textile manufacturers flooded the American market with cheap sheets and towels.

Imposing import quotas and ending the two-price cotton system played well with the textile workers of Cannon Mills. The company continued to be a model of paternalism as it celebrated its seventy-fifth anniversary in 1962. Kannapolis remained the largest unincorporated town in the nation, and the firm still owned more than two thousand mill homes. Workers believed that Charles Cannon cared about them and would protect their jobs. Cannon Mill workers remained among the highest paid textile workers in the South because the firm matched wage increases set by other southern textile firms. For example, when Burlington raised wages in 1955 and J. P. Stevens increased wages in 1956, Cannon matched each increase. In 1959, Cannon Mills set the wage pattern by instituting a new round of increases.[47] From 1959 to 1962, the Cannon Mills minimum wage increased from $1.25 an hour to $1.30.[48] Voluntarily raising wages instilled worker loyalty and provided a strong bulwark against unionization. Indeed, union activity at Cannon Mills had ebbed after the failure of Operation Dixie. A job with Cannon Mills had always meant stable employment and, since World War II, steadily increasing wages.

Even President Kennedy recognized Charles Cannon's ability to provide stable employment and create jobs. On November 29, 1962, Cannon's seventieth birthday, the president sent the manufacturer a birthday telegram of praise:

> Congratulations on a noteworthy birthday which represents over fifty years of service to the textile industry, to the community, and to the nation. I understand that the employment in Cannon Mills, under your direction, has averaged one new job every single day for fifty years. This is a remarkable contribution.[49]

Throughout 1963, industry pressure increased on the administration and Congress to end the two-price cotton system. President Kennedy's farm message of January 31, 1963, highlighted the importance of cotton and urged Congress to pass legislation that would "make this important fiber more competitive and help recapture its market."[50] Cannon believed that the elimination of two-price cotton would achieve most of the president's goals and wrote Under Secretary of Agriculture Charles S. Murphy to express his view.[51]

Cannon Mills workers also sent letters to their members of Congress. After receiving a letter from Cannon Mills worker S. B. Cook, Senator Sam Ervin Jr. wrote the president. Ervin noted that he had seen little improvement in the industry since the administration promised assistance. The senator wanted to know "exactly what the Administration proposes to do to fulfill these promises," and he pressed the president to end the two-price cotton system, which injured the textile industry in his state.[52]

Congress soon began work on ending two-price cotton. House Agriculture Committee chairman Harold Cooley (D-N.C.) introduced HR 6196 on May 9, 1963, to reestablish the one-price cotton system.[53] Cooley combined the cotton bill with a wheat bill to get it passed in the House. The Senate modified the bill before sending it back to the House. Support dwindled for the modified bill, so Cooley and Speaker John McCormack (D-Mass.) lobbied for votes from Democratic representatives by tacking a food stamp provision to the cotton-wheat bill. The new cotton–wheat–food stamp bill passed Congress, and President Lyndon B. Johnson signed it on April 11 as the Agriculture Act of 1964.[54]

Charles Cannon received much of the credit for ending the two-price cotton system. In recognition for his hard work, the *Textile Reporter* named Cannon "Mr. Textile" for 1964. The manufacturer received the award at the Jack Tar Poinsett Hotel in Greenville, South Carolina, on October 11.[55] Cannon predicted that the end of two-price cotton would increase cotton consumption at domestic mills. Daily consumption of cotton was more than 2,200 bales per day higher in August 1964 than in August 1963, and the Department of Agriculture estimated that the consumption would increase more than 1.1 million bales in 1964–65.[56]

Encouraging news also included a drop in textile imports. In May 1964, imports declined by twenty-three million yards from April and eighteen million below May of the previous year. Japan, Hong Kong, Portugal, and India registered sharp declines in textile exports to the United States.[57]

Improving business conditions led to a boom in modernization and expansion in 1964. Dan River Mills built a $5 million plant in Fountain Inn, South Carolina, and a $10 million plant in Benton, Alabama. Scotland Mills of Laurinburg, North Carolina, added two new plants costing a total of $12 million. The P. H. Hanes Knitting Company, based in Winston-Salem, North Carolina, announced the construction of a plant in Lubbock, Texas. In addition, Spartan Mills made plans to build a $7 million plant in Spartanburg, South Carolina.[58]

Confidence also ran high at Cannon Mills. Charles Cannon pointed to the end of two-price cotton, changes in tax laws, and more liberal depreciation allowances on textile equipment as positive moves for the industry.[59] "We are so confident that the force behind one-price cotton will reverse the trend of shrinking textile production," Cannon told a reporter, "that we are embarking on the largest expansion program in the history of the company."[60] In fact, Cannon Mills announced its plans for expansion only days after the government ended the two-price cotton system. Cannon Mills president Don Holt made public the firm's plans to expand and modernize Plant 10 in Concord, adding three hundred jobs. Holt revealed that the firm had developed plans to expand the Concord facility in 1963 but held off pending the outcome of the one-price cotton legislation.[61] The expansion and modernization plans soon went far beyond Concord.

The textile firm announced and began work on numerous improvements. Cannon publicized modernization plans for the facilities in Social Circle and Eatonton, Georgia, along with improvements at Central and York, South Carolina.[62] In addition, Cannon Mills made many improvements at Plant 1. These upgrades included a filter plant, additions to its bleachery operations, and air-conditioned equipment and spinning rooms. The firm also added a towel mill (Mill 7) at Plant 1. Other changes included a new warehouse for Plant 6, an addition to Plant 11, and new air-conditioned equipment and refrigeration rooms at Plant 4.[63]

Cannon Mills also expanded through acquisition. In 1964, the firm acquired Travora Textiles of Graham, North Carolina, which made decorative fabrics. The company also purchased the Hoover Hosiery Company of Concord, added thirty thousand square feet to the facility, and converted it to Plant 6, Mill 4 for spinning synthetics.[64]

The most ambitious part of Cannon's expansion plan, however, was the plan to build the new Swink Plant. As far back as 1924, Charles Cannon had discussed the possibility of building a new mill in Rowan County, but until 1964 the time did not seem right. Reputed by the company to be the largest textile plant constructed since World War II, the Swink Plant, named after deceased Cannon Mills executive William Swink, was built between China Grove and Salisbury, North Carolina. Designed primarily to manufacture sheets from one thousand looms and providing 550 jobs, the facility did not have mill housing. Charles Cannon believed that the plant would draw from the local work force, who could get to the mill by car.[65]

The textile industry emerged from its slump of the early 1960s. Improvement in the industry actually appeared before the end of two-price cotton. By 1965, increasing demand came from two sectors: the baby boomers and United States' involvement in the Vietnam War. Strong apparel demand came from those age fourteen to twenty-four, for whom disposable income continued to increase. Military demand increased sharply in 1965 and 1966. Cloth demand for the military grew from 6.6 million yards to 120 million yards. With GNP growth of 6.8 percent in 1965, some economists believed the United States had entered into a "war-propelled boom."[66]

Demand continued to grow for textile products after 1965, from a total demand of 8.4 billion pounds of textiles at the beginning of 1965 to 9 billion pounds by the end of the year. The market slumped, however, in 1966 through the first quarter of 1967, with demand dropping to approximately 8.8 billion pounds. During the second quarter of 1967, the demand for textile goods increased sharply. In early 1969, demand reached more than 10 billion pounds.[67]

Consumer demand fueled the growth in the textile market in the latter years of the decade. Housing starts and growing disposable income increased the demand for household furnishings. Construction of new homes rose 5.3 percent in 1968, while disposable income rose 5 percent more than in 1967.

Consequently, the demand for home furnishings increased from 2.253 billion pounds of textiles in 1965 to 2.965 billion pounds in 1969.[68] Cannon Mills benefitted from the boom. Sales increased from $270,524,000 in 1964 to $299,380,000 in 1969, and in those same years net operating profits fluctuated from $31,129,000 to $30,510,000. During the period, profits ranged from a low of $24,318,000 in 1967 to a record high of $47,060,000 in 1965.[69]

The firm continued to expand and make capital improvements during the one-price cotton boom. To finance its expansion, the firm increased it working capital to $100 million.[70] In 1965, Cannon Mills purchased Concord Textiles and the old White Parks Mill, both in Concord. The White Parks facility became Plant 17 of the Cannon Mills Company and operated as a spinning mill.[71] By the end of 1965, recent modernization and expansion plans had cost the textile firm more than $100 million. Yet Cannon Mills remained committed to growth and improving its operations into the immediate future. The firm committed $20 million to improve operations in 1966.[72] In 1966, operations began at the new Swink Plant along with work on two other plants. Construction continued on the expansion of the bleachery at Plant 1 housing the new data processing (computer) department. In addition, the textile firm planned to increase decorative fabric production at Plant 6 by constructing a two-hundred-thousand-square-foot facility for packing and finishing its product.[73]

Charles Cannon did not believe in using long-term debt to finance expansion or modernization. He ran the firm as conservatively as he always had, accumulating no long-term debt.[74] By 1967, Cannon Mills Company, the seventh largest textile company in the United States, was the only textile firm of the twelve largest with no long-term debt. In contrast to Cannon, Burlington Mills, the largest textile firm, had long-term debt of more than $297 million, or 34 percent of its invested capital. WestPoint-Pepperell, the fifth largest textile firm, had the least amount of long-term debt, excluding Cannon, at $800,000, or less than 1 percent of its invested capital.[75]

The leadership at Cannon Mills, however, did not receive praise from the financial sector. Market analysts blamed the slow growth of the company's sales on the conservative management of the firm. While sales did grow, they leveled out to increases of approximately 2 percent per year in the latter part of the decade. Other firms, such as Burlington, supported twice as much business on its capital base as Cannon Mills. Some critics also accused Cannon, which primarily produced towels and sheets, of a lack of diversification.[76]

Despite such criticism, dividends remained remarkably stable. Cannon Mills paid between $3.00 and $4.00 per share annually from 1949 to 1967, except for three years. The firm paid $2.25 per share in 1953 and 1962 and $4.60 per share in 1966.[77] Dividends represented steady income for company stockholders, most of whom valued stability over creativity or diversification. Cannon Mills stock performed almost like bonds since the textile company always paid dividends, even during the worst years of the Great Depression. Cannon stock also resembled bonds in that few stockholders had voting rights. Charles Cannon and his insiders controlled the votes of the common stock while the class B stockholders had no voting rights.[78] Few stockholders seemed concerned about having little voice in how the company operated as long as the firm continued to pay dividends.

On May 21, 1967, in the midst of rising sales and company expansion, the town of Kannapolis demonstrated gratitude to its benefactor by holding Appreciation Day for Charles Cannon. The company and town attempted to get as many citizens involved in the special day as possible. Festivities included a photographic display titled "Kannapolis—Today and Yesterday," a display of Cannon products, and an antique car show.[79] The literary committee encouraged townspeople to write letters to Charles Cannon, suggesting they say, "Thank you, Mr. Cannon, for allowing us to live with you in this community."[80] The letters were collected and presented to the textile manufacturer.

The highlight of the day was the afternoon program held at the football stadium. The attendance committee members worked to get six thousand "retired workers, present employees, citizens, and students to attend the program."[81] Governor Dan Moore, the keynote speaker, presented Cannon with a Distinguished Citizen's Award.[82] In his remarks, Cannon honored his "family"—the twenty-five thousand workers of Cannon Mills—and passed on a few words of wisdom to his beloved town. The world, Cannon said, operated on unchangeable laws. Reflecting his conservative thinking, he spoke of laws that persisted in spite of changes in culture, people's thinking, or the "great conflict for the domination of ideas." Among these laws Cannon identified were "you reap what you sow," "keep life simple . . . complexity only confuses," labor contains therapy and dignity, and honesty is always the best policy, in spite of situational ethics.[83]

Although he did not mention God, Cannon's "laws" reflected his conservative Presbyterian upbringing. They also carried over into his business practices. His call for simplicity reflected Cannon Mills' business practice of staying with what it did best, producing towels and sheets. Diversification would only complicate and confuse. Cannon stood against change in both the company and the mill town.

Change, nonetheless, came to Cannon Mills. Already Don Holt held the office of president of Cannon Mills, and though he had been with the firm since 1950, Holt had not been raised in the "Cannon family." More of the operations of the firm fell to Holt, such as heading up the construction of the new distribution center in Kannapolis, but he did not disagree with Cannon's leadership or try to take the firm in any new direction while Charles Cannon lived.

An omen of future change came, however, when Holt's protégé, Harold Hornaday, became a member of the board of directors in 1967. Hornaday, at age twenty-three, had come to Cannon Mills with Holt to work at the faltering Plant 6. In 1965, he had become an assistant vice president, and he rose to vice president in 1966.[84] Holt and Hornaday represented the future of the firm after Charles Cannon.

Economic forces also began to weaken the paternalistic bond of the firm. Charles Cannon and his firm's hold on Cabarrus County gradually weakened. Cannon's influence, economic and political, in the least unionized county in the nation enabled him to keep out industries that would bid up wages. By controlling all essential services, he kept competing firms out of Kannapolis.[85] "Mr. Charlie don't want nobody coming in here and running up wages," one Cannon worker commented.[86] Increasingly, however, industries sought to locate in Cabarrus County. Phillip Morris's interest in the county presented perhaps the greatest threat to the firm's local control as the cigarette manufacturer paid higher wages than Cannon Mills and was unionized. Eventually, Phillip Morris built a plant in the county and began the production of cigarettes in 1983, providing wage competition and, finally, alternative employment for residents of Cabarrus County.[87]

As Cannon's paternalism slowly weakened, it seemed increasingly out of place and archaic in the modern corporate world. Cannon Mills and the company town of Kannapolis eventually drew the attention of Ralph Nader. The consumer advocate sent a team of investigators to the mill town for an unwelcome visit in 1970. Public television nationally aired the investigation of Cannon Mills and its town by "Nader's raiders." The program rendered a broad indictment against "Mr. Charlie's" paternalism, especially the lack of elected officials in the town. In addition, the program highlighted the relatively low wages of workers compared to the national average and the discrimination in housing against black employees.[88]

In spite of government interference, the economic diversity of Cabarrus County, and negative publicity, the paternalistic nature of Kannapolis remained. Charles Cannon embodied the conservative, controlling, and paternalistic attitude of the company's founder. Although his turn-of-the-century paternalistic business practices were out of date in the business world of the 1970s, Charles Cannon ensured that as long as he lived, the business practices of the past continued at Cannon Mills.

The death of Charles Cannon, therefore, marked the demise of the firm's paternalism. Cannon suffered a stroke at 2:40 p.m. on April 1, 1971, while working at his office. The seventy-eight-year-old textile magnate was rushed to Cabarrus Memorial Hospital, which he had helped to establish, and died the next day. After his death, the board of directors elevated Don Holt to chairman of the board of Cannon Mills.[89]

Charles Cannon's death represented the greatest single change in the history of the firm. Charles's governance of Cannon Mills demonstrated a continuity of leadership style and attitude stretching back to the time his father, James W. Cannon, ran the company. Don Holt shared much of Charles's leadership style, but he also brought change to the eighty-four-year-old firm. Rapid change now replaced the continuity that had characterized Cannon Mills for so long.

CHAPTER 14

———————•◆◆◆•———————

THE CIVIL RIGHTS MOVEMENT, FEDERAL INTERFERENCE, AND THE WEAKENING OF PATERNALISM

The civil rights movement eventually had a major impact on Cannon Mills. President Kennedy demonstrated his support for civil rights in the workplace in 1961 by signing Executive Order 10925, which forbad discrimination in hiring and promotion for firms that worked on government contracts. This order became more important as the United States became more involved in the Vietnam War.[1] It was estimated that the war resulted in forty-one thousand textile jobs and therefore the order gave the government leverage on black employment in the textile industry.[2]

The textile industry was hesitant to hire blacks for production jobs. Textile management had many reasons to be leery of changing the racial status quo in the mills. The industry believed that blacks were happy in their current jobs, blacks were not qualified for production jobs, and that some form of quota system would emerge from any change, resulting in reverse discrimination. Furthermore, management was concerned about the reaction of white workers to opening production jobs to black workers. Since the U.S. Supreme Court's *Brown v. Board of Education* decision and the Montgomery bus boycott, support for segregation had increased in mill villages, including segregated Kannapolis.[3]

The percentage of blacks working in the textile industry had only increased to 3.3 percent, up from 2.1 percent in 1940. In 1962, a J. P. Stevens executive complained that the firm could not find qualified blacks for job openings in production. Other southern textile firms made the same claims.

Nevertheless, the lure of government contracts pushed textile firms to begin hiring blacks for production jobs.[4]

Cannon Mills began to hire black women for production jobs in token numbers. Corine Lythe Cannon was one of the first black women hired for production in 1962. She remembered the day she and another black woman reported to the supervisor's office:

> "Good morning, come right on in." He had us to sit down. Then he said, "This is something new and I have to admit I feel like it should have been done earlier, but this is the way it is." He said, "I'll tell you, you'll be an example. Everbody [sic] is going to look at you." . . . And he said, "You were chosen, Cannon Mills have seen so many black people and you were chosen." And all this time he was standing with his back to us. He got up from the desk and turned his back to us and said, "This is new and try to make the best of it. You have been chosen and you are going to be an example." And he stood like this with his back to us, looking out the window. I think he thought his face was going to be red because you could tell from his ears and neck were turning red.[5]

The hiring of the first black women for production jobs in the mill caused a problem for the company: Those few black women would not be allowed to use indoor restrooms (black men had a bathroom facility outside the mill called the "outhouse" by the black workers). Eventually, the textile firm built a new facility for black women workers. Corine Cannon described it as "a little house out there and on one side was 'Colored Men' and the other side 'Colored Women.'"[6]

A greater problem for Cannon Mills was the Civil Rights Act of 1964, which went into effect on July 2, 1965.[7] The act mandated fair hiring practices regardless of race. Title VII of the act, SEC. 2000e-2 Section 703 b, states:

> It shall be unlawful employment practice for an employment agency to fail or refuse to refer for employment, or otherwise to discriminate against, any individual because of race, color, religion, sex, or national origin, or to classify or refer for employment any individual on the basis of his race, color, religion, sex, or national origin.[8]

The segregated textile industry was now threatened. Twenty southern senators under the leadership of Richard Russell (D-Ga.), including North Carolina senator Sam Irvin Jr., had fought the legislation but to no avail.[9]

The NAACP focused on expanding the opportunities for black employment in the textile industry. Kelly Alexander, the North Carolina head of the
NAACP, believed that employment of more blacks in production jobs would
lessen general poverty among blacks. NAACP attorney Julius Chambers,
who believed that the southern textile industry offered higher-paying jobs
with low skill requirements, targeted textile firms for legal action if they did
not comply with Title VII.[10]

Under pressure from both government and the NAACP, Cannon Mills
slowly hired more black workers. Yet those black workers faced a tense working environment. Kay Willis, whose mother was the domestic for Charles
Cannon, was the first black woman hired to work in the washcloth department. She was nervous on her first day and had to endure the stares and
frowns of the white women.[11] Most black workers felt that they were on their
own in their new jobs. Johnny Mae Fields certainly believed she had no support. "The black women don't have nobody to look after her in the mill," she
said. "Really seem like the white men in the mill look after the white women,
and the black men look after the white women, and seem like the black women
ain't got nobody to look after them but themselves."[12] While Fields believed
that even black men did not look after black women in the mills, black men
had their own problems on their new jobs. Cromwell Russell got a job inside
the mill after having worked on the loading dock. While he worked on the
dock, he said, "Old Man Cannon" would speak to him. But once he went
inside the mill to work, "the boss" did not speak to him anymore.[13]

White workers also had to adjust to their new co-workers. Elboyd Deal
admitted that whites were slow to believe that blacks could be successful as
supervisors and that many whites "resented a black man being over them."[14]
While some whites remained resentful of the new workers, other whites
warmed up to their black colleagues. Johnny Mae Fields was asked one day
by a white worker if she wanted to be called "black or colored." Eventually a
friendship emerged between the two, and it grew to the point that Fields felt
that the white woman "fell in love with me."[15]

Most of the major textile firms had problems complying with the Civil
Rights Act of 1964, especially Title VII, which forbade discrimination in
hiring and employment practices. Black plaintiffs sued Dan River Mills, J. P.
Stevens, Cone Mills, Fieldcrest Mills, and Burlington Industries. Cannon
Mills also faced its share of lawsuits stemming from racial discrimination
and company segregation policies.[16]

Blacks working in production jobs at Cannon Mills continued to face
discrimination from management. Johnny Mae Fields believed that white
women at Cannon got the better jobs:

I got along, but now I haven't always been done right. You know, sometimes they don't know the meaning of fair. And that was definitely because I was black. If there are two jobs and one is just a little better the white woman will get the better job. No matter how qualified that black woman is, that's just the way it is.[17]

Fields also experienced discrimination in the form of being assigned "men's work." When she first went on first shift there was no defined job for her so her boss gave jobs she classified as odd jobs—"off the wall" and typically done by men. Fields spoke to her supervisor when she noticed the type of work being assigned to her and that white women in the same employment position were not assigned these odd jobs.[18]

Other black women at Cannon Mills, not just Fields, were assigned to what had traditionally been men's jobs, and thus a pattern of discrimination emerged. Ida Mae Caldwell complained that her job of "sweeping and opening waste machines" had always been a man's job and that she was assigned that position solely because she was a black female. Caldwell also observed that no white women were assigned such jobs.[19]

Mary Black also complained that she was given "men's work" because of her race. She believed that her work was dirty, difficult, and traditionally had been done by men. In a letter to a district court judge concerning one of the discrimination cases against Cannon Mills, Black wrote of the problems of her job and added that management was deliberately making her assignment difficult by speeding up the work. She wrote, "We are over worked. Some had had strokes, heart attacks, and some have even died. We need help very badly."[20]

For black women who did work production jobs there emerged other accusations of discrimination. Some black workers stated that while white women received assistance from their supervisors, black workers did not. Johnny Mae Wilson experienced this on her job at Cannon Mills. Wilson saw how supervisors "gave white women help and wouldn't give us blacks any so I just got tired of it."[21] While some supervisors would not assist their black workers, others went further in directly sabotaging the production of their black workers.

Some supervisors refused to allow black workers to produce more than white workers in the same department. Ruth B. Leazer worked in the spinning room and accused her boss of not letting her produce to the maximum of her ability. She stated that he "would cut off my spinning frames to prevent me from making production. He would put two white spinners on the same job, and expect me to run the job alone. If I asked for any help he would tell me that he could not give me help."[22] Evidently, while the mill was forced to hire more black women to work in production jobs, it did not be believe that it had to allow equality on the job by allowing black workers to make as much as whites.

While working to comply with the Civil Rights Act of 1964, a pattern of discrimination emerged at Cannon Mills. First, when the company hired some black females in jobs traditionally worked by white women, it discriminated in promotion in favor of whites. Second, Cannon Mills assigned many newly hired black women the types of jobs that had been traditionally held by black men and, in many cases, avoided by white men. These jobs were by nature difficult, involved hard physical labor, and were dirty. It seems that if the mill had to hire more black women, it would attempt to limit many of them to jobs traditionally not considered suited for women. Third, some black women complained that their work was speeded up beyond what was reasonable or healthy. And fourth, some supervisors deliberately sabotaged black workers' production to keep it below that of whites. Perhaps the strategy was to have the black women resign out of frustration and thus prove that they were unsuited for work in the cotton mill. Furthermore, this helped to segregate many black women from white women through job assignments.

By 1966, the Equal Employment Opportunity Commission (EEOC) had targeted textile mills in the South to eliminate "institutionalized preference" in advancing workers to supervisory positions. As textile firms now hired blacks to work in the mills, a prospect made more appealing by the continuing labor shortage, the EEOC wanted to make sure that mills were not keeping black workers in lower positions and refusing to advance qualified blacks to supervisory jobs.[23] Slowly, the number of blacks employed by textile mills increased to 94,000, still only 10 percent of the 984,000 textile workers in 1968.[24]

Cannon Mills was distinct because it retained a mill village with mill housing long after other textile companies had disposed of both. Historian John Salmond noted that "the mill village system was in decline" by 1930 and textile firms began to divest themselves of mill villages.[25] Textile companies sold mill housing to workers because maintenance and modernizing the old mill houses was expensive and mill owners believed that homeownership would cut down on labor mobility, but there had arisen much criticism against the paternalistic mill village system.[26] Small Elmore Corporation sold its thirty mill houses in Spindale, North Carolina, in 1934. Burlington Mills sold two entire mill villages in 1935 and then sold four more in North

Carolina and Virginia the following year. In 1937 four textile firms sold off ten mill villages, and in 1939 thirty more mill villages were sold. Between 1940 and 1941, five firms sold an additional fourteen villages.[27] Dan River Mill had 958 houses in 1945 and began selling them to the mill workers in 1949.[28] Sales of mill houses continued in the postwar period with fourteen firms selling thirty-one villages consisting of 5,000 houses between 1945 and 1948.[29] Yet while the textile industry had largely divested itself of company housing, Cannon Mills still had 2,477 houses as late as 1983.[30]

Discrimination in hiring and on the job continued for sometime in the textile industry, but the pattern of discrimination was not uniform throughout the industry. Black women had difficulty getting hired at some textile mills but had similar jobs and experiences to white women workers once they were on the job. This seemed to be the case with J. P. Stevens in its relationship with black females. The attorney for black plaintiffs who sued J. P. Stevens on discrimination charges noted, "We believe that black females find it more difficult to get hired and once hired, we think that their initial assignments tend to be much like those of white females."[31] Evidently, the on-the-job discrimination was more pronounced at Cannon Mills than at many other textile firms.

Most of the large textile companies had discrimination cases filed against them, yet some companies worked to a greater degree than others to make progress toward integrating the mills. Burlington Industries, Dan River Mills and J. P. Stevens were compelled by the Civil Rights Act of 1965, the EEOC, the Fair Housing Act of 1968, and requirements against textile firms discriminating on defense contract work to end discrimination in housing and on the job. One way these mills complied so quickly was to sell off the remainder of their mill housing. These textile companies had been in the process of selling of their residential properties for some time, but now the rest were liquidated. The Nixon administration was a critic of both company housing and many industry leaders. As a result of their efforts to comply with civil rights legislation, the Nixon administration said they were engaged in "affirmative action."[32]

Cannon Mills, however, did not attempt to comply with federal regulations to as great a degree as Burlington, Dan Rivers, and J. P. Stevens. In 1969, the Nixon administration brought suit against Cannon Mills for violation of the 1968 Fair Housing Act, Title VII of the 1964 Civil Rights Act, and Title VIII of the Civil Rights Act of 1968. The administration accused the textile firm of segregation in its approximately two thousand company houses. Furthermore, the suit accused Cannon Mills of giving black families inferior housing and charging them more than white families. Black women also accused the firm of giving them more work than white women and of assigning black women workloads traditionally reserved for men.[33] Other charges cited the practice of giving blacks low-level jobs, intimidating blacks seeking promotion, fighting harder against workman compensation and unemployment claims for blacks, and firing blacks accused of stealing without evidence. The lawsuit filed by the government against the textile company was known a *United States v. Cannon Mills*.[34]

The textile firm stubbornly fought the charges of racial discrimination in the case for eleven years. Finally, in 1982, Cannon Mills decided to work for a settlement. The settlement resulted in Cannon Mills paying sixteen defendants back wages and $4,000 in special relief, an amount totaling $1.65 million.[35] Cannon Mills issued a one-page press release in which the firm denied any discrimination against the defendants:

> Cannon denies that it practiced discrimination in any form prior to the commencement of the suit. Cannon is confident that it would ultimately prevail at trial, however, in order to avoid further unreasonable expenditures of manpower, money and time necessary to continue the litigation, the company has decided it is best to settle the issue.[36]

Some of the defendants were shocked that the case had been settled. Plaintiff Eural Brown believed that "it'd be just like everything else—it'd run awhile and then be thrown out."[37] Many of the plaintiffs had worked for Cannon Mills for a long time. Brown had worked for the company for twenty-three years, while Moses Young had been employed for thirty-six years and John Adams had worked for Cannon Mills since 1940. Adams characterized the settlement as constructive and said workers would "learn to work better between the whites and the colored, doing the same thing and getting paid the same thing."[38]

Not all of the plaintiffs were convinced that discrimination in all of its forms would end at the company. Alexander McCorkle remained concerned over discrimination in promotions. He believed that there were still ways that Cannon Mills could find to overlook blacks in advancement. McCorkle had participated in the suit but remained at the company because he wanted to demonstrate to everyone that he could advance at Cannon Mills.[39]

Cannon Mills had agreed not to take retaliatory action against any of the plaintiffs while the case of *United States v. Cannon Mills* was in litigation. After the settlement, however, the company fired Daisy Crawford, an action that initiated legal action. Crawford's foreman, Jay Campbell, stated that he was instructed by his supervisor to watch Daisy Crawford because "she was a member of the NAACP and a trouble maker." Crawford accused Campbell of limiting her production and said someone had tampered with her looms. A loom fixer, Johnny High, also harassed her, and her foreman taking no action against him. On two occasions High placed mice in her weaving ally looms, knowing that she had a phobia of mice. Crawford was fired for slapping High when he brushed against her breast and called her a "nigger." High received a four-day suspension for the incidents.[40] The EEOC sued for the reinstatement of Daisy Crawford to her former job, for back pay with interest, and to clear her company record of any "adverse comments since April 1970."[41]

The commission continued to find fault with Cannon's employment practices. In 1977 the EEOC stated that Cannon had hired 3 percent more blacks from 1971 to 1974 but that the blacks hired were in "the blue collar job classifications which are the lowest paying job titles," there had been "next to no progress in opening up office and clerical jobs to blacks," and "thirty departments remained all white after 1974." The EEOC promised further legal action unless Cannon Mills made "substantial progress in the next few months" in opening more jobs for blacks.[42]

Cannon Mills' ongoing battle against racial discrimination demonstrated a continuum with regard to race from the leadership of Charles Cannon through three successive chairmen. The firm grudgingly hired more blacks but continued to fight government interference in its right to hire whomever it wanted. Charles Cannon had taken a stand numerous times against the federal government and the later chairmen of the board—Don Holt (1971–74), Harold Hornaday (1974–79), and Otto Stolz (1979–82)—had followed. The pending civil rights litigation was not settled until the firm's board of directors was in buyout talks with California businessman David Murdock.

The trend to hire more black workers had a profound impact on the paternalistic nature of the mill village. As more blacks were hired, paternalism weakened. James and Charles Cannon had limited the paternalistic compact to the whites who worked for them and had deliberately excluded blacks. Now the firm was forced to hire those who had no stake in the paternalistic structure of the mill village. As was feared by mill management, these new workers were much more prone to ally with unions and be in a more adversarial relationship with the firm. The exclusion of the black population in Kannapolis now came back to haunt Cannon Mills management.

Federal law infringed upon Charles Cannon's paternalistic kingdom. The feudal regime, as a 1933 *Fortune* article called Kannapolis, was unraveling.[43] The increasing diversification of Cabarrus County also had an impact on the racial makeup of Cannon workers. As new businesses opened, whites left the mills to seek other employment. This was especially the case with the Phillip Morris cigarette plant, which paid higher wages and had better benefits than Cannon Mills. So as more blacks moved into textile jobs with Cannon, whites left for better jobs, a trend that increased the ratio of blacks to whites in the mill over the next decade.

CHAPTER 15

———◆◆◆◆◆———

CANNON MILLS AFTER CHARLES CANNON:
New Leadership, Union Vote, and the Continuation of Paternalism

While sharing most of the paternalistic beliefs that Cannon had held, Don Holt, the new chairman of the board, was less authoritarian. "The difference between Mr. Cannon and myself is, if he wanted to cross the street, he'd cross it when and where he saw fit," Holt said in an interview with Forbes. "I'd go down to the stop light and wait until it turned green."[1] In addition, Holt was more modern in his approach to business than Cannon had been. Times had changed, but Cannon Mills had not kept up with the times.

Holt's primary problem was the firm's tarnished public image caused by the discrimination lawsuits and the Nader exposé. The new president and chairman of the board realized that the closed-door nature of the firm under Charles Cannon had hurt the company's image. Such a management style had led to its delisting from the New York Stock Exchange and given the firm's critics, especially unions, the impression that Cannon Mills had something to hide. In addition, critics usually overlooked the good works of the firm. Cannon Mills needed to publicize its role as a good corporate citizen more effectively. Holt, therefore, quickly moved to form a public relations department.[2]

On becoming chairman, Holt immediately discovered how the absence of a public relations department had hurt the firm. Following Cannon's death, he found himself swamped with requests for interviews. A public relations spokesman could have handled these interviews, freeing Holt from such tasks. Holt also realized that the firm had not been open to reporters and had not done a good job molding positive stories on the firm. When an editor called expressing the desire to do a story on "the new look at Cannon," Holt responded, "New look? Hell, it's the first look."[3]

To help in the public relations campaign, Holt tapped John Harden of Greensboro, North Carolina. Harden had his own public relations firm when Holt offered him the job at Cannon Mills. Before creating his own firm, Harden had worked for ten years in public relations with Burlington Industries, which many in the textile industry believed to have the finest public relations department in the nation.[4] To improve on Cannon Mills' public image, Holt named Harden special assistant to the president, a new position with a wide range of responsibilities, from special public relations problems, such as Ralph Nader's television program, to community affairs.[5]

Even before Charles Cannon's death, Holt had contemplated a public relations program at Cannon Mills. Several times Holt had spoken with Cannon about public relations at the firm, but Charles saw no need for such a department. Cannon told workers and the public what he thought they should know. John Harden noted, "Mr. Cannon was so much his own public relations man that it would have been completely frustrating to anyone brought in to handle PR."[6]

Harden hired Edward Rankin Jr. on January 1, 1972, to head the new public relations department. Rankin had headed the Raleigh office of John Harden Associates and had also worked at Burlington Industries.[7] The public relations department focused on various groups: employees, the public, customers, and special groups. For workers, the public relations department began publishing a company newspaper known as the *Cannon News* to disseminate news and the firm's position on labor topics.[8] Harden hired James Hale, former head of the public relations department at Bibb Manufacturing Company, as editor.[9]

In Kannapolis, open houses and plant tours by uniformed guides marked the firm's new openness. Cannon Mills executives became more accessible to civic and service organizations and the firm held plant-community meetings. In 1974, the textile firm converted the Sewanee Theater into a visitor's center, which introduced visitors to Kannapolis to Cannon Mills' various products and history. The company town also became the home of the firm's only retail store, selling Cannon sheets and towels directly to the public.[10]

To facilitate communications with the media, the public relations department instituted a system to handle media inquiries and issue press releases.[11] Holt believed that the cost of the public relations work represented an investment that would pay dividends in the future. Positive publicity for the firm would boost its image and increase sales. The chairman of the board also recognized the worth of having a department to deal effectively with damage control when bad publicity did occur.[12]

While creating the public relations department, Holt was optimistic about the business environment for Cannon Mills. In 1972, net income had risen to $353.4 million, an increase of $30 million from 1971 and a record for the firm. Sales of Cannon products outpaced the textile market and even the nondurable goods market between 1961 and 1971. During that period, Cannon sales increased more than 81 percent, while the textile market grew at 64 percent and the nondurable goods market expanded by 71.7 percent.[13] Further, the threat from imports for Cannon's primary products, towels and sheets, remained low.

As Cannon Mills garnered record profits, Holt worked to remove impediments to Cannon stock being relisted on the New York Stock Exchange. In 1973, under Holt's leadership, stockholders approved a five-for-one stock split and the conversion of all stock to voting stock. Cannon Mills now had seven thousand stockholders with more than nine million shares of stock. Shortly, Cannon Mills would be back on the NYSE.[14] More significantly, the Cannon family's control of Cannon Mills stock had been broken.

Even as the textile firm moved into the modern business world, worker discontent simmered below the surface. Some workers complained of low retirement pay. Employee Viola Safrit wrote the company that she had been working for the firm for fifty-two years and was on the verge of retiring with a pension of twenty dollars a month. "Just what do you call this?" Safrit asked referring to her future pension.[15] Estelle Spry, who had been working for Cannon Mills since 1927, also wrote the firm. Spry believed that "they sure do the older people dirty that is in retiring age."[16]

Other workers complained that the "office" remained out of touch with policy in the mills. A thirty-year employee anonymously complained that the actions of her boss encouraged workers in the finishing department to sign union cards:

> If the people in the office only knew half what was going on inside the mill they would understand why cards are being signed. We had to [sic] many bosses that dont [sic] care about the help, afraid their production will go to [sic] high, and the employee will make a little more than they want them. We get about 2 hrs. work on production, the rest is hour wages [of] $2.45 an hour[,] the raise never helped when you don't get the goods to run.[17]

Unsolved grievances also fueled discontent. Lynn Sloop, a Cannon employee for thirty-nine years, wrote Don Holt about being overlooked for advancement:

> A few years ago, I went to see Mr. Elmer Spence as I felt I had been mistreated in advancement. After talking with Mr. Spence and his investigation, it seems the odds of advancement have been totally against me. He visits my department often but I'm afraid to say anything to him for fear of being terminated.

Sloop even asked to speak directly with Holt about the situation.[18]

Attempting to take advantage of worker discontent, the Textile Workers Union of America began another union drive in Kannapolis in 1973. This union drive was different from past drives for two reasons. First, the union did not have to deal with Charles Cannon, only his residual influence on the town and workers. Second, the Cannon Mills work force was now 20 percent black. The firm's paternalism had less hold on blacks than on whites in the firm. Mill owners had segregated blacks in their own section of town and had allowed few to work in the mills, and Cannon had refused to hire blacks for production work until forced to by the federal government. In short, he had denied blacks the benefits of Cannon's paternalism until recently, and, therefore, they had no history of loyalty to the system. The increasingly black work force at Cannon Mills changed the dynamics of the battle between the union and the firm.[19]

The union immediately noticed a difference in its first union drive in Kannapolis since the death of Charles Cannon. This time the union accomplished what had been impossible during Cannon's life: It acquired office space in Kannapolis. Rob Freeman, veteran labor organizer and former Cannon employee, headed the TWUA 1973–74 union campaign.[20]

The National Labor Relations Board called an election in 1974, after 30 percent of Cannon Mills employees had signed union cards. But the actual number of Cannon workers who had signed union cards was in dispute. Bob Freeman of the TWUA claimed that 69 percent, or eleven thousand of the sixteen thousand workers in Cabarrus and Rowan counties, Concord and Kannapolis, had signed cards. Cannon Mills believed that far fewer had signed the cards.[21] Kannapolis, Cannon Mills, and the workers braced for the November 21 election.

Don Holt handled the company campaign against the union very differently than Charles Cannon had done. During Cannon's life a union vote never occurred, so the vote in 1974 broke new ground for Cannon Mills. Holt battled the union more cautiously. He did not want the union to accuse him of unfair labor practices, so he allowed the distribution of union literature at company gates without harassment. Unlike Charles Cannon, Holt answered union charges and attempted to utilize the media for the company's benefit. Part of Holt's cautious approach resulted from the surprising victory the union had secured over J. P. Stevens in August.[22] Holt knew that the days of using brute force to deal with the union had died with Charles Cannon.

In November, the firm made its position on the union vote clear to its employees. Holt sent a letter to all Cannon Mills employees urging the workers to overwhelmingly vote no on November 21. The chairman's letter emphasized the family nature of the firm. "Outside interests," Holt insisted, did not run Cannon Mills. Local people, or at least people from North Carolina, did. He also noted that management lived in the same communities as the workers and all had a stake in keeping the company profitable. Holt characterized Cannon Mills as "an informal, shirt-sleeve organization" in which management remained accessible and open to employees.[23]

Holt and Harold Hornaday, the new president and chief operating officer, sent several more letters to their employees. In these letters the executive officers tried to persuade Cannon workers that they did not need a union and that the family atmosphere of the firm would change if the union won the right to represent them.[24] The firm's officers also made sure that supervisors knew how the company felt about the union and where their loyalties should be:

> The Company is not neutral on this matter [the union vote]. And for all of you in supervision there can be no middle ground—no neutral position for you on this matter. We expect you to stand completely and unqualifiedly where the Company stands on this issue—and that is, against the Union, and against its getting in here.[25]

Although Holt's tactics paid off, the election results did not give Cannon Mills the margin of victory he had wanted. The final vote of 8,473 to 6,801, or 56 percent to 44 percent, demonstrated that Cannon Mills employed a sizable number of discontented workers.[26] Discontentment among workers had existed during the years of Charles Cannon's leadership, but his iron-fisted policies keep it below the surface. Losing the vote so closely raised the union's confidence that it would eventually organize Cannon Mills, just as it had J. P. Stevens. Thus began a period of protracted conflict between the union and the firm.

Perhaps the greatest impact of the union vote was the resignation of Don Holt as chairman of the board. After a mere three years at the helm of Cannon Mills, Holt retired and his protégé, Harold Hornaday, took over.[27] Holt had made a heavy imprint on Cannon Mills during his short three years as chairman. He had introduced public relations to the firm and led the move to convert all Cannon stock to voting stock. While changing Cannon Mills to resemble a modern corporation, Holt attempted to maintain some aspects of Charles Cannon's paternalism. He also wanted to maintain the family atmosphere in the plants and the company town. Indeed, Holt believed that the firm's new openness, characterized by the public relations department, would foster good will and the sense of family between management and workers. Undoubtedly, he felt betrayed by the workers in the close union vote. Besides, if the union had come so close to winning this time, it might win the next time, and Holt did not wish that to happen on his watch.

By the time Harold Hornaday became chairman of the board of Cannon Mills, the firm was at a decisive point. Its revenues had grown 42 percent since 1965 to $395 million, yet its stock dividends did not match those of 1965. Cannon Mills stock was selling at a large discount from its $28.00 per share book value. Compared with other towel makers, Cannon Mills' sales growth had fallen behind that of Fieldcrest, J. P. Stevens, and Springs Mills, and the firm's profitability among the twelve largest textile firms had fallen from third in 1970 to tenth in 1975.[28]

In many ways, Cannon Mills was the same old company. Board members controlled more than 35 percent of the stock and still held practical control of the firm after the stock reform initiated by Don Holt. And the board members still consisted of insiders. When a board member died, William C. Cannon, whom his father had sacked in 1962, became the new member of the board of directors. Furthermore, the firm continued most of the paternalistic policies of Charles Cannon.[29]

The company-owned mill village of Kannapolis also put Cannon Mills outside the mainstream of southern textile companies. Paternalism, characterized by the existence of the mill village, had largely died out—nearly all textile firms had divested themselves of their mill villages by 1970—but as late as 1978, Cannon Mills owned 2,537 houses.[30] The company rented most

of the houses to employees, but it rented 52 to YMCA personnel, teachers, and law enforcement personnel. Instead of selling its houses to comply
with the civil rights acts, as other textile firms had done, Cannon decided to
maintain the homes and worked under a consent decree to open all housing
to both white and black workers.[31] Hornaday had no intention of changing
this aspect of the firm.

Nevertheless, Cannon Mills had the potential for future growth and
success. The textile firm could acquire other textile firms and diversify since
Cannon had no long-term debt and a tremendous amount of cash on hand.
Besides, Cannon Mills still had 50 percent of the domestic towel market and
15 percent of the sheet market.[32]

At a stockholders' meeting in 1977, Hornaday announced his plan for
changes at Cannon Mills. His scheme included reorganizing management
and diversifying the firm's product line. The management reorganization
involved dividing the firm's operations into two groups, each to be headed
by an executive vice president. The nine operating departments came under
thirty-eight-year-old A. B. Adams, who had been with the firm since 1962.
"Finance, general accounting, legal, controller's, purchasing, payroll and cost
departments" fell under the direction of thirty-six-year-old Otto Stolz. This
reorganization plan represented a departure for the firm in two areas. First,
few men as young as Adams and Stolz had gained as much power within the
firm. Second, Otto Stolz was the first outsider to become an officer of the
company. Stolz taught law at Duke University and served in the Nixon and
Ford administrations before coming to Cannon Mills in September 1977.[33]
With the elevation of Stolz to executive vice president, Hornaday began to
open management to outsiders and moved away from advancement from
within the firm that had characterized Cannon Mills during the leadership
of Charles Cannon.

Sales grew to $608.7 million in 1979, up from $395 million in 1974.
Profits also increased, rising to $41.2 million in 1979 from $15.5 million five
years earlier. In addition, the firm returned to the New York Stock Exchange
on February 15, 1979, with its stock selling at $18.25 per share.[34]

Yet the firm faced another unionization attempt. The Amalgamated
Clothing and Textile Workers Union (ACTWU), formed by the 1976 merger
of the Amalgamated Clothing Workers Union of America and the Textile
Workers Union of America, began an organizing drive in Kannapolis. A previous union drive in 1976 had ended without achieving a NLRB vote. This
organizing attempt began, according to a union official, at the urging of
Cannon workers. In early July, the union sent out sixteen thousand copies of

a union paper to Cannon workers announcing its intentions, and later in the month the ACTWU opened a union office in Kannapolis.[35] Union criticism of Cannon Mills concentrated on its antiquated paternalism. Henry Mann, an ACTWU official, stated that Cannon's paternalistic policies represented a "method of handling people" that were a holdover from the past. Living in company houses stifled workers' initiative, Mann said.[36]

While the union organizing continued, more damaging events rocked the textile firm. On October 17 the firm reported a loss of $804,000 for the third quarter, representing a dramatic turnaround from the $7 million profits for the third quarter of the previous year. Chairman Harold Hornaday resigned on the same day. Hornaday cited "personal reasons" for his resignation, but most analysts tied it to the shocking loss. Cannon's new chairman, thirty-eight-year-old Otto Stolz, blamed the drop in profitability on higher cotton costs, higher costs for manufacturing, and a drop in sales of the firm's more profitable products. Stolz also noted that bottlenecks from equipment breakdowns and scheduling problems had contributed to the loss.[37]

Stolz, Cannon's new, youthful chairman, looked to the new decade with optimism. In comments made before Hornaday's resignation, Stolz said that Cannon Mills could become an international company with a billion dollars in sales by 1990 and be transformed from "a medium sized domestic company to a large international company." When asked about the loss in the third quarter at Cannon Mills, Stolz continued to be upbeat. The chairman noted that sales had increased 10.7 percent in January through June compared with 1979 and that the projected decrease of one million dollars in annual profits would not hurt the operations at Cannon. Considering the atmosphere of the prevailing recession, Stolz stated that the decrease in profits would be mild compared with losses incurred by other textile firms. In addition, the projected a loss of eight million dollars from the bad business deal with Peak Textiles, Inc., would "have no effect on the company's operations, and no effect on any one working in the mills."[38]

While bringing a youthful presence to the ninety-three-year-old textile firm, Stolz showed that the paternalistic management style at Cannon Mills would continue. When asked about the status of the company's houses, Stolz replied that "Cannon Mills has no plans to sell these houses. This possibility is not a subject of management discussion. I hope this will put the rumors to rest once and for all." Perhaps because of the union organizing effort, Stolz left open the possible incorporation of Kannapolis. "The subject of incorporation is one to be decided by the citizens of Kannapolis." The textile executive, however, did not discuss the complexity of incorporating the company town while the firm continued to own houses in the town.[39]

Cannon Mills continued its staunchly anti-union position under the leadership of Stolz. The public relations department issued a statement to the press that expressed the firm's stance:

> Cannon has always provided wages and benefits that are among the best in the textile industry. Because of its record in this regard, the company feels that there is no need for unionization of its plants and believes that its employees agree. The company pledges that should an organized campaign be started it will do everything within its legal power and ability to make sure that its employees are fully informed of their rights.[40]

Supervisory and management personnel had already attended workshops on how to deal with the union campaign in the mill. Beginning in August, a series of workshops and manuals educated management on how to discuss the union campaign to "maintain our conduct consistent with the highest standards, practices, and principles of our company's founder." Senior Vice President W. S. Murdoch stressed that management should maintain a good line of communications with workers.[41] "Supervisory training sessions" began on August 27 and managers received a nineteen-page manual on dealing with workers during the union drive.[42]

Anti-union employees also responded to the union activity. Two hundred Cannon workers attended an anti-union rally in October. Later, on December 16, 1980, workers under the leadership of Ray Beaver, a fifteen-year employee from Plant 1, held "Loyalty Day," supposedly without the aid of the firm. Supporters at the event distributed thousands of anti-union buttons, shirts, and jackets, eight thousand in all by one count.[43]

Eventually the union drive died. Workers were probably not interested in pressing the firm for higher pay and benefits in the midst of the company's losses. Besides, the recession had weakened the profitability of most textile firms and employees at Cannon wished to hold on to their jobs and ride out the economic downturn.

Cannon workers had good reason to worry about their jobs. The luster had fallen from Cannon towels. During the late 1970s, other textile manufacturers gained in reputation for style and quality and Cannon towels became associated with "bargain-basement-type goods." In addition, the textile firm had fallen behind in the modernization of its plants. From 1980 to 1981, Cannon spent $20.5 million on new equipment, but this modernization mainly aimed at meeting regulations of the Occupational Safety and Health Administration.[44]

As the recession lowered consumer demand for textile products, firms began to lay off workers. By January 1982, textile companies had laid off thousands of workers in the Carolinas. Springs Mills of South Carolina laid off 2,250 workers, Fieldcrest Mills laid off 4,300, and Burlington Industries closed three plants in North Carolina.[45]

In the middle of the economic turmoil, Cannon Mills became the target of a takeover. Los Angeles financier David H. Murdock, head of Pacific Holding Company, chairman of FlexiVan, and a director of Occidental Petroleum Corporation, began negotiating with Cannon's board of directors in January 1982. The West Coast financier began by offering forty dollars per share of Cannon stock and eventually raised his bid to forty-four dollars. When William Cannon agreed to sell his stock for $4 million, the board and stockholders accepted Murdock's offer. By March, Murdock had purchased 99 percent of Cannon Mills stock for $413 million, and Cannon Mills became a private company.[46]

CHAPTER 16

———◆◆×◆◆———

David Murdock, Modern Management, and the Demise of Paternalism

Immediately, David Murdock made major changes in the operation of the textile firm.[1] He reorganized Cannon management. Stolz resigned as chairman and Murdock became chairman and chief executive officer. Mississippian Harold M. Messmer Jr. came to Cannon with Murdock and became the firm's president and chief operating officer. Much of the rest of the reshuffling occurred within the firm among existing management.[2]

The new chairman immediately began to modernize Cannon Mills and improve the efficiency of the firm's operation. Between 1983 and 1984, the textile company spent $100 million to modernize equipment, including the most advanced textile equipment in the world. Management planned to spend a similar amount in 1985 and 1986. Cannon Mills also worked to improve its public image by revamping its advertising. The advertising department placed new slick advertisements in major magazines featuring celebrities with Cannon towels.[3]

With Cannon Mills operating at a four-million-dollar loss when he took over, Murdock laid off eighty-five hundred workers for six days in March 1982. Public relations officer Ed Rankin characterized the action as a "curtailment in production" and avoided using the term "lay off." Workers' morale dropped. Some noted the bad conditions at Cannon, and one worker told a reporter that "people are scared to death."[4] By the end of the year, Cannon Mills began selling or closing some of its plants. The sale of Plant 14 in Graham, North Carolina, to Culp, Inc., of High Point, North Carolina, cut three hundred workers from the Cannon payroll.[5] Murdock had eliminated more than three thousand jobs by the time he sold Cannon Mills in 1986.[6]

Many Cannon workers were leery of David Murdock. The new chairman represented a break from the family-oriented, paternalistic management of the past. Murdock told workers, "People who don't want to work and don't want to do a good job [won't be allowed to stay]. I'm aware there are some people in the Cannon family who think if they hide in the stairwell they can continue to draw their paychecks and not have to work hard."[7] Cord Winburn, who retired after forty-three years as weaver, did not like Murdock and his new management style. "I'd rather have things the old way," he told the *Charlotte Observer* a year after Murdock took control of Cannon Mills.[8] Workers soon pegged Murdock as a modern businessman, not a paternalistic leader. Johnny Mae Fields viewed Murdock as "a businessman from the top of his head to his toes."[9] Cannon Mills retiree Evis Moore stated that Charles Cannon was family but "Mr. Murdock's the boss."[10] Any sense of family between the management of Cannon Mills and its workers was gone.

Chairman Murdock also brought changes to the mill village. Viewing the company housing as "an enormously losing proposition," Murdock began to sell company houses to the firm's workers.[11] In 1983, Cannon sold three hundred houses to workers at its plants in Concord, Rockwell, China Grove, and Salisbury, North Carolina. Noting that it was "one of the last companies in the United States to provide company-owned housing and that most companies in the textile industry sold all their houses more than 20 years ago," Cannon Mills announced on October 18, 1983, that it would sell its houses in Kannapolis. The firm offered its mill houses to then-current tenants below market prices and provided financing through Countrywide Funding Corporation.[12]

Noticing that Kannapolis looked rundown, Murdock spent $20 million to renovate the downtown district. He created "Cannon Village" out of the downtown district, an attractive shopping area composed primarily of outlet shops.[13] Murdock also sought to divest the firm of the company-sponsored YMCA. The chairman gave land in the GI Town section of Kannapolis for the new center. Thirty GI houses were to be torn down to make room for the new YMCA, and residents, mostly retirees, were moved to other housing. While the Cannon family had paid for the past YMCAs with company funds, Murdock left the building of the new center to the community. YMCA director Jerry Shepherd summed up the Murdock philosophy as "Let's see some initiative out of you folks, rather than just giving a handout."[14] The transfer of the Cannon family's beloved YMCA from company to community control was yet another blow to paternalism.

The Cannon chairman further displayed his belief that paternalism did not fit the new Cannon image by allowing a vote for incorporation in Kannapolis. On November 6, 1984, the voters of the mill town decided to incorporate. Bachman Brown became the town's first mayor on May 7, 1985. Kannapolis, with a population of thirty-four thousand, now became the sixteenth largest city in North Carolina and was no longer a company-owned town.[15]

As Murdock focused on profits by dismantling paternalism, his control over workers was becoming uncertain. In this changing atmosphere, the Amalgamated Clothing and Textile Workers Union tried to organize Cannon Mills again. On July 23, 1984, the union began handing out literature at the gates of Plant 1. Murdock sent a letter to employees stating the company's opposition to unionization and vowing to "resist the unionization attempts by all legal means."[16] In addition, he hired the law firm of Constangy, Brooks, and Smith to run the anti-union campaign.[17] To counter union accusations, the law firm rushed into production a forty-minute film that all employees had viewed by August 2. The cost of the film—thirty-one thousand dollars—showed the company's commitment quickly to inform its workers as to Cannon Mills' position and to defuse rumors circulating in the mills.[18] The chairman stated in the film that

> one of the biggest pleasures I have had while visiting the plants is that so many of you have told me that you are standing with me . . . [to] fulfill the dream we all have for Cannon and for the future. As long as Cannon people stand behind their company . . . I will continue to support Cannon.[19]

Hearing such comments, many workers believed that Murdock would sell the firm if it unionized. In response, the chairman attempted to clarify his position by stating, "I will continue to operate Cannon as long and only as long as I can see that Cannon can be a competitive company."[20] Workers got the message that unionization was equal to uncompetitiveness and believed that defeating the union would prevent the sale of the firm.

The union eventually got enough union cards signed to force an election. The fall 1985 vote was a resounding victory for Murdock. Workers turned down the union 9,958 to 5,982.[21] Nine weeks later, Murdock sold most of Cannon Mills to Fieldcrest Mills of Eden, North Carolina, for $250 million. The transaction was completed on January 1, 1986, and Cannon Mills became Fieldcrest Cannon.[22]

While Murdock sold the textile firm to Fieldcrest, he kept a great deal of real estate. A study conducted in 1986 called "Who Owns North Carolina"

David Murdock meeting with Cannon Mills workers during the union campaign. Courtesy of the Kannapolis History Associates.

by the Southern Studies Institute disclosed that Murdock's holding company, Atlantic American Properties, retained 900 acres in Cabarrus County and 3,250 acres in Rowan County. The study called Kannapolis a "money pump" for Murdock as he took the proceeds from the sale of six hundred mill houses to pay down debt from other corporations he owned. The study noted that Murdock used the real estate as collateral for loans in his other business interests and developed his property in Kannapolis into "higher income-producing property." In addition, he sold some of the property at large profits, such as a lot to Hardee's for $235,000 and sixty-four acres to First Hartford Realty.[23] Yet Murdock's ultimate plans for Kannapolis would be in the next century.

Murdock's impact on Cannon Mills far outweighed the short time he ran the firm. The West Coast financier tore the textile firm from its paternalistic past at breathtaking speed. He downsized the firm, sold and shut down plants, modernized what remained, and eliminated at least three thousand jobs in the process. Murdock began the process of selling mill houses in Kannapolis, a process that would be completed years later, and sold some of the town's real estate. He jerked Cannon Mills into the modern corporate world, and the firm ceased to be the "family" of which Charles Cannon had often spoken with pride. Emerging into the modern corporate world at such speed resulted in much pain, fear, and insecurity among workers.

The cost of Murdock's leadership began to be made public in late 1985. The ACTWU investigated the financier for possible misuse of Cannon Mills pension funds and sued Murdock for allegedly using $197 million of Cannon Mills' pension fund in a takeover of Castle and Cooke, Dole Food's parent company. Murdock settled out of court in 1989 for $1 million.[24]

Another scheme involving the firm's pension fund did not become known to workers until the junk bond crisis of 1990. Murdock bought stock for the pension fund in companies he hoped to take over, especially Occidental Petroleum. Realizing what Murdock was planning to do, the targeted firms bought back the stock from the Cannon Mills pension fund at a higher price. Murdock made a profit of $30 million and invested it. The chairman then terminated the pension fund and purchased annuities with the Los Angeles insurance firm, Executive Life Insurance Company, with the rest of the funds. Having invested heavily in junk bonds during the 1980s, Executive Life was the largest insurance company to fail in the United States. In 1991, insurance regulators took control of the assets of the insurance firm and cut pension payments 30 percent.[25] Cannon Mills retirees found their monthly pension payments cut correspondingly. Nannie Sue Garner complained to a reporter that her pension had dropped to $29.64 per month. Garner believed that "Murdock should be made to pay this pension back. . . . But one thing's for sure, when he faces God he will answer for a great deal and he can't take a dime with him."[26] Retiree Buford Henley, a forty-year employee at Plant 6, found his pension reduced from $40.55 per month to $28.39 in the spring of 1991.[27] Financial writers Karen Ferguson and Kate Blackwell noted that "even former critics of Cannon-style paternalism professed shock at the crassness with which the new owner cast off responsibility for his employees."[28] Perhaps the retirees remembered Charles Cannon's warnings about outsiders sticking their noses into Cannon Mills' business. Instead of dreaded northern union organizers damaging the "family," the real danger came from a western financier.

CHAPTER 17

———————✦✦✦✦———————

FIELDCREST CANNON, PILLOWTEX, BANKRUPTCY, AND THE RETURN OF DAVID MURDOCK

Market conditions, competition, the aftershock of the Murdock period, and bad industrial relations plagued the company's new management. Fieldcrest Cannon struggled with profitability. In 1987, the firm lost $3,660,000 on sales of $1.4 billion. Profits increased the next year to $11,776,000 and to $23,434,000 in 1989. The encouraging trend did not continue into 1990, however, as Fieldcrest Cannon lost $37,834,000 and sales fell to $1.242 billion.[1] During most of 1991, the textile firm continued to lose money but managed to make a profit of $3 million for the year with the strength of the fourth quarter. Company president Chuck Horn blamed the poor performance on the downturn in housing, which caused a loss in Cannon's rug and carpet division. (Cannon Mills had purchased Designer Accents of Tennessee, Inc., in 1982 and renamed the firm the Cannon Rug Company.) Horn also explained that the bed and bath division of Cannon remained strong. The head of the bed and bath division, Robert Dellinger, noted that Cannon still maintained a 50 percent market share for towels. The domestic market was not growing, however, so sales growth had to come through gaining market share from rival firms. Dellinger claimed that the firm had recently gained an additional 2 percent market share at the expanse of its competitors.[2]

The growth of large discounters also changed market conditions for the textile firm. Cannon had been selling products to Kmart and Walmart for years. Those companies' use of electronic inventory systems, which recorded actual sales at each register, tallied total sales at the end of the week, and placed orders accordingly, necessitated changes at Fieldcrest Cannon. Kmart required five days for orders to be filled, while Walmart expected orders in three days. Fieldcrest Cannon had to restructure its manufacturing operations to meet the demands of the large discounters.[3]

Restructuring of the manufacturing operations had been ongoing since the takeover by David Murdock. Cannon had cut fourteen thousand employees from its work force since the early 1980s,[4] and the work force at its core plants in Kannapolis and Concord had fallen to seventy-five hundred production employees.[5] Relations between management and production employees deteriorated in the atmosphere of rapid change. Workers "complained of job overloads, irregular hours, poor benefits and wage cuts." Some workers claimed that the firm had cut employees' wages by sixteen to eighteen dollars a day.[6] While explaining that changes were necessary because of the competitive market, the company also admitted that it had to do a better job at communicating effectively with employees.[7] As chief operating officer James Fitzgibbons noted, "We've got to change, and we know it."[8]

News of the debacle at Executive Life and Murdock's use of Cannon's pension fund contributed to the bad labor relations at Fieldcrest Cannon. Workers felt betrayed by the firm. Company loyalty plummeted as many workers wondered if they could trust the new management. Some employees longed for the good old days of working under Charles Cannon. Pete McIntyre summed up the feelings of many when he said, "Mr. Cannon is not going to walk out of that grave down in Concord and say, 'I'm going to take care of you.' If Fieldcrest treated their employees fairly—give them a fair day's pay for a fair day's work—then there would be no problem."[9]

It was not surprising that in this strained atmosphere the Amalgamated Clothing and Textile Workers Union tried again to organize the firm. What was surprising was the speed at which the union garnered the 30 percent support from workers to force a union vote. One week after the organizing effort began on June 12, 1991, the ACTWU filed with the National Labor Relations Board for a vote. The NLRB set the vote for August 20–21.[10]

Members of the International Association of Machinists from the Philip Morris cigarette plant in Cabarrus County helped the ACTWU. Some Philip Morris organizers merely sympathized with the Cannon workers. Others, however, had been workers at Cannon Mills and had gotten jobs at the unionized cigarette manufacturer after the textile company had eliminated their textile jobs.[11] Although it already had some unionized plants, Fieldcrest Cannon fought the organizing effort.[12] Company officials stated that "Fieldcrest Cannon has resisted all attempts by this union to further organize our company, and we fully intend to do everything legally possible to defeat their efforts now."[13] The firm handed out anti-union literature, posted bulletins, and showed films to workers.[14]

Despite the bad labor relations at Fieldcrest Cannon, the union lost the vote. Initial results gave the company a 199-vote advantage, but 538 ballots remained challenged. The sorting of the first 210 challenged ballots by the NLRB in October gave the firm an insurmountable advantage, and the union dropped its challenge against the remaining votes.[15]

Despite the vote, Mayor Brown of Kannapolis remained concerned about the city's future. Brown knew that the city's dependence on one industry was unhealthy. Twenty-two thousand workers commuted outside Cabarrus County to work daily. Kannapolis needed to attract new industry to make up for the jobs Fieldcrest Cannon had eliminated. To help attract new businesses, Kannapolis annexed new land for industrial sites. Additionally, the town's bond rating would not rise unless it diversified.[16] Labor unrest divided residents and brought bad publicity, thus adding to the city's problems. Unfortunately for Kannapolis, the 1991 labor vote remained unresolved.

Court action regarding the 1991 election continued for six years. Although the union dropped its challenges to the contested votes, it charged that Fieldcrest Cannon had violated labor laws. Agreeing that the firm had unfairly fired union supporters and had intimidated workers, the National Labor Relations Board took Fieldcrest Cannon to court. In 1996, the Fourth United States Circuit Court of Appeals in Richmond, Virginia, voided the election results and issued several remedies for a future election. The court then set a new election for August 12–13, 1997, with polling stations off plant premises.[17]

In early July, the Union of Needletrades, Industrial and Textile Employees (UNITE) began campaigning. UNITE, created by the merger of the Amalgamated Clothing and Textile Workers Union with the International Ladies' Garment Workers' Union in 1995, soon encountered problems with Fieldcrest Cannon.[18] Alleging that the textile firm had violated the remedies mandated by the court, UNITE complained to the NLRB. The board found that Fieldcrest Cannon had disobeyed the court order by not giving the union adequate time to respond to company speeches and not giving UNITE equal time and access to workers to counter the firm's presentations. In response, the court ordered the firm to hold employee meetings in which NLRB representatives read the list of Fieldcrest Cannon violations in the 1991 election and allowed UNITE to hold meetings in the plants.[19]

Results of the election did not settle the labor dispute. Fieldcrest Cannon's 5,530 workers, down 2,000 from 1991, turned down the union by

369 votes. UNITE and the textile firm challenged 378 of those votes and the NLRB voided 15 of them. Realizing that they could not win even if all challenged votes went for the union, UNITE official Bruce Raynor filed complaints on more than fifty election violations committed by the company in the last seventy-two hours leading up to the election.[20]

While the NLRB investigated the allegations made by the union, a Texas-based firm, Pillowtex Corporation, purchased Fieldcrest Cannon for $700 million in late 1997. The Dallas-based firm made various bedding products, including pillows, blankets, comforters, and mattress pads under the brand names Ralph Lauren, Martha Stewart, and Disney. Chairman of the Board Charles M. Hansen Jr. guided the growth of Pillowtex through the acquisition of fourteen firms and was credited with making the firm profitable. One industry analyst characterized the takeover of Fieldcrest Cannon as a coup, and many hoped Hansen could return the company to profitability.[21]

Chuck Hansen and Pillowtex, however, had purchased a firm with problems. Fieldcrest Cannon's sales had fallen to $1 billion and held at that level through 1996. Profits, however, were anything but consistent. The textile firm lost $42,931,000 in 1993, made $30,745,000 the next year, but lost $15,725,000 in 1995. By 1996, profits for Fieldcrest Cannon had risen to a mere $1 million.[22] Hansen seemed to turn things around. For 1998, sales for the expanded Pillowtex Corporation had grown to $1,510,000,000 with profits of $42,855,000.[23]

Meanwhile, litigation from the 1997 trial continued. Eventually, the National Labor Relations Board put aside the results and mandated a new election. The NLRB set the new elections for June 22–23, 1999.[24] Hansen and Pillowtex took a much different approach to the election than had Fieldcrest Cannon in 1985, 1991, and 1997. Pillowtex management interfered little in the election. While tension and confrontation characterized other union elections at the firm, reporters called this one low keyed. Even UNITE representative Michael Zucker dubbed the election legitimate and "without intimidation."[25] Union officials credited the clean election with Pillowtex's experience with unionization, as 40 percent of the company's workers in eleven of its plants belonged to unions.[26]

Election results gave UNITE the victory. The vote was 2,270 to 2,102 with 285 votes contested.[27] UNITE secretary and treasurer Bruce Raynor stated that "today is a great day for North Carolina and for Kannapolis. This is the largest election victory in the southern textile history."[28] Even AFL-CIO president John J. Sweeney acknowledged that the union victory was the greatest in the industry below the Mason-Dixon line.[29]

In November 1999, Pillowtex management decided to recognize the union as the bargaining agent for its Fieldcrest Cannon workers. At a joint news conference with union representative Bruce Raynor, Pillowtex chairman Chuck Hansen publicly stated, "I said in June that Pillowtex would respect the decision of the workers. To continue litigation over the union representation would be counterproductive." Raynor acknowledged that Hansen had been cooperative and that the company had run "a clean campaign." Both men committed themselves to work together for the benefit of the firm and its workers.[30] Negotiations over a union contract began on December 6, 1999. After hard but good-faith negotiations, both sides announced a contract in February 2000. Workers received a 9 percent wage increase over two years, reporting pay, increased company match in workers' 401K plans, and paid sick days.[31]

As Hansen built a working relationship with the union, profits fell for Pillowtex. A series of bad business decisions, pressures from vendors (especially Walmart) to lower costs, and price pressures from growing textile imports brought havoc to the firm. The stock price dropped from a fifty-two-week high of $35.25 to between $8.00 and $10.00 a share. CEO Hanson blamed some of the financial problems on growing too fast and on the installation of new equipment that required training for workers and slowed production. Yet the new computer system was more troublesome. Hanson stated:

> The crushing blow came from the new computer system that we had to install. We thoroughly underestimated the impact of this computer conversion. This spring, for example, the system basically forgot to ship orders—it just left product on the dock. . . . One of our plants was four months late making a delivery.[32]

Losses continued to mount and totaled $11 million in the third quarter of 1999 with another loss expected in the fourth quarter. The firm had $1.1 billion in debt, much of it acquired by the purchase of Fieldcrest Cannon. Pillowtex's stock had dropped to $3.06 per share on November 1, 1999, leading major investment firms to downgrade the stock.[33]

In 2000, the firm continued to lose money. It lost $67 million over five quarters and Hanson resigned as CEO and was replaced with Tony Williams. Pillowtex filed for Chapter 11 bankruptcy soon after Hanson resigned.[34] Williams, the new CEO, worked to bring the firm out of Chapter 11 by closing five plants, including two in Kannapolis, cutting debt, and securing credit. Pillowtex emerged from bankruptcy in 2002, its debt down to $205 million, and launched a new line of Cannon products.[35] Consumer research had confirmed that the Cannon brand was "the most recognized and the most favored brand of home fashion textiles."[36]

The new product line and Cannon brand name, however, could not turn things around for Pillowtex. Williams had believed that the textile manufacturer would make $50 million for fiscal year 2002, yet the firm was in much worse condition than he thought. Pillowtex lost $9 million for the year and had difficulty paying back the credit Williams had secured as part of the strategy in existing bankruptcy.[37]

Instability at the top of Pillowtex continued as Williams was replaced with David Perdue as conditions spiraled out of control. Perdue sought a buyer for Pillowtex, believing that the firm could not pull itself out of its financial hole. In March 2003 negotiations began with Springs Industries but ended unsuccessfully in June. Perdue then sought a buyout with the British company Broome and Wellington, as Pillowtex experienced problems filling orders, paying for raw material, and received extensions on it loan payments. The talks with Broome and Wellington ended and Pillowtex's last CEO, Michael Gannaway, filed for bankruptcy on July 30, 2003, and shut down the company's sixteen facilities. The firm hired the Charlotte company GGST, LLC to sell off its assests.[38] After 116 years, the mills that Cannon built were idle.

The bankruptcy and liquidation of Pillowtex had a devastating impact on Kannapolis. Of the 6,450 company jobs lost throughout the nation, an overwhelming number were in Kannapolis. Of the total numbers of Pillowtex jobs eliminated, 4,800 were in North Carolina and 3,984 were in Kannapolis. In addition, being the largest job loss in state history, the shutdown of Pillowtex was felt all the way to Raleigh.[39]

The loss of Pillowtex jobs accelerated the textile decline in North Carolina. The state lost 193,000 textile jobs from 1994 to May 2007, with only 74,100 remaining.[40] The unemployment rate in Cabarrus and Rowan counties increased dramatically, rising to 6.5 percent in Cabarrus and 6.9 percent in Rowan by June 2003. The rates shot up to 9.1 and 9.6 respectively after the final bankruptcy of Pillowtex.[41]

A vestige of Cannon's paternalism still remained. When Pillowtex purchased Fieldcrest Cannon it also became the operator of the city's water supply. Now the city of Kannapolis was dependant on a defunct textile firm to provide water for its residents. In December 2003, Pillowtex agreed to transfer control of the water treatment plant to the city and the last remnant of industrial paternalism vanished in Kannapolis.[42]

Because the fall of Pillowtex was so public, state and local agencies had been preparing for its demise in advance. Beginning in April 2003, local government and nonprofit agencies met to discuss the implications of a Pillowtex closing. The agencies understood that they would have to coordinate as never before to deal with the onslaught of unemployed workers if the worst happened. The core agencies were the Cabarrus County Department of Social Services, United Way of Central Carolinas, Centralina Workforce Development Board, and Cooperative Christian Ministries. Together these agencies formed the Community Service Center (CSC), which was to be an umbrella organization to receive displaced workers and to funnel them to the correct agencies for assistance.

Kimball Memorial Lutheran Church volunteered to be the site of the CSC, and the new organization began to solicit for funding. The Cannon Foundation, the charitable foundation established by Charles Cannon, provided the core gift of five hundred thousand dollars to the CSC. NorthEast Medical Center also provided funds. NorthEast, formally Cabarrus Memorial Hospital, owed its existence to the work of Charles Cannon, who served as the hospital's chairman of the board from 1926 unit 1967 and was responsible for raising millions of dollars for the hospital.[43] Even after Charles Cannon's death, his legacy, in the form of his institutions, was operating to take care of his workers.

The CSC opened at Kimball Memorial Lutheran Church on August 4, 2003, just five days after Pillowtex closed. Employees only had to fill out a single application to receive all its services. By April 2004, twelve hundred workers had made forty-three hundred visits to the CSC center for assistance.[44]

In addition to the local response, the state of North Carolina formed the Rapid Response Team (RRT), which set up in Kannapolis's abandoned Plant 4 on August 4. The RRT's task was to coordinate the work of state and federal agencies as they helped unemployed workers search for jobs, find career counseling, arrange for tuition payment for retraining, set up extended unemployment insurance payments, and find health care. North Carolina received over $20 million from a national emergency grant, which the RRT used for its operation. From August 7 to 13 a minimum of 3,379 former Pillowtex workers attended orientation sessions offered by the RRT.[45]

Rowan-Cabarrus Community College (RCCC) played a prominent role during the crisis. RCCC received the bulk of a $2.5 million national emergency grant to the community college system to retrain the Pillowtex workers. As of April 2004, sixteen hundred displaced workers had enrolled in classes at the community college. The demographics of the unemployed Pillowtex workers had a bearing on their success in community college. Between 40 and 50 percent had not finished high school, and five hundred, mostly Hispanics, did not speak English. Sixty-two had completed their GED, and sixty-five had finished training to be a nurse's aide.[46]

The sad truth is that many workers never recovered from the Pillowtex closing and the loss of their textile job. By the summer of 2005, only 1,545 of the 3,984 workers were employed.[47] Many did not finish classes at RCCC, and those who found jobs usually were paid less than they had been in the mill. Textile employment was one of the last decent-paying jobs for those without a high school education and that had disappeared in Kannapolis. Ruth Crisco attended RCCC after Pillowtex shut down and received her GED, but she found no jobs making the $19.88 an hour she had made at Pillowtex. She had to take a job making $9.50 an hour working more hours. Five years after the fall of Pillowtex and she was still struggling.[48] Janet Patterson also experienced a diminished standard of living as a result of the company's fall. She had started work at Cannon Mills when she was eighteen, "was the first black hemmer in the sheet department," and worked there thirty-eight years. She made good money to the extent that she could support herself and five grandchildren. But Patterson, interviewed two months after she lost her job, was having difficulty finding another job. All she had was textile experience, and no one now needed that in Kannapolis.[49]

The former mill village now had to strive for a future void of textiles. Town officials created a redevelopment plan known as "Weaving a Shared Future." As a part of that plan, Kannapolis annexed ten square miles to the southwest and constructed a business park there. Gradually, companies came to the town, investing $25 million and creating 350 jobs.[50]

Kannapolis, however, needed more than 350 jobs to replace those lost with the fall of Pillowtex. The much-needed help came from an unexpected source. David Murdock had maintained a presence in the former mill village. His real estate holdings included the downtown area and he had built his East Coast home at For Pity's Sake, Charles Cannon's country property on Kannapolis Lake. North Carolina state senator and Concord attorney Fletcher Hartsell became convinced that Murdock's large real estate holdings gave him a stake in the future of the town and that he had the resources to make a big impact on the community. Hartsell contacted Lynne Scott Safrit, the head of Murdock's real estate holdings in North Carolina through a firm now known as Castle and Cooke. Senator Hartsell began conversations with Safrit over the possibility of Murdock purchasing the mill property at auction and doing something with it to create jobs in Kannapolis. Murdock, Safrit said, was open to discussing plans for the property.[51]

With Murdock willing to discuss the possibly of purchasing and developing the mill property, Hartsell meet with state legislators and town officials about economic development plans. Murdock became convinced by Safrit and Hartsell that the property had great potential and its redevelopment became known as Project Phoenix. When the property went to auction as part of the Pillowtex liquidation, Murdock traveled to New York in December 2004 to bid on the property. The West Coast developer purchased the former Pillowtex property for $6.4 million. Yet there still was no plan for the use of the property. Murdock called Safrit and said, "Well, what are we going to do with it? I can't tell them I don't know, but I can say one thing, that I want to create jobs for the people in that community."[52]

Health had become an obsession for Murdock since the death of his wife Gabriele in January 1985. Gabriele had battled cancer and her husband had taken her to the best doctors to no avail. His attention now on health and the elimination of disease, Murdock stopped eating meat and consuming saturated fats. Nutrition, as a means of eliminating and fighting disease, became an important interest for Murdock. In addition, his interest in nutrition coincided with his taking control of Dole Food Company in 2003.[53]

The purpose for his new acquisition now came into focus. After meetings with North Carolina governor Mike Easley, Molly Broad, head of the University of North Carolina (UNC) system, and officials from the UNC School of Public Health, the idea of creating a biotechnology center in Kannapolis emerged. On September 12, 2005, Murdock traveled to Kannapolis and announced the creation of the North Carolina Research Campus in the presences of state and local officials:

> The most exciting part of this project is to be able to create sustainable, better-paying jobs for the people of Kannapolis and the region. The creation of this scientific community centered on biotechnology will allow a transformation of this economy from a manufacturing-based one to one centered on scientific knowledge and research. Through collaboration of the university scientists, the biotechnology research, and the state-of-the-art laboratories, new discoveries will be made that will further my goal of teaching people about proper health, nutrition, and wellness.[54]

Before construction could begin on the North Carolina Research Campus, the old mill buildings had to be razed and the debris removed. The

Preparation for the demolition of the smokestacks. Courtesy of the Kannapolis History Associates.

The fall of the Cannon smokestack, symbolizing the end of the once mighty Cannon Mills. Courtesy of the Kannapolis History Associates.

demolition firm of D. H. Griffin of Greensboro was hired to implode the massive mill buildings. Total square footage of the buildings demolished was 5.5 million, more than twice that of the Empire State Building and more than a Boeing assembly plant. In fact, demolition of the old Cannon Mills plants became the third largest demolition project in American history. The work began in November 2005 with the demolition of Plant No. 1 and the draining of the lake alongside it and continued with the toppling of the iconic Fieldcrest Cannon smokestacks on August 10, 2006. The water tower was brought down in November 2006.[55]

The new research campus is a collaboration with Duke University, North Carolina State University, North Carolina Central University, North Carolina A&T University, UNC–Chapel Hill, UNC–Greensboro, UNC–Charlotte, Rowan-Cabarrus Community College, and private biotechnology firms. The cost of the 350 acres campus is estimated at $1.5 billion, with billionaire Murdock contributing $150 million to create a nonprofit agency to purchase equipment. The main building is the Murdock Core Laboratory Building, for which Murdock purchased a 950-MHz nuclear magnetic resonance spectroscopy.[56]

Job projections for the Kannapolis research campus are five thousand technology jobs and thirty-five thousand ancillary jobs. The educational breakdown for these jobs, according to the North Carolina Biotechnology Center, are 67 percent requiring a high school education or an associate's degree, 27 percent requiring a college education, and 6 percent requiring a graduate degree.[57] How long it will take for these jobs to appear, especially the jobs that require less education, is unclear. But as of this date, the building of the North Carolina Research Campus has not helped former textile workers like Ruth Crisco and Janet Patterson. Will it ever?

CONCLUSION

———◆◆×◆◆———

Paternalism emerged as part of the textile industry in the South after the Civil War. As mills were built away from existing towns, mill owners had to provide everything for their workers. In return, the owners expected hard work, obedience, and loyalty from their work force. Reciprocity formed an integral part of the paternalistic structure of the mill community, as it had been throughout the rural South with landlords and tenant farmers or share-croppers after the Civil War.[1]

In many ways Cannon Mills was no different from the other textile mills that arose in the New South. James William Cannon's rise as an industrialist in the 1880s was part of the trend to industrialize the South. The Cotton Mill Campaign spread across the southern Piedmont, and textile mills were constructed in large numbers. Mill owners built mill villages and operated their firms in a paternalistic manner. These early mills employed poor whites and people leaving the farms for a better way of life. Few blacks were employed, none at all in production jobs, and mill villages were segregated—as was the greater society. Furthermore, James Cannon's attitude toward organized labor reflected that of other mill owners. He fought to keep his textile mills free of unions.

Yet Cannon's mills were different in several ways. James William Cannon was a southerner who built his cotton mills in North Carolina, unlike some northern mill owners who moved to the South, such as J. P. Stevens. Because Cannon lived close to the cotton mills and was visible in them, he was able to establish a paternalistic structure in Kannapolis that was absent in mills that had absentee ownership. Local ownership and Cannon's constant presence created a paternalistic, family-like bond between the workers in Kannapolis and James Cannon. Cannon's power over his workers was almost complete.

While another southern-owned and -managed mill, Dan Rivers Mills, turned to industrial democracy to manage its workers, James Cannon would not deal with his workers that way. He would not allow industrial democracy or unionization to weaken his control over his mills or employees. James Cannon and later his son, Charles Cannon, dealt harshly with workers who turned against them to the unions. Employees who violated the paternalistic bond and turned against the Cannons lost the mill owner's protection and benevolence.

The deeply rooted structure of James Cannon's paternalism transcended the death of its founders and became stronger under his son Charles Cannon. Indeed, the Cannon myth—that idea that Charles Cannon understood his workers and provided material prosperity in exchange for a compliant work force—was noted by union organizer Dean Culver. By the 1940s, this material prosperity translated into automobile ownership, cheap rental housing, high textile wages, job security, a good school system, recreational facilities, and theaters. Workers understood that the prosperity they enjoyed came from Charles Cannon and could be withdrawn if they were disloyal to him. Workers who agitated for unionization were fired, kicked out of company housing, thrown out of Kannapolis, and blacklisted. The way in which Charles dealt with the strike of 1921 early in his career demonstrated the consequences for workers who challenged the established power structure. This episode provided a powerful collective memory in the mill village that worked to retarded any serious union threat to the power structure until after Charles Cannon's death.

By 1921 Cannon workers had developed a collective identity, but that identity had limitations. First, it bound some workers in sporadic opposition and attempts at labor organizing, but it did not include all or even the majority of Cannon workers. Second, it did not overcome the loyalty or fear experienced by many employees toward Charles Cannon or the textile management. The iron fist in the velvet glove proved effective. While the welfare work practiced by the firm gained the loyalty of some workers and gave the impression that the Cannons cared for them, the efficient use of force against wayward workers instilled a degree of fear among many employees. The boundaries of the paternalistic compact were clearly defined. Third, no labor union had the staying power to combat James or Charles Cannon in the sort of sustained organizing effort it would have taken to overcome the pervasive power of the type of paternalism created in Kannapolis. Without the ability to convince most Cannon workers that any union was there to stay, no union could tap into the collective identity of employees to organize most of them against the Cannons. And finally, the collective identity formed in

Kannapolis was too weak for even popular culture or influences from outside the mill village to galvanize into opposition. Cannon Mills workers traveled, went on vacations, read newspapers, saw movies, and had radios and, later, televisions, but these influences did not motivate the majority of Kannapolis residents to rise up against the paternalistic power structure.

Charles Cannon also resisted pressure outside of Kannapolis to its paternalism. He stood up to the New York Stock Exchange when it threatened his control of the board of directors in 1960. Concerned over the nonvoting 3.3 million class B shares of Cannon Mills stock issued in 1947, and worried that Cannon was not getting proxy votes from voting shareholders who did not attend shareholders' meetings, the NYSE demanded that Cannon Mills grant voting rights to class B stock and solicit proxy votes. Stockholders routinely rubber stamped recommendations of the board of directors, and complying with the NYSE demands would have weakened Charles's hold of the firm. Therefore, Cannon refused to fulfill the demands and the firm decided to stop trading on the NYSE. This action, unparalleled in the textile industry, demonstrated the extent he was prepared to go to preserve the power structure inherited from his father.

Cannon also resisted federal government pressure to change the segregated mill village. Control of mill housing was integral to the structure of paternalism in Kannapolis and segregation was a longstanding practice. While most textile firms had sold or were in the process of selling their mill houses when federal housing policies opposed segregation in 1960s, Cannon Mills Company maintained company housing. The trend of textile firms selling their housing began in the 1930s, and the few companies that had some in the 1960s quickly sold them to comply with federal housing laws. Cannon Mills represented a unique case in that it did not begin to sell its company-owned housing until the 1980s. Kannapolis was still a paternalistic mill town working to comply with federal housing and employment laws in the 1980s. Even then, it took the sale of the firm to an outsider with a different perspective to begin the transition of Kannapolis from a company-owned mill village to an incorporated town.

Under the leadership of Charles Cannon, the firm battled civil rights legislation and litigation. Even with the passing of Charles, three successive chairmen of the board continued to uphold the paternalistic compact and fight discrimination cases. Not until the takeover discussions with David Murdock did management settle the discrimination cases against the firm.

The buyout of Cannon Mills by David Murdock sounded the death knell for the paternalistic structure in Kannapolis. Once Murdock took the firm private, the rapid transition from paternalism to modern management took place. He ended paternalistic practices that cost the firm money and viewed Cannon Mills as a part of his numerous business ventures. Having taken the firm private, his control of it was a throwback to the past, but Murdock also was pushing Kannapolis and the company into the future. The sale of the textile firm to Fieldcrest and later to Pillowtex continued the process of uprooting paternalism. The symbolic end of paternalism came with the transfer of control of the water system to the city of Kannapolis. It took from the 1960s until 2003 for Cannon's paternalism to be totally uprooted. What passed away in the mill community was not only a degree of oppression but also a "neighborliness, spirituality, community and . . . a distinctive and sustaining culture."[2]

NOTES

INTRODUCTION

1. T. J. Jackson Lears, "The Concept of Cultural Hegemony: Problems and Possibilities," *American Historical Review* 90 (June 1985): 568.

2. Wilbur J. Cash, *The Mind of the South* (New York: Alfred A. Knopf, 1941; reprint, New York: Vintage Books, 1991), 200–201; James Cobb, *Industrialization and Southern Society*, 1877–1984 (Lexington: Univ. Press of Kentucky, 1984), 43.

3. Michael D. Schulman and Cynthia Anderson, "The Dark Side of the Force: A Case Study of Restructuring and Social Capital," *Rural Sociology* 63 (Sept. 1999): 354.

4. Gavin Wright, *Old South, New South: Revolutions in the Southern Economy Since the Civil War* (New York: Basic Books, 1986); and Cathy L. McHugh, *Mill Family: The Labor System in the Southern Cotton Textile Industry*, 1880-1915 (New York: Oxford Univ. Press, 1988).

5. Peter Stewart, "Paternalism in a New England Mill Village," *Textile History Review* 6 (Apr. 1968): 59.

6. Ibid., 59–60.

7. Stephen Jay Kennedy, *Profits and Losses in Textile: Cotton Textile Financing Since the War* (New York: Harper and Brothers, 1936), 115–18; Harriet L. Herring, *Passing of the Mill Village: Revolutions in a Southern Institution* (Chapel Hill: Univ. of North Carolina Press, 1949).

8. Michael D. Schulman and Jeffrey Leiter, "Southern Textiles: Contested Puzzles and Continuing Paradoxes," in *Hanging by a Thread: Social Change in Southern Textiles*, ed. Jeffrey Leiter, Michael D. Schulman, and Rhonda Zingraff (Ithaca, N.Y.: ILR Press, 1991), 9.

9. Donald F. Roy, "Change and Resistance to Change in the Southern Labor Movement," in *The South in Continuity and Change*, ed. John C. McKinney and Edgar T. Thompson (Durham, N.C.: Duke Univ. Press, 1965), 238.

10. Ibid., 238–40.

11. Oliver J. Dinius and Angela Vergara, "Company Towns in the Americas: An Introduction," in *Company Towns in the Americas: Landscape, Power, and Working-Class Communities*, ed. Oliver J. Dinius and Angela Vergara (Athens: Univ. of Georgia Press, 2011), 7.

1. James William Cannon

1. On the southern low-wage economy, see Wright's *Old South, New South*.

2. Broadus Mitchell, *The Rise of Cotton Mills in the South* (Baltimore: Johns Hopkins Univ. Press, 1921; reprint, New York: Da Capo Press, 1968), 59.

3. Cash, *Mind of the South*, 200–201.

4. Wright, *Old South, New South*, 145. Southern industrialist William Gregg set the example of using the paternalistic mill village to uplift poor whites in South Carolina in the 1840s. See Mitchell, *Rise of Cotton Mills*, 168–69.

5. David Goldfield cited in Cobb, *Industrialization and Southern Society*, 22; Mitchell, *Rise of Cotton Mills*, 106–7.

6. Ralph McGill cited in Cobb, *Industrialization and Southern Society*, 149. For a study on the industrial leaders in North Carolina, see J. Carlyle Sitterson, "Business Leaders in Post-War North Carolina, 1865–1900," in *Studies in Southern History*, ed. J. Carlyle Sitterson (Chapel Hill: Univ. of North Carolina Press, 1957), 111–21.

7. James Lewis Moore and Thomas Herron Wingate, *Cabarrus Reborn: A Historical Sketch of the Founding and Development of Cannon Mills Company and Kannapolis* (Kannapolis, N.C.: Kannapolis Publishing, 1940), 50; W. M. McLaurine, *James William Cannon (1852–1921): His Plants, His People, His Philosophy* (New York: Newcomen Society of North America, 1951), 22; Gary Richard Freeze, "Master Mill Man: John Milton Odell and Industrial Development in Concord, North Carolina, 1877–1907" (master's thesis, Univ. of North Carolina at Chapel Hill, 1980), 86; Paul R. Kearns, *Weavers of Dreams* (Barium Springs, N.C.: Mullein Press, 1995), 5.

8. *Commerce and Finance* 37 (Sept. 14, 1921): 1327.

9. Moore and Wingate, *Cabarrus Reborn*, 53–57; McLaurine, *James William Cannon*, 23; Freeze, "Master Mill Man," 86.

10. Freeze, "Master Mill Man," 87.

11. *Concord Standard*, Jan. 28, 1888.

12. Gary Richard Freeze, "Model Mill Men of the New South: Paternalism and Methodism in the Odell Cotton Mills of North Carolina, 1877–1908" (Ph.D. diss., Univ. of North Carolina at Chapel Hill, 1987), 189–91.

13. Ibid.

14. Ibid., 188.

15. Quotation in ibid., 189. For information of Concord's chapter of the WCTU, see n. 66, 196.

16. Ibid., 197.

17. Ibid., 210.

18. Ibid., 213.

19. Ibid., 6.

20. Cannon Manufacturing Company, 2, Folder 336, Histories: "Cannon Manufacturing Co.," Cannon Collection, Charles A. Cannon Memorial Library, Foy and Gertrude Hinson History Room, Kannapolis Branch, Kannapolis, N.C. (hereafter cited as Cannon Collection).

21. Charter of the Cannon Manufacturing Company, Sept. 23, 1887, Secretaries' Office Series, Box 60, Cannon Mills Collection, Special Collections Library, Duke University, Durham, N.C. (hereafter cited as Cannon Mills Collection).

22. Freeze, "Master Mill Man," 87–88; Moore and Wingate, *Cabarrus Reborn*, 60–65; McLaurine, *James William Cannon*, 24; Edward L. Rankin Jr., *A Century of Progress: Fieldcrest Cannon, Inc. Salutes Cannon Mills Company and Its Employees, Past and Present* (n.p.: Fieldcrest Cannon, 1987), 5; Herbert Collins, "The Idea of Cotton Textile Industry in the South, 1870–1900," *North Carolina Historical Review* 34 (July 1957): 370; Mildred Gwin Andrews, *The Men and the Mills: A History of the Southern Textile Industry* (Macon, Ga.: Mercer Univ. Press, 1987), 28. Andrews's account of the founding of Cannon Manufacturing contains several inaccuracies. She places James Cannon's first mill in Kannapolis. The first mill was located in Concord on Franklin Street. Kannapolis was not founded until 1907.

23. Cannon Manufacturing Company, 3.

24. Ibid.; *Concord Standard*, Mar. 18, Aug. 31, 1888. Cannonville was annexed by the Concord in 1889. *Laws and Resolutions of North Carolina, 1887–1889*, cited in Freeze, "Model Mill Men," fn. 67, 197.

25. Interview of Jones I. Freeze, Sept. 26, 1938, Federal Writers' Project, Library of Congress.

26. Interview of Alina Caudle, Sept. 2, 1938, Federal Writers' Project, Library of Congress.

27. Mill Rules, Series I.4, Mill Rules, c. 1910, Folder 208, Cannon Collection.

28. Ibid.

29. Cannon Manufacturing Company, 3; John W. Harden, "Cannon: The Story of Cannon Mills Company—90 Years of Textile Leadership and Innovation, 1887–1977," unpublished history, Profile 4, Folder 299, Cannon: The Story of Cannon Mills, 1977, Cannon Collection; Joseph D. Bacon to Mrs. James W. Cannon, Nov. 18, 1937, James William Cannon Series, Box 2, Cannon Mills Collection.

30. Cannon Manufacturing Company, 3.

31. Ibid., 3–4; Bacon to Cannon, Nov. 18, 1937.

32. Financial Statement for the Cannon Manufacturing Company, Aug. 1, 1888, to 1908, glued on the inside cover of the Minute Book, Aug. 1, 1888–Feb. 1898, Cannon Manufacturing Company Series, Box 143, Cannon Mills Collection; Cannon Manufacturing Company, 3.

33. Cannon Manufacturing Company, 5; *Concord Standard*, Oct. 11, 1889.

34. Cannon Manufacturing Company, 5–6; Harden, "Cannon," Product 2; McLaurine, *James William Cannon*, 17; Freeze, "Master Mill Man," 90; Moore and Wingate, *Cabarrus Reborn*, 68.

35. Cannon Manufacturing Company, 6.

36. Ibid., 5–7; Rankin, *Century of Progress*, 12.

37. It is unclear whether these towels were full-size bath towels, smaller hand towels, or washcloths. Cannon Manufacturing Company, 6.

38. Ibid., 8; Histories of the Cannon Plants, 3, Folder 352, Histories: "Histories of Cannon Plants," Cannon Collection.

39. The prosperity of the Cannon and Odell mills in Concord during the 1890s depression is discussed in Freeze, "Model Mill Men," 200–203; Raleigh *News and Observer*, Oct. 9, 1899.

40. "Business," *Textile World and Industrial Record* 17 (Nov. 1899): 28.

41. Patrick J. Hearden, *Independence and Empire: The New South's Cotton Mill Campaign, 1865–1901* (DeKalb: Northern Illinois Univ. Press, 1982), 66.

42. Ibid., 116. Slightly different figures appeared in "The Chinese Question," *Textile World and Industrial Record* 19 (Aug. 1900): 224.

43. Between 1893 and 1896, British and Dutch shipments of cloth sheeting to Shanghai remained stable at about 705,024 pieces while American shipments increased from 1,189,224 to 1,618,815 pieces. By 1905, however, U.S. textile exports to China began to fall because of increased Japanese textile exports. Sung Jae Koh, "A History of Cotton Trade Between the United States and the Far East," *Textile History Review* 4 (July 1963): 137–38; C. Vann Woodward, *Origins of the New South, 1877–1913* (Baton Rouge: Louisiana State Univ. Press, 1951; reprint, Baton Rouge: Louisiana State Univ. Press 1971), 264, 305.

44. McLaurine, *James William Cannon*, 17; Freeze, "Master Mill Man," 90; Moore and Wingate, *Concord Standard*, 68; Jan. 5, 1893.

45. Articles of Incorporation of the Patterson Manufacturing Company, Apr. 27, 1893, Patterson Manufacturing Company Series, Box 204, Cannon Mills Collection; Moore and Wingate, *Cabarrus Reborn*, 68; Freeze, "Master Mill Man," 91; McLaurine, *James William Cannon*, 17.

46. The Buying and Care of Terry (Turkish) Towels, 3, Series I.8, Folder 407, Cannon Collection.

47. Rankin, *Century of Progress*, 5 and 12; McLaurine, *James William Cannon*, 17.

48. "Mill News," *Textile World and Industrial Record* 17 (Nov. 1899): 114; McLaurine, *James William Cannon*, 17–18; Moore and Wingate, *Cabarrus Reborn*, 68.

49. Data Concerning Officers and Directors of Cannon Manufacturing Company, Aug. 24, 1887–February 21, 1905, 1, Folder 110, "Cannon Mills, History," Cannon Collection.

50. Gary R. Freeze, "Patriarchy Lost: The Preconditions for Paternalism in the Odell Cotton Mills of North Carolina, 1882–1900," in *Race, Class and Community in Southern Labor History*, ed. Gary M. Fink and Merle E. Black (Tuscaloosa: Univ. of Alabama Press, 1994), 31.

51. "Mill News," *Textile World and Industrial Record* 22 (Oct. 1902): 735; Cannon Manufacturing Company, 10.

52. Quotation in Rankin, *Century of Progress*, 5; McLaurine, *James William Cannon*, 18.

53. Moore and Wingate, *Cabarrus Reborn*, 70.

54. Interviews: Fairfield, John, Series I.6, Folder 376, Cannon Collection.

55. Rankin, *Century of Progress*, 5; J. W. Cannon to F. H. Freeze, Jan. 5, 1920, Box 331, J. W. Cannon Sr. Correspondence, Charles A. Cannon Collection, Wingate University Library, Wingate, N.C. (hereafter cited as Charles A. Cannon Collection). The sales agency, Cannon Mills, Inc., originally sold the products of J. W. Cannon's various mills. Eventually the sales agency sold the goods of other mills at a 5.5 percent commission. It had sales of $42 million in 1919.

56. Cannon Manufacturing Company, 11; Data Concerning Officers and Directors of Cannon Manufacturing Company, 1.

2. The Founding of Kannapolis

1. Helen Arthur-Cornett *Remembering Kannapolis: Tales from Towel City* (Charleston, S.C.: History Press, 2006), 13–17; Clarence Horton, *An Empire of Looms: A History of Kannapolis, North Carolina 1906–1921*, in "Supplement to Historical Moments—Videos," Cannon Collection. Copies of handwritten options for the land north of Glass are in the Patterson Papers Folder, Cannon Collection.

2. *Cannon News* 4, no. 8 (Apr. 15, 1974). Reprint of an article in the *Daily Independent*, Jan. 20, 1934, Cannon Collection.

3. Harden, "Cannon," Product 5; Rankin, *Century of Progress*, 9; "History for Amortization of Machinery with Regard to WWI," Charles Albert Cannon Series, Box 15, Cannon Mills Collection. The Cannon Manufacturing Company in Concord became known as Mill No. 1 in Concord, while the Cannon Manufacturing Company in Kannapolis was also known as Mill No. 1 in Kannapolis.

4. Rankin, *Century of Progress*, 9.

5. *Concord Times*, July 6, 1906; T. T. Smith to Victor M. Gordon, Mar. 28, 1930, Origin of Name, Folder 187, Cannon Collection.

6. James William Cannon to the Honorable Board of Commissioners of Cabarrus County, June 3, 1907, in "Supplement to Historical Moments—Videos," Cannon Collection. In his letter of March 28, 1930, T. T. Smith stated that "Kannapolis means "Cannon—Town," the first letter "C" being changed to "K" and the letter "O" being changed to "A" and "polis," as I understand it, being the Greek word meaning town." Why this changed was made is only speculation. Sometime later, the name was construed to mean "City of Looms."

7. Ibid.; Moore and Wingate, *Cabarrus Reborn*, 77.

8. Margaret Crawford, "Earle S. Draper and the Company Town in the American South," in *The Company Town: Architecture and Society in the Early Industrial Age*, ed. John Garner (New York: Oxford Univ. Press, 1992), 144.

9. Rankin, *Century of Progress*, 5, 9–10; Moore and Wingate, *Cabarrus Reborn*, 75–79; McLaurine, James William Cannon, 18.

10. John Harrison Cook, *A Study of Mill Schools of North Carolina* (New York: Teachers College, Columbia Univ., 1925), 4–5. The average education of adult mill workers was five and one-half grades, Herbert J. Lahne, *The Cotton Mill Worker* (New York: Farrar and Rhinehart, 1944), 62.

11. Moore and Wingate, *Cabarrus Reborn*, 79–80; Rankin, *Century of Progress*, 9–10; Clarence Horton, Outline of Kannapolis History, Cannon Collection.

12. Vincent J. Roscigno and William F. Danaher, *The Voice of Southern Labor: Radio, Music, and Textile Strikes, 1929–1934* (Minneapolis: Univ. of Minnesota Press, 2004), 7. Transcribed interview from the film *The Uprising of '34*, prod. George Stoney, Judith Helfand, and Susanne Rostock, First Run/Icarus Films, Brooklyn, N.Y.

13. McLaurine, *James William Cannon*, 16; Rankin, *Century of Progress*, 3. Baseball was so important to life in North Carolina mill towns that a semiprofessional league operated from 1936 to 1938. The Concord Weavers and Kannapolis Towelers were linchpin teams of the Carolina League which drew talent from the mills and unemployed major and minor

league players. The league was deemed such a threat to the minor league that the National Association of Professional Baseball Leagues labeled the Carolina League an "outlaw" league and blacklisted its players. See R. G. (Hank) Utley and Scott Verner, *The Independent Carolina Baseball League, 1936–1938* (Jefferson, N.C.: McFarland, 1999).

14. J. W. Cannon to Fuller E. Calloway, Mar. 8, 1917, J. W. Cannon Series, Box 2, Cannon Mills Collection; Rankin, *Century of Progress*, 10; McLaurine, *James William Cannon*, 26–27. For a comprehensive view of the welfare work of North Carolina mills, see Harriet L. Herring, *Welfare Work in Mill Villages: The Story of Extra-Mill Activities in North Carolina* (Chapel Hill: Univ. of North Carolina Press, 1929).

15. Roscigno and Danaher, *Voice of Southern Labor*, 18.

16. Cannon provided insurance for his employees through Aetna Life Insurance Company, *Concord Times*, Jan. 6, 1919; H. W. Owen, of the YMCA, to Cannon Mfg. Co., Mar. 20, 1917; and J. W. Cannon to Clyde M. King, Jan. 1, 1917, both in Box 329, Correspondence, January–March 1917, James W. Cannon Sr. Collection.

17. Rates Paid Per Week, Charles A. Cannon Series, Box 22, Cannon Mills Collection; Lahne, *Cotton Mill Worker*, 133 and 165; Tom Tippett, *When Southern Labor Stirs* (New York: Jonathan Cape and Harrison Smith, 1931), 26–27. For the idea that the family wage system was first used in the textile industry in England before its use in American cotton mills, see William Lazonick, "The Subjection of Labour to Capital: The Rise of the Capitalist System," *Review of Radical Political Economics* 10 (Spring 1978): 6–9.

18. Cobb, *Industrialization and Southern Society*, 43.

19. J. W. Cannon to L. N. Mills, May 28, 1917, J. W. Cannon Series, Box 3, Cannon Mills Collection.

20. Roscigno and Danaher, *Voice of Southern Labor*, 8.

21. Randy Hodson, "Management Citizenship Behavior: A New Concept and an Empirical Test," *Social Problems* 46, no. 3: 1999, 461–62.

22. Ibid., 461.

23. Ibid.

24. Ibid., 461–62.

3. Cannon Mills, Kannapolis, and Blacks

1. It is unknown whether J. W. Cannon read any of Dixon's novels. But it is difficult to conceive the he did not know of Dixon and his writings. Concerning the themes in Thomas Dixon's writings, see F. Garvin Davenport Jr., "Thomas Dixon's Mythology of Southern History," *Journal of Southern History* 36, no. 3 (Aug. 1970): 350–67. For a treatment of Dixon's film career see Anthony Slide, *American Racist: The Life and Films of Thomas Dixon* (Lexington: Univ. Press of Kentucky, 2004).

2. William S. Powell, *North Carolina Through Four Centuries* (Chapel Hill: Univ. of North Carolina Press, 1989), 423–39.

3. Gregory P. Downs, "University Men, Social Science, and White Supremacy in North Carolina," *Journal of Southern History* 75, no. 2 (May 2009): 267–304.

4. Erin Elizabeth Clune, "From Light Copper to the Blackest and Lowest Type: Daniel Tompkins and the Racial Order of the Global South," *Journal of Southern History* 76, no. 2 (May 2010): 282–91.

5. Ibid., 313.

6. Ibid., 297–98, 301.

7. For the background of Thompson, see Freeze, "Model Mill Men," 7–8. For the account of Warren Coleman's mill adventure, see Holland Thompson, *From the Cotton Field to the Cotton Mill* (Norwood, Mass.: Norwood Press, 1906), 253–62. Quotation from Thompson, *From the Cotton Field*, 264–65.

8. Thompson, *From the Cotton Field*, 267.

9. Richard Rowan, "The Negro in the Textile Industry" in Herbert R. Northrop and Richard L. Rowan, *Negro Employment in Southern Industry: A Study of Racial Policies in Five Industries* (Philadelphia: Industrial Research Unit, Wharton School of Finance and Commerce, Univ. of Pennsylvania, 1970), 32.

10. Ibid., Table 18. Textile Mill Products Industry Total Employed Persons by Race and Sex United States, 1890–1960, 54.

11. *Kannapolis: A Pictorial History* (Kannapolis, N.C.: City of Kannapolis, 2008), 13. Copies of handwritten options for the land north of Glass are in Patterson Papers Folder, Cannon Collection.

12. Paulette F. Brewington, "The 'Colored Page': A History of African-American Communities of Centerview, Bethel, Texas, and Happy Holler in Kannapolis, North Carolina: An Account Based on Oral Narratives and Other Sources" (master's thesis, North Carolina A&T Univ., 1996), 7.

13. Ibid., 9–10; T. H. Wingate, "Early Black Churches in Kannapolis," *Daily Independent*, Feb. 14, 1992, n.p., clipping, African Methodist Episcopal Church Box, Cannon Collection.

14. Brewington, "The 'Colored Page'," 13.

15. Ibid., 18.

16. Ibid., 20–28.

17. Ibid., 35 and 39.

18. The First Census of the Village of Kannapolis, As Enumerated by George W. Lee, Enumerator, from May 2, 1910, through May 9, 1910 (Supervisor's District Number 8, Enumerator's District Number 36), Taken from Volume 12 of the 1910 North Carolina Census, A Part of the Thirteenth Census of the United States. Abstracted by Clarence E. Horton Jr. with an Index by Marlene J. Horton, Cannon Collection.

19. Brewington, "The 'Colored Page'," 39.

20. Ibid., 43.

21. Ibid., 44.

22. Ibid., 47–48.

23. *Kannapolis: A Pictorial History*, 8.

24. Ibid., 33.

25. Ibid., 48; "Churches Helped Fill Void Before First Black School Built," *Daily Independent*, Oct. 19, 1981, Education Section, p. 8; "History and Development of Public Education

for Blacks in Kannapolis, North Carolina," in *George Washington Carver School Alumni Association Reunion 2008* program, George Washington Carver Box, Cannon Collection. *Kannapolis: A Pictorial History* states that the black school moved from the Baptist church to the Presbyterian church on East E Street, but others accounts have no mention of this move.

26. *Kannapolis: A Pictorial History*, 82 and 186; "History and Development of Public Education for Blacks."

27. *Kannapolis: A Pictorial History*, 124. The G. W. Carver band is pictured on page 120. "History and Development of Public Education for Blacks."

28. Timothy J. Minchin, *Hiring the Black Worker: The Racial Integration of the Southern Textile Industry*, (Chapel Hill: Univ. of North Carolina Press, 1999), 11–12.

29. Brewington, "Colored Page," 44

30. Robert Sidney Smith, *Mill on the Dan: A History of Dan River Mills*, (Durham, N.C.: Duke Univ. Press, 1960), 164.

31. Brewington, "Colored Page," 39.

32. Victoria Byerly, *Hard Times Cotton Mill Girls: Personal Histories of Womanhood and Poverty in the South* (Ithaca, N.Y.: IRL Press, 1986), 39. Katie Geneva Cannon claimed that her ancestors had been slaves to the Cannons in Mecklenburg County before the Civil War and then sharecroppers after the war, 26–27.

33. Ibid., 98–100.

34. Rowan, "Negro in the Textile Industry," 54.

35. Minchin, *Hiring the Black Worker*, 68–75.

36. Stephen H. Norwood, *Strikebreaking and Intimidation: Mercenaries and Masculinity in Twentieth-Century America* (Chapel Hill: Univ. of North Carolina Press, 2002), 238.

37. Ibid., 27–28; Smith, *Mill on the Dan*, 509–10.

38. Minchin, *Hiring the Black Worker*, 17.

4. A Time of Upheaval

1. For a general work on progressivism, see Robert M. Cruden, *Ministers of Reform: The Progressives' Achievements in American Civilization, 1889–1920* (New York: Basic Books, 1982).

2. Melton A. McLaurin, *Paternalism and Protest: Southern Cotton Mill Workers and Organized Labor* (Westport, Conn.: Greenwood Press, 1971), 22.

3. Elizabeth H. Davidson, *Child Labor Legislation in the Southern Textile States* (Chapel Hill: Univ. of North Carolina Press, 1939), 114–15; Minutes of a Meeting of Cotton Mill Owners and Managers in Greensboro N.C., Jan. 16, 1901, William Alexander Smith Papers, Special Collections Library, Duke University, Durham, N.C.; "Employer and Employed in the South," *Textile World and Industrial Record* 22 (Feb. 1901): 251.

4. Davidson, *Child Labor Legislation*, 149–77; "Child Labor in Southern Cotton Mills," *Textile World and Industrial Record* 24 (Feb. 1903): 273.

5. Jacquelyn Dowd Hall, James Leloudis, Robert Korstad, Mary Murphy, Lu Ann Jones, and Christopher B. Daly, *Like a Family: The Making of a Southern Cotton Mill World* (New York: W. W. Norton, 1987), 58.

6. George B. Tindall, *The Emergence of the New South, 1913–1945* (Baton Rouge: Louisiana State Univ. Press, 1967), 322.

7. Ibid., 16–17.

8. J. W. Cannon to David Clark, May 26, 1917, J. W. Cannon Series, Box 3, Cannon Mills Collection.

9. David Clark to J. W. Cannon, May 29, 1917, J. W. Cannon Series, Box 3, Cannon Mills Collection.

10. J. W. Cannon to David Clark, May 30, 1917, J. W. Cannon Series, Box 3, Cannon Mills Collection.

11. David Clark to J. W. Cannon, July 10, 1917, J. W. Cannon Series, Box 3, Cannon Mills Collection.

12. J. W. Cannon to David Clark, July 18, 1917, J. W. Cannon Series, Box 4, Cannon Mills Collection.

13. "Child Labor Law Unconstitutional," *Textile World Journal* 53 (June 8, 1918): 25.

14. Financial Statement for the Cannon Manufacturing Company, Aug. 1, 1888 to 1908, Cannon Mills Collection.

15. Ibid.

16. Stockholders meeting, Sept. 24, 1908, Cannon Manufacturing Company Minute Book, 1908–1928, Cannon Manufacturing Company Series, Box 143, Cannon Mills Collection (hereafter cited as Cannon Manufacturing Company Minute Book, 1908—1928).

17. Cannon Manufacturing Company, 25–26.

18. Stockholders meeting, Sept. 24, 1908.

19. Stockholders meeting, Feb. 15, 1910, Cannon Manufacturing Company Minute Book, 1908–1928.

20. Cannon Manufacturing Company, 14.

21. Stockholders meeting, Jan. 31, 1909, Cannon Manufacturing Company Minute Book, 1908–1928.

22. Cannon Manufacturing Company, 15.

23. Stockholders meeting, Feb. 15, 1910, and Feb. 21, 1911, Cannon Manufacturing Company Minute Book, 1908–1928.

24. Stockholders meeting, Feb. 20, 1912, Jan. 23, 1913, and Jan. 22, 1914, Cannon Manufacturing Company Minute Book, 1908–1928.

25. Board of Directors meeting, Sept. 30, 1914, Cannon Manufacturing Company Minute Book, 1908–1928.

26. Stockholders meeting, Jan. 27, 1916, Cannon Manufacturing Company Minute Book, 1908–1928; Sales—Cannon Manufacturing Co., Charles Albert Cannon Series, Box 15, Cannon Mills Collection.

27. J. W. Cannon to T. N. Crowell, May 17, 1916, J. W. Cannon Series, Box 3, Cannon Mills Collection.

28. Stockholders meeting, Jan. 25, 1917, Cannon Manufacturing Company Minute Book, 1908–1928; Cannon Manufacturing Company, 16–17.

29. Board of Directors meeting, Jan. 27, 1916, Cannon Manufacturing Company Minute Book, 1908–1928.

30. Stockholders meeting, Jan. 25, 1917.

31. J. W. Cannon to N. B. Mills, Aug. 11, 1916, J. W. Cannon Series, Box 3, Cannon Mills Collection.

32. Tindall, *Emergence of the New South*, 121–23.

33. J. W. Cannon to N. B. Mills, Oct. 10, 1916, J. W. Cannon Series, Box 3, Cannon Mills Collection.

34. Claude Kitchen to William Jennings Bryan, Sept. 10, 1915, cited in Tindall, *Emergence of the New South*, 42.

35. Ibid., 43–44.

36. J. W. Cannon to Fuller E. Calloway, Jan. 1, 1917, J. W. Cannon Series, Box 3, Cannon Mills Collection.

37. J. W. Cannon to H. G. Chatham, July 20, 1917, J. W. Cannon Series, Box 3, Cannon Mills Collection.

38. Hudson C. Miller, Secretary of the Cotton Manufacturers Association of North Carolina, to J. W. Cannon, July 11, 1917, J. W. Cannon Series, Box 3, Cannon Mills Collection.

39. J. W. Cannon to T. C. Thompson, May 25, 1917, J. W. Cannon Series, Box 2, Cannon Mills Collection.

40. J. W. Cannon to Carolina-Portland Cement Co., Sept. 12, 1917, J. W. Cannon Series, Box 3, Cannon Mills Collection.

41. The Transportation Act of 1920 returned railroads to private operation under federal regulation under the ICC. K. Austin Kerr, *American Railroad Politics, 1914–1920: Rates, Wages, and Efficiency* (Pittsburgh: Univ. of Pittsburgh Press, 1968). Also see Albro Martin, *Enterprise Denied: Origins of the Decline of American Railroads, 1897–1917* (New York: Columbia Univ. Press, 1971); and John Ford Stover, *The Life and Decline of the American Railroad* (New York: Oxford Univ. Press, 1970).

42. Stockholders meeting, Jan. 24, 1918, Cannon Manufacturing Company Minute Book, 1908–1928; Sales—Cannon Manufacturing Co.

43. Cannon Manufacturing Company at Present Time Working on the Following Contracts for Various Departments of the Government, Feb. 14, 1918, Charles Albert Cannon Series, Box 15, Cannon Mills Collection.

44. Balance of Towels and Toweling Due Various Departments of the Government by Cannon Mfg. Co., Kannapolis, N.C., May 25, 1918, Charles Albert Cannon Series, Box 15, Cannon Mills Collection; Balance of Towels and Toweling Due Various Departments of the Government by Cannon Mfg. Co., Kannapolis, N.C., Aug. 6, 1918, Charles Albert Cannon Series, Box 15, Cannon Mills Collection.

45. Balance of Towels and Toweling Due Various Departments of the Government, May 25, 1918.

46. Sales–Cannon Manufacturing Co.; Stockholders meeting, Jan. 23, 1919, Cannon Manufacturing Company Minute Book, 1908–1928.

47. Board of Directors meeting, Dec. 2, 1918, Cannon Manufacturing Company Minute Book, 1908–1928.

48. Clarence Horton, Outline of Kannapolis History.

49. Board of Directors meeting, July 17, 1918, Cannon Manufacturing Company Minute Book, 1908–1928; Cannon Manufacturing Company, 17; "Cannon Manufacturing Company," *Chesapeake Pilot* 16 (Oct. 20, 1924): 5; "Halls' Here Real Homes for Many," *Daily*

Independent (July 7, 1950), 15. In addition, in 1920 Cannon built Cabarrus Hall, a dormitory for female workers in Concord that housed 130.

50. Cannon Manufacturing Company, 17.

51. J. W. Cannon to Thomas R. Goodlatte, June 4, 1917, Box 329, J. W. Cannon Sr. Correspondence, April–June 1917, Charles A. Cannon Collection.

52. J. W. Cannon to Thomas F. Bryne, Sept. 31, 1918, Box 330, J. W. Cannon Sr. Correspondence, July–September 1918, Charles A. Cannon Collection.

53. J. W. Cannon to H. M. Anning, Jan. 21, 1919, Box 330, J. W. Cannon Sr. Correspondence, January–March 1919, Charles A. Cannon Collection.

54. J. W. Cannon to H. M. Anning, Nov. 4, 1918, Box 330, J. W. Cannon Sr. Correspondence, October–December 1918, Charles A. Cannon Collection.

55. Clarence Horton, Outline of Kannapolis History.

56. J. W. Cannon to Mr. Leo Loeb, Dec. 3, 1918, Box 330, J. W. Cannon Sr. Correspondence, October–December 1918, Charles A. Cannon Collection.

57. Cannon to Anning, Jan. 21, 1919.

5. Postwar Downturn, Labor Unrest, and New Management

1. "Govt. Contract Policies," *Textile World Journal* 54 (Nov. 23, 1918): 37.

2. Cannon to Loeb, Dec. 3, 1918.

3. Consolidated Balance Sheet, Dec. 31, 1919, Treasurers' Office Series, Box 43, Cannon Mills Collection.

4. Ibid.

5. J. W. Cannon to Judge B. F. Long, Feb. 3, 1919, Box 330, J. W. Cannon Sr. Correspondence, January–March 1919, Charles A. Cannon Collection.

6. "Overhead," *Textile World Journal* 55 (Feb. 15, 1919): 40.

7. J. W. Cannon to H. M. Hooker, Feb. 4, 1919, and J. W. Cannon to H. R. Fitzgerald, Feb. 13, 1919, Box 330, J. W. Cannon Sr. Correspondence, January–March 1919, Charles A. Cannon Collection.

8. J. W. Cannon to H. R. Fitzgerald, Jan. 10, 1919, Box 330, J. W. Cannon Sr. Correspondence, January–March 1919, Charles A. Cannon Collection.

9. J. W. Cannon to H. R. Fitzgerald, Dec. 16, 1918, Box 330, J. W. Cannon Sr. Correspondence, October–December 1918, Charles A. Cannon Collection; Cannon to Fitzgerald, Jan. 10, 1919.

10. J. W. Cannon to H. R. Fitzgerald, Feb. 17, 1919, Box 330, J. W. Cannon Sr. Correspondence, January–March 1919, Charles A. Cannon Collection.

11. H. R. Fitzgerald to Cannon, Feb. 14, 1919, Box 330, J. W. Cannon Sr. Correspondence, January–March 1919, Charles A. Cannon Collection.

12. J. W. Cannon to Mr. Gamewell, General Manager of Erlanger Mills, Feb. 17, 1919, Box 330, J. W. Cannon Sr. Correspondence, January–March 1919, Charles A. Cannon Collection; quotation in J. W. Cannon to H. R. Fitzgerald, Feb. 21, 1919, Box 330, J. W. Cannon Sr. Correspondence, January–March 1919, Charles A. Cannon Collection.

13. Smith, *Mill on the Dan*, 262–68.

14. George Sinclair Mitchell, *Textile Unionism and the South* (Chapel Hill: Univ. of North Carolina Press, 1931), 42–43; "The Eight-Hour Day Again," *Textile World Journal* 54 (Dec. 28, 1918): 26; John Golden, "The Eight-Hour Day: Meaning of the Campaign of United Textile Workers of America," *Textile World Journal* 55 (Jan. 18, 1919): 21.

15. *Concord Times*, June 9, 1921.

16. *Concord Times*, June 9, 1919; Mitchell, *Textile Unionism and the South*, 46–47.

17. For a discussion of the consequences of management breaking workplace norms, see Hodson, "Management Citizenship Behavior," 462; and Mitchell, *Textile Unionism and the South*, 47–48.

18. Dennis R. Nolan and Donald E. Jones, "Textile Unionism in the Piedmont, 1901–1932," in *Essays in Southern Labor History: Selected Papers, Southern Labor History Conference, 1976*, ed. Gary Fink and Merl Reed (Westport, Conn.: Greenwood Press, 1976), 55.

19. "Report of the Annual Convention of the United Textile Workers," 32, Charles Albert Series, Box 22, Cannon Mills Collection.

20. "What About Textile Mill Wages," *Textile World Journal* 58 (Nov. 6, 1920): 93; "Textile Wage Reduction Starts," *Textile World Journal* 58 (Dec. 18, 1920): 39.

21. J. W. Cannon to T. C. Thompson, Dec. 2, 1920, J. W. Cannon Series, Box 2, Cannon Mills Collection.

22. "Sales of Cannon Manufacturing Co., Kannapolis, N.C.," Charles Albert Cannon Series, Box 15, Cannon Mills Collection.

23. *Concord Times*, Jan. 31, 1921.

24. Rick Fantasia, *Cultures of Solidarity: Consciousness, Action, and Contemporary American Workers* (Berkley and Los Angeles: Univ. of California Press, 1998), 170–74.

25. W. G. Walter, Secretary of Local 1238, to C. A. Cannon, Feb. 23, 1921, Charles Albert Cannon Series, Box 22, Cannon Mills Collection.

26. Mitchell, *Textile Unionism and the South*, 52n63.

27. *Concord Times*, May 5, 1921.

28. Mitchell, *Textile Unionism and the South*, 52.

29. *Concord Times*, June 9, 1921.

30. *Concord Times*, June 2, 1921; "N.C. Mill Men Not Worrying Over Strike: About 10,000 Operatives Out in Charlotte District as Protest Against Wage Cuts," *Textile World* 59 (June 11, 1921): 20.

31. *Concord Times*, June 27, 1921.

32. *Concord Times*, July 11, 1921, reprint from the *Gastonia Gazette*.

33. Termination and Eviction Notices, Charles Albert Cannon Series, Box 22, Cannon Mills Collection.

34. Smith, *Mill on the Dan*, 279–80.

35. J. W. Cannon to C. A. Cannon, Aug. 8, 1921, Charles Albert Series, Box 22, Cannon Mills Collection.

36. *Concord Times*, July 25, 1921.

37. *Concord Times*, Aug. 8, 1921.

38. *Concord Times*, Aug. 11, 1921.

39. *Concord Times*, Aug. 13, 1921.

40. Fantasia, *Cultures of Solidarity*, 189; J. W. Cannon to C. A. Cannon, Aug. 18, 1921, Charles Albert Cannon Series, Box 22, Cannon Mills Collection.

41. J. W. Cannon to C. A. Cannon, Aug. 19, 1921, Charles Albert Cannon Series, Box 22, Cannon Mills Collection.

42. *Concord Times*, Aug. 22, 1921.

43. J. W. Cannon's obituary is in the December 22, 1921, issue of the *Concord Times*; "Death of James W. Cannon," *Textile World* 60 (Dec. 24, 1921): 20. For a bibliographical article on Cannon, see Steve Usselman, "James William Cannon," *American National Biography*, ed. John A. Garraty and Mark C. Carnes (New York: Oxford Univ. Press, 1999), 335–36.

44. Sales of Common Stock Announcement, July 10, 1928, Treasurers' Office Series, Box 42, Cannon Mills Collection.

45. Michael Mann, *Consciousness and Action Among the Western Working Class* (London: Macmillan, 1973), 13.

46. For works on collective identity theory, see Fantasia, *Cultures of Solidarity*, and Mann, *Consciousness and Action*. Fantasia uses the term "cultures of solidarity" and describes it as "more or less bounded groupings that may or may not develop clear organizational identity and structure, but represent the active expression of worker solidarity within an industrial system and a society hostile to it" (19). This also fits workers' situation in Kannapolis. Collective identity theory resembles the ideas of class conscience developed by British historian E. P. Thompson. Thompson wrote that class consciousness is based on shared experiences and a perceived difference in status from the management, based in time, and differs from group to group. There are no uniform laws defining its exact structure or formation for each occupational group. See E. P. Thompson, *The Making of the English Working Class* (New York: Vintage, 1966), 9–11. Also see William H. Sewell Jr., "How Classes Are Made: Critical Reflections on E. P. Thompson's Theory of Working-Class Formation," in *Thompson: Critical Debates*, ed. Harvey J. Kaye and Keith McClelland (Oxford: Basil Blackwell, 1990), 50–77. On the ideas of trust, legitimacy, reciprocity, and workplace justice as important aspects of the management-labor relations, see Hodson, "Management Citizenship Behavior," 460–78.

47. Fantasia, *Cultures of Solidarity*, 169–70.

6. New Leadership, Market Decline, and Consolidation

1. James R. Young, *Textile Leaders of the South* (Columbia, S.C.: R. L. Bryan, 1963), 41; "Cannon of Kannapolis," *Cotton* 109 (June 1945): 106.

2. F. C. Niblock to C. A. Cannon, July 21, 1947, Box 189, First Presbyterian Church, Concord, N.C., Correspondence 1946–49, Charles A. Cannon Collection.

3. Cannon to Mills, May 28, 1917.

4. Information Regarding Cost of Operating an Automobile, Charles Albert Cannon, Box 22, Personal Files: 1921, H–Y, Cannon Mills Collection.

5. Officer and Directors of Cannon Manufacturing Company, 1915–1921, n.d., Cannon Manufacturing Company Series, Box 146, Cannon Mills Collection.

6. According to an unpublished draft of a *Fortune* article about the Cannon family, which Charles Cannon refuted, Joseph Cannon fell out of favor with his father over a cotton transaction. Joseph was managing the Wiscasset Mills and had purchased $2 million of

cotton for twenty cents per pound. His father declared Joseph a "fool" for buying cotton for so much, but when cotton went to forty cents, James asked to buy some of Joseph's cotton for the original price. The oldest son refused. James Cannon promptly disinherited Joseph for Charles. Except for Charles, James's sons were a disappointment to him. Charles Cannon to Eleanor Hard of *Fortune* magazine, Oct. 2, 1933, Card Box 1, C. A. Cannon and Family, Cannon Collection.

7. J. W. Cannon to William Post, president of Central National Bank, Jan. 7, 1918, J. W. Cannon Series, Box 4, Cannon Mills Collection; Will of James W. Cannon Sr., J. W. Cannon Series, Box 2, Cannon Mills Collection. James Cannon probably excluded Joseph from the will because of his drinking problem. While Joseph was treasurer of the Wiscassett Mills Company, his drinking and lack of attention to his job prompted a letter from the superintendent of Wiscassett to the elder Cannon. J. N. Barnhardt, the superintendent, reported to Cannon that over the last twelve months Joseph's actions "have become notorious," that there had been much talk about him at the mill, and that "no man can attend to business and drink as much as he does." J. N. Barnhardt to J. W. Cannon, July 3, 1919, Box 330, J. W. Cannon Sr. Correspondence, July–December 1919, Charles A. Cannon Collection.

8. Kennedy, *Profits and Losses*, 128.

9. Ibid., 122. Cloth that is unfinished, not in a condition to be sold to the consumer, is considered gray goods. Converters purchase gray goods from mills and finish these goods for the consumer market. Claudius T. Murchison, *King Cotton Is Sick* (Chapel Hill: Univ. of North Carolina Press, 1930), 61–62.

10. Kennedy, *Profits and Losses*, 122–24, 128–29.

11. Jules Backman and M. R. Gainsbrugh, *Economics of the Cotton Textile Industry* (New York: National Industrial Conference Board, 1946), appendix table 45, "Income and Taxes of All Corporations, All Manufacturing Corporations, and Cotton Manufacturing Corporations," 210. A breakdown of the number of mills reporting profits and deficits for the years 1926 to 1933 is in "Income and Deficit of Mills as Reported by the Bureau of Internal Revenue," in Kennedy, *Profits and Losses*, 129.

12. Backman and Gainsbrugh, *Economics*, 168.

13. Kennedy, *Profits and Losses*, 196.

14. Ibid., 197.

15. Hall et al., *Like a Family*, 199–200.

16. Interview of Glenn Kanipe, Sept. 29, 1939, Federal Writers' Project, Library of Congress.

17. Kennedy, *Profits and Losses*, 162; Hall et al., *Like a Family*, 200–201. Scientific management was built on the ideas of Frederick W. Taylor, who advocated the rationalization of the manufacturing process. Taylor pioneered time-and-motion studies to determine the efficiency of workers in an attempt to improve worker productivity. See Thomas P. Hughes, *American Genesis: A Century of Invention and Technological Enthusiasm* (New York: Penguin, 1989), 188–203.

18. H. D. Martin, "Preventable Losses in Textile Mills," *Southern Textile Bulletin*, Apr. 20, 1922, 1, cited in Hall et al., *Like a Family*, 200.

19. Hall et al., 202, 204.

20. Ibid., 203–4.

21. Ibid., 206; Schuman and Leiter, "Southern Textiles," 13–14. For two good articles on the importance of skill to industrial workers, their concept of work, and attempts to maintain their skilled positions, see William Lazonick, "Industrial Relations and Technical Change: The Case of the Self-Acting Mule," *Cambridge Journal of Economics* 3 (1979): 231–62; and John Rule, "The Property of Skill in the Period of Manufacture," in *The Historical Meaning of Work,* ed. Patrick Joyce (Cambridge: Cambridge Univ. Press, 1987), 99–118.

22. On the difficult transition from rural life to factory workers, especially on the concept of rural versus factory time, see E. P. Thompson, "Time, Work-Discipline, and Industrial Capitalism," *Past and Present* 35 (1967): 56–97. On the impact of industrialization on the American work ethic, see Daniel T. Rodgers, *The Work Ethic in Industrial America, 1850–1920* (Chicago: Univ. of Chicago Press, 1978).

23. Kennedy, *Profits and Losses,* 158; Backman and Gainsbrugh, *Economics,* 181; H. E. Michl, *The Textile Industries: An Economic Analysis* (Washington: Textile Foundation, 1938), 177.

24. Kennedy, *Profits and Losses,* 159: Michl, *Textile Industries,* 179. The advantages of Japanese textile manufacturers included lower wages and standard of living, increases in worker productivity and the use of new machinery, better grades of cotton, the formation of large units of production by merging smaller and less productive mills, and the low value of the yen compared to the dollar. Kennedy, *Profits and Losses,* 159; Michl, *Textile Industries,* 180. Kennedy, 158–59, also notes as an advantage the apprentice or indentured system used in Japan. Under this system, parents sent children to work in the mills for an advance of usually between one hundred and two hundred dollars against the wages of their children (usually a daughter). After two years or so of "apprenticeship," the children were discharged from the mill and new apprentices hired.

25. Kennedy, *Profits and Losses,* 178.

26. Ibid., 178–79.

27. The Cannon Manufacturing Company had become the Cannon Mills Company through merger in 1928. This merger is discussed later in the chapter. How Fashion Towels Began, Folder 355, Histories: "How Fashion Towels Began," Cannon Collection; Rankin, *Century of Progress,* 12–13.

28. Kennedy, *Profits and Losses,* 182–94.

29. Ibid., 183.

30. Ibid., 188–89; Murchison, *King Cotton Is Sick,* 161–62; Michl, *Textile Industries,* 170–72.

31. Kennedy, *Profits and Losses,* 187.

32. Ibid., 191.

33. Louis Galambos, *Competition and Cooperation: The Emergence of a National Trade Association* (Baltimore: Johns Hopkins Univ. Press, 1966), 20–36.

34. Ibid., 104; Louis Galambos, "The Cotton-Textile Institute and the Government: A Case Study in Interacting Value Systems," *Business History Review* 38 (Summer 1964): 187; "Cotton-Textile Institute Hold Annual Meeting," *Textile World* 70 (Oct. 23, 1926): 27–28.

35. Galambos, "Cotton-Textile Institute," 189–90; Galambos, *Competition and Cooperation,* 106; Kennedy, 203; Murchison, 125–26.

36. Galambos, *Competition and Cooperation*, 107; Galambos, "Cotton-Textile Institute," 189–90; Kennedy, 203.

37. Kennedy, *Profits and Losses*, 204; Galambos, 107; Galambos, "Cotton-Textile Institute," 190; Murchison, *King Cotton Is Sick*, 126.

38. Cannon Mills, the Bibb Manufacturing Company, and Avondale Mills had joined the Cotton Textile Institute by June 1, 1931. Boris Siniavsky, "The Cotton-Textile Institute, Inc., a Stabilizing Agency in the Cotton Textile Industry" (master's thesis, Univ. of North Carolina at Chapel Hill, 1931), 150; Charles Cannon later served on the CTI executive board. Untitled article on local textiles by Hazel Mizelle in the *Uplift* (published at the Stonewall Jackson Manuel Training School in Cabarrus County) 25 (July 17, 1937): 3.

39. Galambos, *Competition and Cooperation*, 134–38.

40. Advertising Contract Between N. W. Ayers and Son and J. W. Cannon for Cannon Manufacturing Company, June 11, 1907, Box 245, Topical Files, N. W. Ayers and Son, 1907–1958, Charles A. Cannon Collection.

41. Ralph M. Hower, *The History of an Advertising Agency: N. W. Ayer and Son at Work, 1869–1939* (Cambridge: Harvard Univ. Press, 1939), 590.

42. Rankin, *Century of Progress*, 16.

43. Ibid.

44. "Comparative Advertising Expenditures," Charles Albert Cannon Series, Box 11, Cannon Mills Collection.

45. Kennedy, *Profits and Losses*, 115–17.

46. Ibid., 117.

47. *Concord Daily Tribune*, May 25 and June 4, 1928; "Mill News," *Textile World* 74 (July 14, 1928): 65; "Cannon Merger Approved," *Southern Textile Bulletin* 34 (July 12, 1928): 25.

48. Sales of Common Stock Announcement, July 10, 1928; *Concord Daily Tribune*, May 25, 1928.

49. Untitled newspaper clipping, July 5, 1928, Charles Albert Cannon Series, Box 16, Cannon Mills Collection.

50. *Concord Daily Tribune*, May 26, 1928.

51. Kennedy, *Profits and Losses*, 117–18. The ratio of exchange was .580952 for Cannon Mfg. Co., 2.60 for Cabarrus Cotton Mills, 3.633061 for Barringer Mfg. Co., 3.33 for Gibson Mfg. Co., 4.46 for Kesler Mfg. Co., 2.50 for Patterson Mfg. Co., 2.46063 for Norcott Mills Co., and 2.66 for Hobarton Mfg. Co. The conversion of Franklin Cotton Mills is not listed, as it had been wholly owned by J. W. Cannon. Charles Cannon's shares of the other companies converted into 149,199.31239 shares or almost 15 percent of Cannon Mills. Stock Conversion Chart for Charles A. Cannon, Charles Albert Cannon Series, Box 17, Cannon Mills Collection.

52. Kennedy, *Profits and Losses*, 118; Sales of Common Stock Announcement, July 10, 1928.

53. Kennedy, Profits and Losses, 118.

54. Untitled newspaper clipping, July 5, 1928, Charles Albert Cannon Series, Box 16, Cannon Mills Collection; Sales of Common Stock Announcement, July 10, 1928.

55. The selling house for the new firm would be Cannon Mills, Inc., of New York City, which had served as the selling house for the nine individual companies. Cannon Mills, Inc.,

was also the selling agent for six mills in which the Cannon family had controlling interest and sixteen other mills. *Concord Daily Tribune*, May 26, 1928; Kennedy, *Profits and Losses*, 117.

56. Murchison, *King Cotton Is Sick*, 51.

57. Ibid., 62.

58. Ibid., 51.

59. Walker D. Hines, president of the Cotton-Textile Institute, believed that consolidations and mergers in the textile industry were desirable and followed the pattern set in other industries. "Mergers of Cotton Mills Desirable, in Opinion of Walker D. Hines," *Concord Daily Tribune*, Apr. 2, 1929, 6.

60. Murchison, *Cotton Is Sick*, 161–62.

61. Nolan and Jones, "Textile Unionism in the Piedmont," 58–59: Hall et al., *Like a Family*, 213–14. For a detailed account from a labor viewpoint of the Elizabethton strike, see Tippett, *When Southern Labor Stirs*, 54–75.

62. Nolan and Jones, "Textile Unionism in the Piedmont," 59–60: Hall et al., *Like a Family*, 214–15. Also see Tippett, *When Southern Labor Stirs*, 76–108. The best early account of the Gastonia strike is Liston Pope, *Millhands and Preachers: A Study of Gastonia* (New Haven, Conn.: Yale Univ. Press, 1942), 207–84. A more recent account is John Salmond, *Gastonia 1929: The Story of the Loray Mill Strike* (Chapel Hill: Univ. of North Carolina Press, 1995). The governor was himself a mill owner. He owned the Cleveland Cloth Mills, Inc., a rayon plant, since 1925. Joseph L. Morrison *Governor O. Max Gardner: A Power in North Carolina and New Deal Washington* (Chapel Hill: Univ. of North Carolina Press, 1971), 42.

63. Tippett, *When Southern Labor Stirs*, 109–155; Gary Fink and Merl Reed, *Essays in Southern Labor History: Selected Papers, Southern Labor History Conference*, (Westport, Conn.: Greenwood Press, 1976), 61–62: Hall et al., *Like a Family*, 215–17. Governor Gardner made a distinction between the strike in Gastonia and the labor dispute in Marion. He told a newspaper reporter that he might meet with the AFL leaders about the situation in Marion but would not confer with the communist union leaders in Gastonia. Referring to the union leaders in Gastonia, Gardner said, "If they believed in our form of constitutional government and institutions I could and would talk with them, but their whole teaching is against the American form of government and our most cherished institutions. I do not know how to confer with such a group." Morrison, *Governor O. Max Gardner*, 61.

64. Hall et al., *Like a Family*, 214.

65. The best work on the familial nature of southern textile communities is Hall et al., *Like a Family*.

66. Kennedy noted that "the principal products of Cannon Mills, towels, require special looms, of which there are a limited number in the industry." Kennedy, *Profits and Losses*, 118.

67. Alfred D. Chandler Jr., *Strategy and Structure: Chapters in the History of the Industrial Enterprise* (Cambridge, Mass.: MIT Press, 1962).

7. Paternalism Expanded

1. Stuart D. Brandes, *American Welfare Capitalism, 1880–1940* (Chicago: Univ. of Chicago Press, 1976), 6–7.

2. Ibid. For other general works on welfare capitalism, see Gaston V. Rimlinger, "Welfare Policy and Economic Development: A Comparative Historical Perspective," *Journal of Economic History* 26 (Dec. 1966): 556–71; and Homer J. Hagedorn, "A Note on the Motivation of Personnel Management: Industrial Welfare 1885–1910," *Explorations in Entrepreneurial History* 10 (Apr. 1958): 134–39. On how welfare capitalism operated in an individual company, see Gerald Zahovi, "Negotiated Loyalty: Welfare Capitalism and the Shoeworkers of Endicott Johnson, 1920–1940," *Journal of American History* 70 (Dec. 1983): 602–20.

3. Rankin, *Century of Progress*, 11.

4. Herring, *Welfare Work in Mill Villages*, 156–58; C. A. Cannon to Mr. F. R. Shepherd, Superintendent of Cannon Manufacturing Company and J. H. Talbert, Superintendent of Franklin Cotton Mills, Feb. 27, 1924, Circular Letters, 1924–40, 60, Charles A. Cannon Collection.

5. Cabarrus County Tuberculosis Nurse Fund (mill totals for 1926–27), and T. T. Smith to G. B. Lewis, Treasurer of Cannon Mills Company, Oct. 17, 1929, both in Box 195, Gifts to Churches, etc., 1925–32, Charles A. Cannon Collection.

6. Rankin, *Century of Progress*, 11; G. B. Lewis to C. A. Cannon, June 25, 1930, Box 195, Gifts to Churches, etc., 1925–32, Charles A. Cannon Collection.

7. Freeze, "Model Mill Men," 199.

8. Cited in A. P. Donajgrodzki, "Introduction," in *Social Control in Nineteenth Century Britain*, ed. A. P. Donajgrodzki (Totowa, N.J.: Rowman and Littlefield, 1977), 10. A good article on social control is F. M. L. Thompson, "Social Control in Victorian Britain," *Economic History Review* 34 (May 2, 1981): 189–208.

9. Pope, *Millhands and Preachers.*

10. Daniel Nelson and Stuart Campbell, "Taylorism Versus Welfare Work in American Industry: H. L. Gantt and the Bancrofts," *Business History Review* 46 (Spring 1972): 2. Nelson and Campbell mention that the southern textile industry was one of the leading industries in welfare work before 1910.

11. Paul R. Kearns, *Mullen Leaves and Brown Sugar: Memories to Make Our Hearts Smile* (Barium Springs, N.C.: Mullein Press, 1993), 12–13; Horton, Outline of Kannapolis History.

12. Interview with C. M. Deal Jr., Sept. 1, 1939, Federal Writers' Project, Library of Congress.

13. C. A. Cannon to F. R. Shepherd, Superintendent of Cannon Manufacturing Company, Concord, and E. A. Hall, Superintendent of Cannon Manufacturing Company, York, S.C., Nov. 9, 1921; and Banquet Program, Nov. 18, 1921, both in Cannon Manufacturing Company Series, Box 137, Cannon Mills Collection.

14. Caudle interview, Federal Writers' Project.

15. Rankin, *Century of Progress*, 19.

16. Cynthia D. Anderson, *The Social Consequences of Economic Restructuring in the Textile Industry: Change in a Southern Mill Village* (New York: Garland, 2000), 56.

17. Kearns, *Mullen Leaves and Brown Sugar*, 12–13.

18. Ibid.

19. Debate still rages among labor historians over the success of welfare capitalism to win the hearts and minds of workers. David Brody, "The Rise and Decline of Welfare Capitalism," in *Change and Continuity in the Twentieth-Century: The Twenties*, ed. John Braeman et al.

(Columbus: Ohio State Univ. Press, 1968), 178, argues that welfare capitalism had won the hearts of most workers and only the Great Depression, not worker ambivalence, put an end to it. Zahovi, in "Negotiated Loyalty," takes the position that workers did not wholeheartedly support or reject welfare work but were agents negotiating with employers. On the other hand, Don Lescohier and Elizabeth Brandies agree with Brandes that welfare capitalism did not win the hearts of workers. See Lescohier and Brandies, *History of Labor in the United States, 1896–1932* (New York: Macmillan, 1935).

8. The Great Depression, the New Deal, and Cannon Mills

1. Backman and Gainsbrugh, *Economics*, 211; Kennedy, *Profits and Losses*, 129.

2. Kennedy, *Profits and Losses*, 123; Backman and Gainsbrugh, *Economics*, 137.

3. Kennedy, *Profits and Losses*, 127.

4. Brent D. Glass, *The Textile Industry in North Carolina: A History* (Raleigh: Division of Archives and History, North Carolina Department of Cultural Resources, 1992), 74.

5. Rankin, *Century of Progress*, 18.

6. Ibid.; Morrison, *Governor O. Max Gardner*, 104.

7. *Moody's Manual* (New York: Moody's, 1931, 1932, 1933), 1931, 585; 1932, 205; 1933, 396 (*Moody's Manual* was known at various times as *Moody's Manual of Industrial and Miscellaneous Securities, Moody's Manual of Railroads and Corporation Securities,* and *Moody's Analyses of Investments* but herein it is cited as followed by the manual's date).

8. Cannon Mills Board of Directors meeting, Mar. 4, 1929, and June 2, 1930, Cannon Mills Company Minute Book, 1928–1949, Cannon Manufacturing Company Series, Box 144, Cannon Mills Collection (hereafter cited as Cannon Mills Company Minute Book, 1928–1949).

9. "Comparative Advertising Expenditures."

10. F. A. Williams, Vice-President of Cannon Mills, Inc., "Advertised Brands Proved to Be Best Profits Makers," *Printers' Ink* 160 (Sept. 29, 1932): n.p., Folder 70, Advertising, Cannon Collection; "Cannon Leads in Modern Textile Merchandising," Kannapolis *Daily Independent,* June 2, 1938, n.p., Folder 70, Advertising, Cannon Collection; Harden, "Cannon"; "Cannon: I," *Fortune,* Nov. 1933, 50.

11. Williams, "Advertised Brands," n.p.

12. "Comparative Advertising Expenditures."

13. *Moody's,* 1933, 396; *Moody's,* 1937, 362.

14. "Advertising Recommendations for 1946." Total sales were $30,495,252 for 1935 and $65,151,914 for 1941. *Moody's,* 1936, 1042; *Moody's,* 1942, 1987.

15. "Comparative Advertising Expenditures." Advertising figures for towels differ in "Comparative Advertising Expenditures" and "Analysis of Advertising Expenditures to Sales—Years 1935–1945 and 1946 Estimated." The figures are lower in "Comparative Advertising Expenditures." No reason is evident for the disparity.

16. Board of Directors meetings, July 6, 1928, Apr. 14, 1931, Apr. 11, 1933, and Apr. 10, 1934, Cannon Mills Company Minute Book, 1928–1949.

17. Board of Directors meeting, Dec. 4, 1933, Cannon Mills Company Minute Book, 1928–1949.

18. Charles Cannon to Stockholders, Apr. 15, 1936, Box 144, Cannon Mills Co., Correspondence, July 1935–1946, Charles A. Cannon Collection.

19. Board of Directors meetings, June 1 and Dec. 31, 1936, Cannon Mills Company Minute Book, 1928–1949.

20. Board of Directors meeting, Mar. 6, 1939, Cannon Mills Company Minute Book, 1928–1949.

21. "No Loss in 30s," Kannapolis *Daily Independent*, May 21, 1967, p. 4d.

22. K. P. Lewis, President of the Cotton Manufacturers' Association of North Carolina, to Charles Cannon, Oct. 31, 1931, Cotton Manufacturers Association of North Carolina, 1924–31, 38, Charles A. Cannon Collection.

23. Galambos, *Competition and Cooperation*, 142–43. Charles Cannon later served on the board of New York Life Insurance with Hoover. Box 211, Herbert Hoover Oral History Interview, 1966–70, 2–3, Charles A. Cannon Collection.

24. Galambos, *Competition and Cooperation*, 143.

25. Ibid., 143–44.

26. Ibid.; Michl, *Textile Industries*, 261–62; Kennedy, *Profits and Losses*, 204.

27. Board of Directors meeting, Apr. 8, 1930, Cannon Mills Company Minute Book, 1928–1949.

28. Tindall, 362; Galambos, *Competition and Cooperation*, 145–47. Assistant Secretary of Commerce Julius Klein assured the CTI that the administration did not view the 55-50 plan as a restraint of trade and therefore no antitrust action would be taken against the institute.

29. Galambos, *Competition and Cooperation*, 149–150; Michl, *Textile Industries*, 262; Kennedy, *Profits and Losses*, 204; Tindall, *Emergence of the New South*, 362.

30. Kennedy, *Profits and Losses* 204; Michl, *Textiles Industries*, 262. North Carolina passed a law, in 1931, preventing women from working more than eleven hours daily and fifty-five hours weekly. Lahne, *Cotton Mill Worker*, 140.

31. Galambos, *Competition and Cooperation*, 176–78; Galambos, "Cotton-Textile Institute," 201.

32. Title I of the NIRA provided for the code and Section 7(a) and Title II created the Federal Emergency Administration of Public Works. Irving Bernstein, *Turbulent Years: A History of the American Worker, 1933–1941* (Boston: Houghton Mifflin, 1970), 33–34; William E. Leuchtenburg, *Franklin D. Roosevelt and the New Deal, 1932–1940* (New York: Harper and Row, 1963), 57–58; James A Hodges, *New Deal Labor Policy and the Southern Cotton Textile Industry, 1933–1941* (Knoxville: Univ. of Tennessee Press, 1986), 44–45. Ellis Hawley, in *The New Deal and the Problem of Monopoly: A Study in Economic Ambivalence* (Princeton, N.J.: Princeton Univ. Press, 1966), argued that a chief weakness of the New Deal was inconsistency in its relationship with business. It was a convoluted mixture of the New Nationalism, the New Freedom, and the "new competition" or a mix of industry self-regulation under government supervision (new competition), "government supported cartelization" (New Nationalism), and trust busting (New Freedom).

33. Galambos, *Competition and Cooperation*, 204; Hodges, *New Deal Labor Policy*, 49.

34. Actually, the CTI already had indication that most of the industry agreed with the 40-40 plan. Galambos, *Competition and Cooperation*, 206; Hodges, *New Deal Labor Policy*, 49.

35. Galambos, *Competition and Cooperation*, 207.

36. Ibid., 220; Hodges, *New Deal Labor Policy*, 53.

37. Hodges, *New Deal Labor Policy*, 53.

38. Ibid., 55; Galambos, *Competition and Cooperation*, 225.

39. Hodges, *New Deal Labor Policy*, 75; Cannon Mills expense letters for Charles Cannon's attendance at a Code Authority meeting, May 17 and Dec. 10, 1934, Box 106, Charles A. Cannon Collection. It is likely, although archives material do not prove it, that Charles Cannon served on the CTIC and became a Code Authority member when the CTIC became the Code Authority. "Timeline Through 1930's," 2–3; *Uplift* 25 (July 17, 1937): 13. In addition, Cannon also served as the vice chairman of the Fifth Federal Reserve District's bank and industrial committee. "Banking Group Elects Cannon," *Charlotte Observer*, June 8, 1932, p. 1.

40. Tindall, *Emergence of the New South*, 436; Hodges, *New Deal Labor Policy*, 57; Hall et al., *Like a Family*, 292–93.

41. Hodges, *New Deal Labor Policy*, 56–57.

42. Ibid.; Leuchtenburg, *Franklin D. Roosevelt*, 48–49; Tindall, *Emergence of the New South*, 437.

43. "Charles A. Cannon Advises House Group, 12/6/32," Card Box 2, Cannon Collection.

44. "Cannon Speaker at Banquet for Franklin, 1/28/35," Card Box 2, Cannon Collection.

45. Hall et al., *Like a Family*, 293–98.

46. Hodges, *New Deal Labor Policy*, 57–58; Galambos, *Competition and Cooperation*, 249.

47. Galambos, *Competition and Cooperation*, 258; Hodges, *New Deal Labor Policy*, 58; Hall et al., *Like a Family*, 328; "Piedmont Mills on Short Hours: Curtailing as Part of the 30-Hour Schedule Approved by NRA," *Concord Daily Tribune*, June 4, 1934, p. 1.

48. Hall et al., *Like a Family*, 325.

49. Bernstein, *Turbulent Years*, 302–4; Hodges, *New Deal Labor Policy*, 70–71.

50. Hodges, *New Deal Labor Policy*, 70; Hall et al., *Like a Family*, 326–27.

51. Hall et al., *Like a Family*, 328–29; Hodges, *New Deal Labor Policy*, 98–99; Lahne, *Cotton Mill Worker*, 225; Bernstein, *Turbulent Years*, 306.

52. "Some Comments on the General Strike in the Textile Industry," *Cotton* 98 (Sept. 1934): 40; Hall et al., *Like a Family*, 329; Hodges, *New Deal Labor Policy*, 104–6; Lahne, *Cotton Mill Worker*, 224; F. Ray Marshall, *Labor in the South* (Cambridge: Harvard Univ. Press, 1967), 166–67; Bernstein, *Turbulent Years*, 306–9. The actual total number of strikers remains uncertain. Marshall stated 450,000, Lahne wrote of 420,000, Hall believed 400,000, and Bernstein counted 375,000.

53. Hodges, *New Deal Labor Policy*, 108. For an account of the general strike in a northern textile town, Woonsocket, Rhode Island, see Gary Gerstle, *Working-Class Americanism: The Politics of Labor in a Textile City, 1914–1960* (New York: Cambridge Univ. Press, 1989), 127–40.

54. Francis Hampton, "New Leisure: How Is It Spent? A Study of What One Hundred Twenty-Two Textile Workers of Leaksville, Spray, and Draper Are Doing with the New Leisure Created by the N.R.A., as Applied to Certain Types of Activities" (master's thesis, Univ. of North Carolina at Chapel Hill, 1935), cited in Roscigno and Danaher, *Voice of Southern Labor*, 27.

55. Roscigno and Danaher, *Voice of Southern Labor*, 71–80.

56. Ibid., 28.

57. Ibid., 44–45 and 76.

58. "Four Mills Are Closed; Strike Leaders Heard," *Concord Daily Tribune*, Sept. 3, 1934, p. 1.

59. "Little Change in Strike Situation," *Concord Daily Tribune*, Sept. 4, 1934, p. 1; "Pickets Enlarge Activities Here," *Concord Daily Tribune*, Sept. 5, 1934, p. 1.

60. "Kannapolis Not Picketed So Far," *Concord Daily Tribune*, Sept. 7, 1934, p. 1.

61. Freeze interview, Federal Writers' Project.

62. Hodges, *New Deal Labor Policy*, 109; Hall et al., *Like a Family*, 332; "Troops from Statesville Arrived Early This Morning and Charlotte Co. at Later Hour," *Concord Daily Tribune*, Sept. 6. 1934, p. 1.

63. "Kannapolis Was Picketed Today but Plants Run," *Concord Daily Tribune*, Sept. 10, 1934, p. 1.

64. "Strikers Again Stage Parades in Kannapolis," *Concord Daily Tribune*, Sept. 11, 1934, p. 1.

65. "Paraders Peaceful and Hope for Support of People but Mills Are Running with Full Personnel," *Concord Daily Tribune*, Sept. 13, 1934, p. 2.

66. "Trooper Stabbed by Picket During Riot," *Concord Daily Tribune*, Sept. 15, 1934, p. 1.

67. Freeze interview, Federal Writers' Project.

68. Ibid.

69. Hall et al., *Like a Family*, 349–50; Hodges, *New Deal Labor Policy*, 114; Bernstein, *Turbulent Years*, 310.

70. "Cannon Witness at Washington," *Concord Daily Tribune*, Sept. 11, 1934, p. 1.

71. "Textile Labor Board Appointed After Winant Report and End of Strike," *Cotton* 98 (Oct. 1934): 57–60; Hodges, *New Deal Labor Policy*, 114; Hall et al., *Like a Family*, 350; Galambos, *Competition and Cooperation*, 263–64; Bernstein, *Turbulent Years*, 313–14.

72. *Concord Daily Tribune*, Sept. 17, 1934, p. 1.

73. "Literature of Communists Is Seized in Raid," *Concord Daily Tribune*, Sept. 21, 1934, p. 1.

74. Hodges, *New Deal Labor Policy*, 115; Hall et al., *Like a Family*, 350; Marshall, *Labor in the South*, 168; Bernstein, *Turbulent Years*, 314; "Agrees to Halt Strike on Plan Made by Board," *Concord Daily Tribune*, Sept. 22, 1934, p. 1.

75. Hodges, *New Deal Labor Policy*, 115.

76. Hall et al., *Like a Family*, 353–54.

77. "Local Mills Opened as Usual This AM," Sept. 24, 1934, unidentified newspaper clipping, Card Box 2, Cannon Collection.

78. Termination and Eviction Notices, Charles Albert Cannon Series, Box 22, Cannon Mills Collection.

79. Freeze interview, Federal Writers' Project.

80. Bernstein, *Turbulent Years*, 313–15; Hodges, *New Deal Labor Policy*, 121–22.

81. Hodges, *New Deal Labor Policy*, 133–34.

82. Hugh Johnson had resigned in September 1934 and Roosevelt replaced him with the National Industrial Recovery Board to oversee the NRA. Galambos, *Competition and Cooperation*, 268.

83. Hodges, *New Deal Labor Policy*, 136–37.

84. Ibid., 137–38; Galambos, *Competition and Cooperation*, 288.

85. Galambos, *Competition and Cooperation*, 288; Hodges, *New Deal Labor Policy*, 138.
86. Hodges, *New Deal Labor Policy*, 180–83.
87. Ibid., 185; "Timeline Through 1930's," 6.
88. "Cannon Testimony Makes Strong Impression," New York *Daily News Record*, June 30, 1939, Card Box 2, Cannon Collection; Hodges, *New Deal Labor Policy*, 186–88.
89. Ibid., 188.
90. *Moody's*, 1939, 1108; *Moody's*, 1940, 2823; *Moody's*, 1941, 2101; *Moody's*, 1943, 1987.

9. CANNON MILLS IN WORLD WAR II

1. "Textile Half-Year Incredible," *Textile World* 91 (Aug. 1941): 51.
2. "A Break Down of Cotton-Textile Purchases for Defense Needs," *Cotton* 104 (Oct. 1940): 90; Paul David Richards, "The History of the Textile Workers Union of America, CIO, in the South, 1937 to 1945" (Ph.D. diss., Univ. of Wisconsin–Madison, 1978), 151.
3. "Break Down of Cotton-Textile Purchases," 91.
4. "Defense Purchases Accelerated," *Textile World* 90 (Sept. 1940): 66.
5. Ibid.
6. Backman and Gainsbrugh, *Economics*, 150.
7. Ibid.
8. Harold G. Vatter, *The U.S. Economy in World War II* (New York: Columbia Univ. Press, 1985), 89 and 97; David Novick, Melvin Anshen, and W. C. Truppner, *Wartime Production Controls* (New York: Columbia Univ. Press, 1949), 242–43.
9. *Moody's*, 1939, 1108; *Moody's*, 1940, 2823; *Moody's*, 1941, 2101; *Moody's*, 1943, 1987.
10. "Cannon Timeline—1940's," 7, Folder 369, Cannon Collection.
11. *Moody's*, 1946, 1885.
12. "Advertising Expenditures, Towel Manufacturers, Sheet Manufacturers and Hosiery Manufacturers," Charles Albert Cannon Series, Box 11, Cannon Mills Collection.
13. Tindall, *Emergence of the New South*, 694.
14. Ibid.
15. Wright, *Old South, New South*, 241.
16. Richards, "History of the Textile Workers Union of America," 152.
17. "The Textile Manpower Problem," *Cotton* 108 (June 1944): 109; "American Association Urged to 'Put Out—Produce,'" *Cotton* 108 (May 1944): 95–98; *Daniel J. Clark, Like Night and Day: Unionization in a Southern Mill Town* (Chapel Hill: Univ. of North Carolina Press, 1997), 33; Richards, "History of the Textile Workers Union of America," 151–52.
18. Rankin, *Century of Progress*, 9.
19. Board of Directors meeting, Aug. 31, 1945, Cannon Mills Company Minute Book, 1928–1949.
20. "Cannon Timeline—1940's," 2 and 4.
21. Ibid., 5; *Cannon News*, Feb. 1945, 4, Card Box 2, Cannon Collection.
22. "Cannon Timeline—1940's," 5. The percentage of women working in the textile industry rose from 43 percent in 1940 to 51.5 percent in 1945. See Richards, "History of the Textile Workers Union of America," 152.

23. "Cannon Timelime—1940's," 3.

24. Ibid., 4.

25. Ibid.

26. Ibid., 7; Rankin, *Century of Progress*, 23.

27. Gordon Cole to Charles Cannon, Mar. 5, 1942, Box 11, Cannon Mills Collection.

28. Ibid.

29. John Philip Jones, *What's in a Name? Advertising and the Concept of Brands* (Lexington, Mass.: Lexington Books, 1986), 6.

30. Cole to Cannon, Mar. 5, 1942.

31. Bernstein, *Turbulent Years*, 400–402; Hodges, 148.

32. Hodges, *New Deal Labor Policy*, 149; Bernstein, *Turbulent Years*, 617–18; Tindall, *Emergence of the New South*, 517; Richards, "History of the Textile Workers Union of America," 40–41; Marshall, *Labor in the South*, 169.

33. Marshall, *Labor in the South*, 169; Barbara Griffith, *Crisis of American Labor: Operation Dixie and the Defeat of the CIO* (Philadelphia: Temple Univ. Press, 1988), 19.

34. Griffith, *Crisis of American Labor*, 19.

35. 1943 Survey, CIO Organizing Committee, North Carolina, TWUA Cabarrus Area: Cannon Mills: 1943 Survey, 1943, 1946, and n.d., Box 85, Folder 3, Cannon Mills Collection (hereafter cited as 1943 Survey); Board of Directors meeting, Sept. 6, 1938, Cannon Mills Company Minute Book, 1928–1949.

36. Hodges, *New Deal Labor Policy*, 151.

37. Tindall, *Emergence of the New South*, 518; Griffith, *Crisis of American Labor*, 19; Richards, "History of the Textile Workers Union of America," 58.

38. Griffith , *Crisis of American Labor*, 19–20.

39. Marshall, *Labor in the South*, 171; Lahne, *Cotton Mill Worker*, 270; Hodges, *New Deal Labor Policy*, 176.

40. Hodges, *New Deal Labor Policy*, 177–78; Marshall, *Labor in the South*, 173.

41. Hodges, *New Deal Labor Policy*, 178.

42. Marshall, *Labor in the South*, 173.

43. Hodges, *New Deal Labor Policy*, 178.

44. Joseph Brooks, President of Local 633 of the TWUA, to "Dear Friend," n.d., in Katherine F. Martin, ed., *Operation Dixie: The CIO Organizing Committee Papers*, (New York: Microfilming Corporation of America, 1980), 75 reels of 35-mm microfilm (hereafter cited as *Operation Dixie*), reel 7. Local 633 of the Amazon plant had 466 dues-paying members. North Carolina Local Unions, *Operation Dixie*, reel 11.

45. Richards, "History of the Textile Workers Union of America," 167; Griffith, *Crisis of American Labor*, 190n3; Clark, *Like Night and Day*, 35; Timothy J. Minchin, *What Do We Need a Union For? The TWUA in the South, 1945–1955* (Chapel Hill: Univ. of North Carolina Press, 1997), 16.

46. Minchin, *What Do We Need a Union For?* 47.

47. 1943 Survey.

48. Bernard W. Cruse to J. D. Pedigo, Oct. 25, 1943; 1943 Survey.

49. Cruse to Pedigo, Oct. 25, 1943, 2.

50. James A. Jones Jr., Director of Public Relations for J. A. Jones Construction Company to Charles Cannon, June 30, 1944, and International Freight Corporation to Charles A. Cannon, Nov. 28, 1944, both in Box 297, Topical Files, S. S. James W. Cannon, 1944–46, 61, Charles A. Cannon Collection.

51. Article on Charles A. Cannon Jr., Charles A. Cannon Jr. Military Service, etc., January–March 1945, Box 151, Charles A. Cannon Collection.

52. A. L. Hudson, Secretary of the Charles A. Cannon Jr., Scholarship Committee to T. C. Haywood, Treasurer of the Cannon Foundation, Aug. 12, 1971, Charles A. Cannon Jr. Military Service, etc., June 1946–71, Box 153, Charles A. Cannon Collection.

10. Cannon Mills and Postwar America

1. *Moody's*, 1946, 1385. In addition, Cannon Mills received an excess profit tax refund of $1.1 million in 1945.

2. Board of Directors meeting, Apr. 9, 1946, Cannon Mills Company Minute Book, 1928–1949.

3. Board of Directors meeting, Sept. 1, 1939, Cannon Mills Company Minute Book, 1928–1949.

4. *Moody's*, 1946, 1385.

5. Harden, "Cannon."

6. "C. A. Cannon, W. P. Jacobs State Views," *Charlotte Observer*, Jan. 20, 1946, n.p.; "OPA Cotton Policies Hit by Cannon," *Charlotte Observer*, Mar. 1, 1946, n.p., both in Card Box 2, Cannon Collection; "This Small, Dapper Man Wanted to Dry the Backs of the World," Kannapolis *Daily Independent*, May 21, 1967, p. 8D.

7. "C. A. Cannon, W. P. Jacobs State Views"; "Government Investigates Black Market Operations in Textiles," *Concord Tribune*, Sept. 12, 1946, p. 1. Part of the shortage resulted from textile mills shifting production to more profitable goods under the "crazy-quilt" price controls of the OPA. Sanford S. Parker, "1947 Textile Volume Will Be Close to 1946's Good Record," *Textile World* 97 (Feb. 1947): 103.

8. "C. A. Cannon, W. P. Jacobs State Views"; "OPA Cotton Policies Hit by Cannon"; "This Small, Dapper Man."

9. "C. A. Cannon, W. P. Jacobs State Views."

10. "This Small, Dapper Man." In the face of increasing opposition, the Office of Price Administration ended price controls on most goods in late 1946.

11. Hazel M. Trotter, "Cannon Mills Offers Help to Veterans," *Textile World* 96 (June 1946): 125 and 194. Joseph Harris Cannon was born in Rock Hill, South Carolina, on September 19, 1916. He attended Clemson University and joined the Cannon Mills Company in 1944. John Harden, "Cannon," Profile 13; obituary, Kannapolis *Daily Independent*, Apr. 14, 1992, p. 1.

12. S. W. Sewell, "Adjusting Problems of Returning Veterans," *Cotton* 109 (Jan. 1945): 91.

13. Ibid.

14. Ibid.

15. Ibid.; Trotter, "Cannon Mills Offers Help to Veterans," 194.

16. "Cannon Timeline—1940's," 7.

17. Board of Directors meeting, Dec. 3, 1945, Cannon Mills Company Minute Book, 1928–1949.

18. Rankin, *Century of Progress*, 23.

19. Parker, "1947 Textile Volume," 102.

20. C. W. Bendigo, "Mill Purchases Reach New High Level," *Textile World* 97 (Feb. 1947): 105.

21. *Moody's*, 1946, 1385; *Moody's*, 1947, 2686–87.

22. "Cannon Timeline—1940's," 5.

23. The hourly earnings for cotton textile workers averaged 78.8 cents in 1946. Joseph M. Gambatese, "Textile Wages Move Up, While Others Are Moving Down," *Textile World* 96 (June 1946): 141.

24. Board of Directors meeting, Dec. 2, 1946, Cannon Mills Company Minute Book, 1928–1949.

25. "Cotton Will Survive Say C.T.I. Speakers," *Textile World* 96 (Nov. 1946): 135.

26. Ibid.

27. Ibid., 135, 224 and 228.

28. "Cannon Timeline—1940's," 5.

29. Ibid.

30. Sanford S. Parker, "Textile Production Plateau Will Run for Another Year," *Textile World* 98 (Feb. 1948): 104.

31. The 1923–25 average was 100. Parker, "Textile Production Plateau," 102.

32. C. W. Bendigo, "Mill Purchases Reach New High Level," *Textile World* 98 (Feb. 1948): 104.

33. *Moody's*, 1948, 2209.

34. Board of Directors meeting, Mar. 3, 1947, and Dec. 1, 1947, Cannon Mills Company Minute Book, 1928–1949.

35. Parker, "1947 Textile Volume," 102.

36. "Mill Profits Aids [*sic*] Workers: Wages Double in Five Years," Kannapolis *Daily Independent*, Apr. 8, 1947, p. 1.

37. C. W. Bendigo, "Higher Operator Production," *Textile World* 99 (Aug. 1949): 4; Richard C. Scott, "Principal Capital Outlay Is for Modernization," *Textile World* 99 (Nov. 1949): 103–4 and 238; "Mills Spend Money to Save on Operating Costs," *Textile World* 99 (Nov. 1949): 105–9 and 242.

38. "Cannon Mills, Inc., Advertising, Terry Towels—Dish Towels, July 1947," 2, Charles Albert Cannon Series, Box 12, Cannon Mills Collection.

39. Board of Directors meeting, Aug. 6, 1947, Cannon Mills Company Minute Book, 1928–1949. The issuance of this nonvoting stock would lead to a conflict with the New York Stock Exchange in the early 1960s.

40. Harden, "Cannon," Profile 14.

41. The 1923–25 average was 100. Sanford S. Parker, "1949 Textile Output Should Run Close to 1948 Figures," *Textile World* 99 (Feb. 1949): 104.

42. William B. Dall, "1948's Textile Achievements Can Be Matched in 1949," *Textile World* 99 (Feb. 1949): 103.

43. Parker, "1949 Textile Output Should Run Close to the 1948 Figures," 104.

44. *Moody's*, 1949, 2357.

45. Annual Report to Stockholders for 1948, Secretaries' Office Series, Box 63, Cannon Mills Collection.

46. *Moody's*, 1966, 720.

47. Board of Directors meeting, Mar. 1, and Dec. 3, 1948, Cannon Mills Company Minute Book, 1928–1949.

48. "Approved Estimated Advertising Appropriations for 1947" and "Projected 1948 Space and Production," Box 12, Cannon Mills Collection.

49. "Approved Estimated Advertising Appropriations for 1947" and "Projected 1948 Space and Production"; "Cannon Timeline—1940's," 6.

50. "Approved Estimated Advertising Appropriations for 1947" and "Projected 1948 Space and Production."

51. Ibid.

52. The 1923–25 average was 100. Robert P. Ulin, "1950 Production: More Sustained than in 1949," *Textile World* 100 (Feb. 1950): 109.

53. Ibid.

54. Ibid., 110.

55. C. W. Bendigo, "1949 Purchases Higher than Expected," *Textile World* 100 (Feb. 1950): 111.

56. "1949 Advertising Budget," Charles Albert Cannon Series, Box 12, Cannon Mills Collection.

57. *Moody's*, 1950, 2368. A more accurate comparison in profits is between the years 1947 and 1949, for which the 1949 profits fell $11 million.

58. Ibid.

59. *Moody's*, 1951, 2431.

60. Board of Directors meeting, Nov. 27, 1950, Cannon Mills Company Minute Book, 1950–1971, Manufacturing Company Series, Box 144, Cannon Mills Collection (hereafter cited as Cannon Mills Company Minute Book, 1950–1971).

61. Robert P. Ulin, "1950 Production Tops Records of 1941–45," *Textile World* 101 (Feb. 1951): 110.

62. Not including the unusual year of 1948, in which the cost of production compared to sales totaled 69 percent. *Moody's*, 1951, 2433.

63. "Cannon Mills, Inc., Towel Advertising, 1950," prepared by N. W. Ayer & Son, Aug. 1949, 14–16, Charles Albert Cannon Series, Box 13, Cannon Mills Collection.

64. "1950 Advertising Budget, March 23, 1950," Charles Albert Cannon Series, Box 13, Cannon Mills Collection. The company public advertising records for hosiery and sheet advertising are spotty beginning in 1950 and public records for all advertising end in the mid-1950s.

65. Tim Vanderburg, "Advertising, Brand Loyalty, and Market Maturity: A Case Study of Cannon Mills, 1935–1950" (master's thesis, Univ. of North Carolina at Charlotte, 1994), 97–100.

66. "Cannon Timeline—1950's," Folder 370, Chronology 1950's, Cannon Collection.

11. Cannon Mills and Operation Dixie

1. CIO Organizing Committee press release, July 21, 1946, 2, *Operation Dixie*, reel 11; Minchin, *What Do We Need a Union For?* 29–30; Griffith, *Crisis of American Labor*, 25; Glass, *Textile Industry in North Carolina*, 86; Marshall, *Labor in the South*, 256.

2. Griffith, *Crisis of American Labor*, 25; Marshall, *Labor in the South*, 254; Minchin, *What Do We Need a Union For?* 27–28.

3. Griffith, *Crisis of American Labor*, 26.

4. CIO Organizing Committee press release, July 21, 1946, 1.

5. Ibid., 2.

6. Griffith, *Crisis of American Labor*, 49.

7. Theodore Adams, Weekly Activity Report, June 29, 1946, *Operation Dixie*, reel 10; Clyde Jenkins, Weekly Activity Report, June 30, 1946, *Operation Dixie*, reel 10; Harry S. Stroud, Weekly Activity Report, June 30, 1946, *Operation Dixie*, reel 10; Dean Culver, Report and Summary of Concord—Kannapolis, June 30, 1946, *Operation Dixie*, reel 10.

8. William Smith to All Field Representatives in North Carolina, June 18, 1946, *Operation Dixie*, reel 7.

9. Minchin, *What Do We Need a Union For?* 61.

10. Marvin Lewelly Searborough, letter to the editors of the Kannapolis *Daily Independent*, June 28, 1945, *Operation Dixie*, reel 11.

11. Joe Kirk Jr., Weekly Activity Report, June 30, 1946, *Operation Dixie*, reel 10.

12. Marcelle Malamas, Weekly Activity Report, June 15, 1946, *Operation Dixie*, reel 10.

13. Marcelle Malamas, Weekly Activity Report, June 29, 1946, *Operation Dixie*, reel 10.

14. Minchin, *What Do We Need a Union For?* 57.

15. Marcelle Malamas, Weekly Activity Report, June 8, 1946, *Operation Dixie*, reel 10; L. L. Shepherd, Weekly Activity Report, June 8, 22, 1946, *Operation Dixie*, reel 10; Fleming Bracewell, Weekly Activity Report, June 21, 1946, *Operation Dixie*, reel 10; Culver, Report and Summary of Concord—Kannapolis, June 30, 1946.

16. Lears, "Concept of Cultural Hegemony," 568.

17. L. L. Sheperd, Weekly Activity Report, June 15, 1946, *Operation Dixie*, reel 10.

18. Malamas, Weekly Activity Report, June 8, 1946.

19. Sheperd, Weekly Activity Report, June 8, 1946, *Operation Dixie*, reel 10.

20. Fred Wingard, Weekly Activity Report, June 29, 1946, *Operation Dixie*, reel 10.

21. Paul Faucette, Weekly Activity Report, June 30, 1946, *Operation Dixie*, reel 10.

22. Statement of Zeb James Plott, n.d., *Operation Dixie*, reel 11.

23. Malamas, Weekly Activity Report, June 22, 1946, *Operation Dixie*, reel 10.

24. Malamas, Weekly Activity Report, June 29, 1946.

25. Nancy Blaine, Report on YMCA, July 26, 1946, *Operation Dixie*, reel 10.

26. "The first job to be done is to set up active, operating committees inside of the plant." William Smith to "All Field Representatives in North Carolina," June 18, 1946, 2, *Operation Dixie*, reel 7.

27. Harry S. Stroud, Weekly Activity Report, July 5, 22, 1946, *Operation Dixie*, reel 7.

28. Robert Freeman, Weekly Activity Report, July 28, 1946; Joe Kirk Jr., Weekly Activity Report, July 22, 1946; and Paul Faucette, Weekly Activity Report, July 22, 1946, all in *Operation Dixie*, reel 7.

29. Harry S. Stroud, Weekly Activity Report, July 11, 1946, *Operation Dixie*, reel 7.

30. Dean Culver, Initial Report on [the] Kannapolis Situation, July 9, 1946, 2, *Operation Dixie*, CIO Organizing Committee, North Carolina, TWUA Cabarrus Area: Administrative Reports: Weekly Progress of 1946 Drive, 1946, Box 85, Folder 2, Operation Dixie Archives, Special Collections, Perkins Library, Duke University, Durham, N.C. (hereafter cited as ODA).

31. Ibid., 3; Griffith, *Crisis of American Labor*, 49.

32. Griffith, *Crisis of American Labor*, 49.

33. Culver, Initial Report on [the] Kannapolis Situation, July 9, 1946, 3.

34. Ibid.

35. Ibid., 3–5

36. Dean Culver, Report on Activity Concord—Kannapolis Situation, July 21, 1946, 3, *Operation Dixie*, reel 7.

37. D. D. Wood to William Smith, July 29, 1946, reel 7.

38. Culver, Report on Activity Concord—Kannapolis Situation, July 21, 1946, 4.

39. Dean Culver to William Smith, July 31, 1946, *Operation Dixie*, reel 7.

40. William Smith to Dean Culver, Aug. 2, 1946, *Operation Dixie*, reel 7.

41. William Smith to Dean Culver, Aug. 30, 1946, *Operation Dixie*, reel 7.

42. Dean Culver to William Smith, Aug. 3, 1946, 2, *Operation Dixie*, reel 7.

43. Ibid.

44. "CIO Leaders Confer Here: 'No Comment' They Say After Meeting Lawyer for Discussion of Alleged Unfair Treatment," *Concord Tribune*, Sept. 11, 1946 (this clipping is probably mislabeled and should be August 11), Box 85, Folder 9, ODA.

45. "CIO Agents Are Found Guilty: Magistrate's Court Fine Two Men $10 and Costs for Violating Ordinance," *Concord Tribune*, Sept. 12, 1946, ibid.

46. CIO Organizing Committee press release, n.d., *Operation Dixie*, reel 11; "Cases Against CIO Agents Are Not Pressed in Superior Court," *Concord Tribune*, Oct. 16, 1946, Box 85, Folder 9, ODA; "Halt Action in CIO Case," *Charlotte News*, Oct. 15, 1946, Box 85, Folder 7, ODA; "CIO Workers' Cases Shelved," *Charlotte Observer*, Oct. 15, 1946, Box 85, Folder 8, ODA.

47. Dean Culver to Draper Wood, Aug. 28, 1946, *Operation Dixie*, reel 11.

48. "Textile Wages in Local Area Dixie's Highest," *Concord Tribune*, Sept. 16, 1946, Box 85, Folder 9, ODA; Minchin, *What Do We Need a Union For?* 59.

49. Minchin, *What Do We Need a Union For?* 59.

50. Ibid.

51. Dean Culver, Observations, 2, Sept. 17, 1946, Box 85, Folder 2, ODA.

52. Dean Culver, Suggestions, 4–5, Sept. 17, 1946, Box 85, Folder 2, ODA.

53. Ibid.; Minchin, *What Do We Need a Union For?* 57–58.

54. "Van Bittner to Speak at Concord CIO Meet: CIO Organizer, George Baldanzi, Other Leaders to Address Big Rally Saturday," *Concord Tribune*, Sept. 19, 1946, Box 85, Folder 9, ODA.

55. Draper to Howard Parker, Sept. 9, 1946, *Operation Dixie*, reel 11.

56. "CIO Men Hold Open Meeting," *Concord Tribune*, Sept. 21, 1946 (this clipping is probably mislabeled and should be dated September 22), Box 85, Folder 9, ODA.

57. T. H. Wingate to George Baldanzi, Sept. 23, 1946, *Operation Dixie*, reel 11. As mentioned in chapter 3, in 1940 Thomas Wingate and the publisher of the *Daily Independent*, James L. Moore, published the book *Cabarrus Reborn: A Historical Sketch of the Founding and Development of Cannon Mills and Kannapolis*, which gave an uncritical account of the founding of the firm and company town.

58. Rowan, "Negro in the Textile Industry," 54.

59. John A. Salmond, *Southern Struggles: The Southern Labor Movement and the Civil Rights Struggle* (Gainesville: Univ. Press of Florida, 2004), 6; Timothy J. Minchin, *Fighting Against the Odds: A History of Southern Labor Since World War II* (Gainesville: Univ. Press of Florida, 2005), 28.

60. George Baldanzi to T. H. Wingate, n.d., *Operation Dixie*, reel 11.

61. "Freedom or CIO? Union Sets Up Certain Dictatorship to Control Members' Work and Pay," *Concord Tribune* (reprinted from the *Southern Textile News*), Oct. 1, 1946, Box 85, Folder 9, ODA.

62. "An Executive Views the News in Textiles," *Textile Industries*, n.p., Textile Committee on Public Relations, Correspondence, December 1951, Box 26, Cannon Mills Collection.

63. C. A. Cannon to Elliot Springs, Feb. 21, 1951, Textile Committee on Public Relations, Correspondence, February–April 1951, Box 25, Cannon Mills Collection; William A. Newell, "Good Work—Let's Keep It Up," *Textile World* 101 (July 1951): 4.

64. Newell, "Good Work," 4.

65. From May 15, 1950, to April 18, 1950, Cannon Mills contributed $4,345, the largest single contribution of the 193 member mills. J. P. Stevens contributed the next largest amount at $2,939. Contributions to Textile Committee on Public Relations from May 15, 1950, to September 30, 1950 and Contributions to Textile Committee on Public Relations from Oct. 1, 1950 to April 18, 1951, both in Textile Committee on Public Relations, Correspondence, May–June 1951, Box 25, Cannon Mills Collection.

66. Newell, "Good Work—Let's Keep It Up," 4.

67. Dean Culver, Activity Report, Oct. 9, 1946, 4–5, *Operation Dixie*, reel 11.

68. Ibid., 9.

69. Ibid., 1; Dean Culver, Survey Report, Sept. 21, 1946, 1, *Operation Dixie*, reel 11.

70. William J. Smith to "Brothers and Sister," Oct. 7, 1946, *Operation Dixie*, reel 11.

71. Dean Culver, Suggestions, 1, Sept. 17, 1946, Box 85, Folder 2, ODA. The North Carolina director, William Smith, filed a complaint with the Federal Communication Commission concerning the Concord radio station WEGO. William Smith to Jerome Cooper, Oct. 19, 1946, *Operation Dixie*, reel 7.

72. Joel Leighton to Larry Rogin, Dec. 11, 1946, *Operation Dixie*, reel 11.

73. "New CIO Leader Is Sent into Cabarrus," *Concord Tribune*, Oct. 23, 1946, Box 85, Folder 9, ODA; William Smith to D. L. Culver, Nov. 12, 1946, *Operation Dixie*, reel 7.

74. Griffith, *Crisis of American Labor*, 57.

75. Ibid.

76. "Textile Organizers Find Going Tough," *Concord Tribune*, Oct. 28, 1946, Box 85, Folder 9, ODA.

77. "Textile Workers Win Long Service Awards," *Concord Tribune*, Oct. 4, 1946, p. 1.

78. "Truman Also Orders Purge of Communists: House Committee Says Presidential Agency Will Not Deter Its Aims," *Concord Tribune*, Nov. 26, 1946, Box 85, Folder 9, ODA.

79. Marshall, *Labor in the South*, 257.

80. William Smith to North Carolina Staff Members, Nov. 26, 1946, *Operation Dixie*, reel 11.

81. S. H. Dalrymple, Secretary-Treasurer, CIO Organizing Committee, to William Smith, "Initiation Fee Membership Record" from North Carolina for 1946, *Operation Dixie*, reel 7.

82. "The New Textile Wage Pattern," *Charlotte News*, Feb. 17, 1947, 1.

83. Joel Leighton to "Dear Friend," Apr. 22, 1947, *Operation Dixie*, reel 10.

84. "Announcing Saturday–April 26, Big Labor Rally for All Workers in Your Plant," Apr. 23, 1947, *Operation Dixie*, reel 10.

85. Joel Leighton to Larry Rogin, Apr. 25, 1947, *Operation Dixie*, reel 11.

86. Joel Leighton to "Dear Bill" (William Smith), May 8, 1947, *Operation Dixie*, reel 11. Joel Leighton to "Dear Friend" (committee members), n.d., *Operation Dixie*, reel 10.

87. Contest Announcement, n.d., *Operation Dixie*, reel 10.

88. William Smith to Claude R. McCall (letter of termination), June 27, 1947, *Operation Dixie*, reel 11.

89. Joel Leighton to William Smith, July 15, 1947, *Operation Dixie*, reel 11.

90. Joel Leighton to William Smith, Aug. 6, 1947, *Operation Dixie*, reel 11.

91. Joel Leighton to William Smith, Oct. 1, 1947, *Operation Dixie*, reel 11.

92. "Vote to Stage Strike Monday," *Charlotte Observer*, Mar. 2, 1947, Box 85, Folder 8, ODA.

93. Minchin, *What Do We Need a Union For?* 74.

94. Ibid., 92.

95. S. H. Dalrymple, Secretary-Treasurer, CIO Organizing Committee, to William Smith, "Initiation Fee Membership Record" from North Carolina for 1947, *Operation Dixie*, reel 7.

96. S. H. Dalrymple, Secretary-Treasurer, CIO Organizing Committee, to William Smith, "Initiation Fee Membership Record" from North Carolina for 1948, *Operation Dixie*, reel 7.

97. Marshall, *Labor in the South*, 259.

98. Ibid.; Minchin, *What Do We Need a Union For?* 110–11.

99. Minchin, *What Do We Need a Union For?* 110–11; Marshall, *Labor in the South*, 259–60;

100. Marshall, *Labor in the South*, 259–63.

101. Griffith, *Crisis of American Labor*, 46.

102. Griffith's chapter on Kannapolis and Operation Dixie in her work *Crisis of American Labor*, emphasizes the role of paternalism in defeating the organizing effort. But she ignores the role of rising wages. For an examination of the role of rising textile wages in the defeat of the drive, see Minchin, *What Do We Need a Union For?*

103. P. M. Thomas, "Cotton Mills Cut Costs at Every Step," *Textile World* 99 (Nov. 1949): 114–15 and 234; "Mills Spend Money to Save on Operating Costs," 105–9 and 224.

104. "Textile Mills Need Workers in Production: Jacobs Says Employees Must Be Secured If Mills Are to Keep Pace with Markets," *Concord Tribune*, Nov. 2, 1946, Box 85, Folder 9, ODA. According to McGraw-Hill economists, a shortage of textile workers still existed in 1951. C. W. Bendigo, "Manpower Shortage," *Textile World* 101 (Jan. 1951): 4.

105. With regard to rising wages, Minchin focused on its economic function and ignored its paternalistic function that reinforced Charles Cannon's control.

106. Brandes, *American Welfare Capitalism*, 6–7.

107. Nelson and Campbell, "Taylorism Versus Welfare Work," 3–4. Also Rimlinger, "Welfare Policy and Economic Development," 556–71; Hagedorn, "Note on the Motivation," 134–39; Zahovi, "Negotiated Loyalty," 602–20.

108. On the rise of government regulation of business, see Louis Galambos and Joseph Pratt, *The Rise of the Corporate Commonwealth: U.S. Business and Public Policy in the Twentieth Century* (New York: Basic Books, 1988).

109. Minchin, *What Do We Need a Union For?* 59.

110. Rodgers, *Work Ethic in Industrial America*. Also T. J. Jackson Lears, "From Salvation to Self-Realization: Advertising and the Therapeutic Roots of the Consumer Culture, 1880–1930," in *The Culture of Consumption: Critical Essays in American History, 1880–1980*, ed. Richard W. Fox and T. J. Jackson Lears (New York: Pantheon Books, 1983), 101–41.

111. Culver, Initial Report on [the] Kannapolis Situation, July 9, 1946, 2.

112. Freeze interview, Federal Writers' Project.

113. Interview of Dolph Parsons, Aug. 28, 1939, Federal Writers' Project, Library of Congress.

114. Culver, Suggestions, 5, Sept. 17, 1946.

12. The Danger of Larger Forces

1. Charles A. Cannon, "Planning, Production = Power, Preparedness," New York *Daily News Record*, Jan. 25, 1951, 42.

2. Ulin, "1950 Production Tops Records," 108–10. How Cannon Mills fared in 1950 is discussed in chapter 10.

3. C. W. Bendigo, "1950 Mill Purchases Hit All-Time High," *Textile World* 101: 111–12.

4. Textile Profits Decline, Textile Committee on Public Relations, Correspondence, December 1951, Box 26, Cannon Mills Collection.

5. "Production Cuts Aimed to Achieve Stability," *Textile Neighbor* 7 (Aug.–Sept. 1951): 1.

6. Bill Boring, "Drop in Textile Trading Forces Some Mill Closings," *Atlanta Constitution*, Oct. 24, 1951, 2-A.

7. "Production Cuts Aimed to Achieve Stability."

8. Outlook for 1952, Dec. 21, 1951, Textile Committee on Public Relations, Correspondence, December 1951, Box 26, Cannon Mills Collection.

9. A Compilation of Statistics and Background Information on the Cotton Textile Industry for the Year 1951, Textile Information Service, n.d., Textile Committee on Public Relations, Correspondence, December 1951, Box 26, Cannon Mills Collection.

10. Administrative History, Records of the Office of Price Stabilization, National Archives and Records Administration, http://www.archives.gov/research/guide-fed-records/groups/295.html.

11. Press release, Textile Information Service, May 8, 1951, Textile Committee on Public Relations, Correspondence, May–June 1951, Box 25, Cannon Mills Collection.

12. Press release, Textile Information Service, May 31, June 17, 1951, Textile Committee on Public Relations, Correspondence, May–June 1951, Box 25, Cannon Mills Collection.

13. "Raw Cotton Ceiling Removal, Textile Decontrol Sought," *Columbia Record*, Oct. 19, 1951, 10-D.

14. Harden, "Cannon," Cotton 2.

15. Minutes of the Meeting of the Board of Directors of National Cotton Council of America, Sept. 15, 1950, 2, Executive Office Files, 1950, Series, Box 83, Cannon Mills Collection; Committee Assignments 1949–1950, North Carolina Cotton Manufacturers' Association, Inc., Executive Office Files, 1950, Series, Box 84, Cannon Mills Collection.

16. Tom Yutzey to Charles A. Cannon, Oct. 22, 1951, Textile Committee on Public Relations, Correspondence, October 1951, Box 25, Cannon Mills Collection. See "OPS Action Held an 'Invitation to Misuse of Taxpayers' Money,'" *Textile Neighbor* 7 (Aug.–Sept. 1951): 2, Textile Committee on Public Relations, Correspondence, October 1951, Box 25, Cannon Mills Collection.

17. *Moody's*, 1952, 1796.

18. *Moody's*, 1952, 1795; *Moody's*, 1955, 1483; *Moody's*, 1960, 2030.

19. "Cannon Timeline—1950's," 1–4, Folder 370, Cannon Collection.

20. *Moody's*, 1956, 1130; *Moody's*, 1958, 2198. Cannon Mills' internal records show that Brown Manufacturing Company "became a wholly-owned subsidiary" in 1956 and that Central Mills, also known as Issaquena Cotton Mills, merged with Cannon in 1954. Histories of Cannon Plants, Folder 352, Cannon Collection.

21. Board of Directors meeting, Apr. 12, 1949, Cannon Mills Company Minute Book 1928–1949; and Board of Directors meeting, Apr. 12, 1955, Cannon Mills Company Minute Book, 1950–1971.

22. Martin Luther Cannon remained involved in the textile industry as president of the Carolina Textile Corporation and chairman of the board of Davidson Mills, Inc. "Cannons Make Textile Deal," *Concord Tribune*, Oct. 2, 1946, n.p., CIO Organizing Committee, North Carolina, UTWA Cabarrus Area: Clippings: *Concord Tribune*, 1946, Box 85, Folder 9, ODA; "Addition Planned by Davidson Mills," Jan. 12, 1947, n.p., CIO Organizing Committee, North Carolina, UTWA Cabarrus Area: Clippings: *Concord Tribune*, 1946–1947, Box 85, Folder 8, ODA.

23. Board of Directors meeting, Nov. 7, 1952, Cannon Mills Company Minute Book, 1950–1971.

24. Board of Directors meeting, Apr. 14, 1953, Cannon Mills Company Minute Book, 1950–1971.

25. Board of Directors meeting, Apr. 14, 1959, Cannon Mills Company Minute Book, 1950–1971.

26. A. W. Jessup, "Japanese Textile Will Be Slow in Revival," *Textile World* 98 (Jan. 1948): 101–2; A. W. Jessup, "More Production of Japanese Textiles," *Textile World* (May 1949): 242.

27. Claudius Murchison was past president of the Cotton-Textile Institute. The American Cotton Manufacturers' Association and the Cotton-Textile Institute merged to create the American Cotton Manufacturers Institute on August 23, 1949, with its headquarters in Charlotte, North Carolina. Smith, *Mill on the Dan*, 538.

28. Herbert Koshetz, "U.S. Textile Men Worried by Japan," *Textile Neighbor* 7 (Oct.–Nov. 1951): 4.

29. R. Buford Brandis, *The Making of Textile Trade Policy, 1935–1981* (Washington, D.C.: American Textile Manufacturers Institute, 1982), 8.

30. P. M. Thomas, "The Tariff Pressure Is On," *Textile World* 105 (Feb. 1955): 65; William G. Ashmore, "'We Are Not Expendable,' U.S. Mills Insist," *Textile World* (Apr. 1955): 98–99.

31. Thomas, "The Tariff Pressure Is On," 65; Brandis, *Making of Textile Trade Policy*, 8–9.

32. Andrews, *Men and the Mills*, 109.

33. Brandis, *Making of Textile Trade Policy*, 12.

34. Sherman Adams to Donald Comer, May 14, 1956, Charles Albert Cannon Series, Box 14, Cannon Mills Collection.

35. Charles A. Cannon to Fulton Lewis Jr., June 6, 1956, Charles Albert Cannon Series, Box 14, Cannon Mills Collection.

36. C. A. Cannon to F. S. Love, June 29, 1956, Charles Albert Cannon Series, Box 14, Cannon Mills Collection.

37. Robert C. Jackson to C. A. Cannon, May 28, 1956, Charles Albert Cannon Series, Box 14, Cannon Mills Collection. Also see Robert Jackson to Bill Workman of the *Daily Independent*, May 28, 1956, Charles Albert Cannon Series, Box 14, Cannon Mills Collection.

38. Trudy Huskamp Peterson, *Agricultural Exports, Farm Income, and the Eisenhower Administration* (Lincoln: Univ. of Nebraska Press, 1979), 3.

39. Ibid., 4.

40. Ibid., 42; Edward L. Schapsmeier and Frederick H. Schapsmeier, *Ezra Taft Benson and the Politics of Agriculture: The Eisenhower Years, 1953–1961* (Danville, Ill.: Interstate Printers and Publishers, 1975), 98.

41. Peterson, *Agricultural Exports*, 74.

42. Ibid., 102.

43. Ibid.

44. Schapsmeier and Schapsmeier, *Ezra Taft Benson*, 167.

45. Ibid., 165; "1-Price Cotton Means Savings to Consumers," *Daily Independent*, Dec. 14, 1962, 4; "One-Price Cotton Has Benefitted Everyone," *Greenville (S.C.) News*, Oct. 11, 1964, 4-A.

46. Brandis, *Making of Textile Trade Policy*, 11.

47. "A Statement for American Cotton Manufacturers Institute Filed by Mr. C. A. Cannon," North Carolina Collection, Wilson Library, University of North Carolina at Chapel Hill.

48. "The Textile Industry and Cotton Policy," Feb. 2, 1960, 2–3, Executive Office Files Series, Box 66, Cannon Mills Collection.

49. Ibid., 5; "1-Price Cotton Means Savings to Consumers," *Daily Independent*, Dec. 14, 1962, 1.

50. Peterson, *Agricultural Exports*, 36.

51. Figures for farm income and price supports for cotton both in Wesley McCune, *Ezra Taft Benson: Man with a Mission* (Washington, D.C.: Public Affairs Press, 1958). Farm income figures on page 119, and the figures on cotton price supports are on page 88.

52. Peterson, *Agricultural Exports*, 17; Schapsmeier and Schapsmeier, *Ezra Taft Benson*, 55.

53. Brandis, Making of Textile Trade Policy, 16.

54. Henry Kearns to John O. Pastore, Apr. 24, 1959, 4, Box 151, Charles A. Cannon Collection.

55. Ibid., 1.

56. Statement of C. A. Cannon Before the Special Sub-Committee of Senate Interstate and Foreign Commerce Committee, Sept. 30, 1958, 2, Executive Office Files Series, Box 66, Cannon Mills Collection.

57. Ibid., 8–9.

58. Ibid., 17.

59. Ibid., 19.

60. Ibid.

61. Brandis, *Making of Textile Trade Policy*, 16–17.

62. Ibid., 14.

63. A Summary of the National Cotton Council's Petition to the Secretary of Agriculture, June 29, 1959, Cotton Manufactures Association, June, 1959–1970, Box 106, Charles A. Cannon Collection.

64. Peterson, *Agricultural Exports*, 117.

65. Brandis, *Making of Textile Trade Policy*, 14.

66. C. A. Cannon to General Wilton Persons, Mar. 17, 1960, Charles A. Cannon Topical Files, Tariff Commission Hearings, 1960–62, Box 308, Cotton Manufactures Association, June, 1959–1970, Box 106, Charles A. Cannon Collection (hereafter cited as Box 308, Charles A. Cannon Collection).

67. Wilton B. Persons to Mr. Cannon, Mar. 29, 1960, Box 308, Charles A. Cannon Collection.

68. C. A. Cannon to Charles K. McWhorter, Mar. 2, 1960, first letter, Box 308, Charles A. Cannon Collection.

69. C. A. Cannon to Charles K. McWhorter, Mar. 2, 1960, second letter, Box 308, Charles A. Cannon Collection.

70. Charles K. McWhorter to Charles A. Cannon, Mar. 18, 1960, Box 308, Charles A. Cannon Collection.

71. Brandis, *Making of Textile Trade Policy*, 14.

72. Press release of James C. Hagerty, press secretary to the president, Aug. 23, 1960, Box 308, Charles A. Cannon Collection.

13. Cannon Mills in the 1960s

1. "Cotton-Imports Problem Awaits March Hearings," *Textile World* 110 (Feb. 1960): 8.

2. "Failures Continue Upward," *Textile World* 110 (Feb. 1960): 8; "Textile Stocks Drop as Market Wavers," *Textile World* 110 (Feb. 1960): 5.

3. Annual stockholders meeting, Apr. 12, 1960, Cannon Mills Company Minute Book, 1950–1971, Manufacturing Company Series, Box 144, Cannon Mills Collection; "The Passing of Mr. Charlie," *Forbes* 110 (July 15, 1972): 22.

4. "Passing of Mr. Charlie," 22.

5. *Moody's*, 1960, 2031.

6. "Passing of Mr. Charlie," 22.

7. Annual stockholders meeting, Apr. 12, 1960; Board of Directors meeting, Oct. 30, 1961, Cannon Mills Company Minute Book, 1950–1971.

8. Cannon Timeline—1960 to Present, 2, Folder 371, Chronology 1960–1975, Cannon Collection; "Passing of Mr. Charlie," 22.

9. "Living in the Past," *Forbes* 115 (June 1, 1975): 46–47.

10. *Moody's*, 1962, 2508; Harden, "Cannon," Profile 15–16.

11. *Moody's*, 1961, 1917; *Moody's*, 1962, 2509; *Moody's*, 1963, 826; *Moody's*, 1964, 799; *Moody's*, 1965, 786.

12. Harden, "Cannon"; Cannon Timeline—1960 to Present, 2.

13. "Spot News at Home," *Textile World* 111 (May 1961): 19.

14. "Washington Outlook," *Textile World* 111 (Jan. 1961): 20; "Washington Outlook," *Textile World* 111 (Feb. 1961): 22.

15. "Washington Outlook," *Textile World* 111 (Mar. 1961): 24; Luther Hodges to Charles Cannon, Mar. 9, 1961, Topical Files, U.S. Department of Commerce, 1961, Box 311, Charles A. Cannon Collection (hereafter cited as Box 311, Charles A. Cannon Collection).

16. *Meet the Press* transcript, Apr. 1961, Box 311, Charles A. Cannon Collection.

17. C. A. Cannon to Honorable Luther Hodges, Feb. 7, 1961, Box 311, Charles A. Cannon Collection.

18. Luther Hodges to Charles A. Cannon, Feb. 16, 1961, Box 311, Charles A. Cannon Collection.

19. Hodges to Cannon, Mar. 9, 1961.

20. C. A. Cannon to Luther Hodges, Apr. 4, 1961, Box 311, Charles A. Cannon Collection.

21. Luther Hodges to Charles A. Cannon, Apr. 11, 1961, Box 311, Charles A. Cannon Collection.

22. "At Last, Action on Imports," *Textile World* 111 (June 1961): 42; Brandis, *Making of Textile Trade Policy*, 18–19.

23. "What Textile World Asked Industry Leaders," *Textile World* 111 (June 1961): 42–45.

24. "Action Bogs Down on Imports," *Textile World* 111 (July 1961): 20; "Agreement at Geneva," *Textile World* 111 (Aug. 1961): 20; Brandis, *Making of Textile Trade Policy*, 20–22.

25. "Imports—They're Still in the Headlines," *Textile World* 111 (Oct. 1961): 20.

26. "Big Win—and Hottest News in Textile: Depreciation Speed-Up," 111 (Nov. 1961): 17A–17H.

27. Ibid., 17A.

28. "How Textile Men See the New Rates," *Textile World* 111 (Nov. 1961): 17B–17C.

29. Ibid., 17D.

30. "Eyewitness Report: Threat from the Far East," *Textile World* 111 (Nov. 1961): 38–41.

31. C. A. Cannon to Honorable Luther Hodges, June 20, 1961, Topical Files, U.S. Department of Commerce, 1961, Box 311, Charles A. Cannon Collection.

32. Luther Hodges to Charles A. Cannon, Apr. 11, 1961.

33. Richard M. Scammon, Director of the Bureau of the Census, to C. A. Cannon, June 26, 1961; Francis J. Martinez, Foreign Commerce Business Analyst, to C. A. Cannon, Sept. 11, 1961; and Norwood J. Cheek, Business Analyst, to C. A. Cannon, Oct. 16, 1961, all in Box 311, Charles A. Cannon Collection.

34. Brandis, *Making of Textile Trade Policy*, 15.

35. C. A. Cannon to the Members of Congress from the States of North Carolina and South Carolina, Dec. 19, 1961, Box 308, Charles A. Cannon Collection.

36. Strom Thurmond to C. A. Cannon, Dec. 28, 1961, Box 308, Charles A. Cannon Collection.

37. Sam J. Ervin Jr. to C. A. Cannon, Dec. 20, 1961, Box 308, Charles A. Cannon Collection.

38. Carl Vinson to C. A. Cannon, Dec. 27, 1961, Box 308, Charles A. Cannon Collection. Also see Leeman Anderson, Administrative Assistant for Richard B. Russell, to Charles Cannon, Dec. 26, 1961, Box 308, Charles A. Cannon Collection.

39. Brandis, *Making of Textile Trade Policy*, 24, 27–28.

40. The American Cotton Manufacturers Institute changed its name to the American Textile Manufacturers Institute.

41. "In the Balance," n.d., 1, Charles Albert Cannon Series, American Textile Manufacturers Institute, Special Cotton Policy Committee, 1971 and n.d., Box 15, Cannon Mills Collection. The draft for the report is dated January 10, 1962, and is found in Charles Albert Cannon Series, American Textile Manufacturers Institute, Special Cotton Policy Committee, 1958–1964, Box 14, Cannon Mills Collection.

42. "In the Balance," 1–2.

43. Ibid., 7.

44. "1-Price Cotton Means Savings to Consumers," *Daily Independent*, Dec. 14, 1962, 4.

45. Ibid., 1.

46. Kathryn Christensen, "New Ear for Textile Firm: Cannon Mills Courts Wall Street," *Charlotte News*, Feb. 24, 1979, 16B.

47. Minchin, *What Do We Need a Union For*, 156; "Cannon Timeline—1950's," 4, Folder 370, Cannon Collection.

48. "Cannon Timeline—1950's," 4, Folder 370, Cannon Collection; Wage Increases, n.d., Executive Office Files Series, Box 71, Cannon Mills Collection.

49. Telegram read at the Board of Directors meeting, Apr. 9, 1963, Cannon Mills Company Minute Book, 1950–1971.

50. C. A. Cannon to Honorable Charles S. Murphy, Under Secretary of Agriculture, Feb. 12, 1963, Charles Albert Cannon Series, American Textile Manufacturers Institute, Special Cotton Policy Committee, 1958–1964, Box 14, Cannon Mills Collection.

51. Ibid.

52. "Senator Ervin Writes to President: Eliminate Two-Price Cotton System," *Daily Independent*, Mar. 14, 1963, 1; Sam J. Ervin Jr. to the Honorable John F. Kennedy, Mar. 6, 1963, Charles Albert Cannon Series, American Textile Manufacturers Institute, Special Cotton Policy Committee, 1958–1964, Box 14, Cannon Mills Collection.

53. North Carolina Textile Manufacturers Association, Inc., Annual Report of Cotton Committee, [1963], Charles Albert Cannon Series, Box 15, Cannon Mills Collection.

54. News and Comment, *Textile World* 114 (May 1964): 20; Washington Outlook, *Textile World* 114 (May 1964): 22; "Johnson Mows Down the Opposition, Gets Wheat-Cotton Price Support Bill," *National Observer*, Apr. 13, 1964, 3.

55. T. H. Wingate, "Cannon Be Given [*sic*] Title 'Mr. Textiles of 1964,'" *Greenville* (S.C.) *News*, Oct. 11, 1964, 1A.

56. "One-Price Cotton Has Benefitted Everyone," 4A.

57. News and Comment, *Textile World* 114 (Aug. 1964): 20.

58. "One-Price Cotton Has Benefitted Everyone," 4A.

59. Bill Workman, "Industry Prepares: New Cotton Price Battle Foreseen," *Daily Independent*, Oct. 13, 1964, 1A.

60. "One-Price Cotton Has Benefitted Everyone," 4A.

61. T. H. Wingate, "Cannon Mills Plans Major Expansion," *Daily Independent*, Apr. 14, 1964, 1.

62. Workman, "Industry Prepares," 1A.

63. Board of Directors meeting, Nov. 2, 1964, Cannon Mills Company Minute Book, 1950–1971; Cannon Timeline—1960 to Present, 3–4.

64. Harden, "Cannon," Profile 15–16; Cannon Timeline—1960 to Present.

65. Workman, "Industry Prepares," 1A; Board of Directors meeting, Nov. 2, 1964; Harden, "Cannon," Profile 15; Charles Cannon's speech before the Salisbury–Rowan County Chamber of Commerce, Jan. 11, 1965, Executive Office Files Series, Quotes, Sayings, etc., Box 75, Cannon Mills Collection.

66. "The Outlook for 1966: Big, Bright, Booming," *Textile World* 116 (Feb. 1966): 17–26.

67. Priscilla Gang, "The Look for '69: Home Furnishings' Strength Will Help the Textile Industry to a Good Year," *Textile World* 119 (Feb. 1969): 53.

68. Ibid., 51–53.

69. *Moody's*, 1965, 736; *Moody's*, 1970, 779.

70. Board of Directors meeting, Apr. 13, 1965, Cannon Mills Company Minute Book, 1950–1971.

71. The White Parks facility was originally opened in 1898 by the Lippard and Shealy Manufacturing Company as a cotton thread mill. The White Parks Company bought the property some time later. Histories of Cannon Plants, 7–8, Cannon Collection; Cannon Firsts, Folder 352, Histories: "Histories of Cannon Plants," Cannon Collection; Cannon Timeline—1960 to Present, 4; Board of Directors meeting, July 22, 1965, Cannon Mills Company Minute Book, 1950–1971.

72. Cannon Timeline—1960 to Present, 4.

73. Ibid.

74. "Textile World '71–'72 Fact File," *Textile World* 121 (July 1971): 25.

75. Ibid., 24.

76. "Passing of Mr. Charlie," 22–24.

77. *Moody's*, 1968, 593.

78. Ibid.; "Passing of Mr. Charlie," 22.

79. Kannapolis Appreciation Day, revised Mar. 25, 1967, 2, Appreciation Day, Kannapolis, 1967, Box 108, Charles A. Cannon Collection.

80. Ibid., 3. Actually, Cannon never lived in Kannapolis; rather, he lived on Union Street in Concord.

81. Ibid.

82. Dan Moore to Honorable C. A. Cannon, May 4, 1967, Appreciation Day, Kannapolis, 1967, Box 108, Charles A. Cannon Collection; Cannon Timeline—1960 to Present, 5.

83. Charles Cannon's Speech on Appreciation Day, May 21, 1967, 1–3, Appreciation Day, Kannapolis, 1967, Box 108, Charles A. Cannon Collection.

84. Harden, "Cannon," Management 11.

85. Cobb, *Industrialization and Southern Society*, 43 and 81.

86. David R. Goldfield, *Promised Land: The South Since 1945* (Arlington Heights, Ill.: Harlan Davidson, 1987), 149.

87. Ibid.

88. "Passing of Mr. Charlie," 24.

89. "Local Textile Magnate C. A. Cannon Succumbs," *Concord Tribune*, Apr. 2, 1971, 1; "Follows Cannon in Post," *Daily Independent*, Apr. 14, 1971, 1; Board of Directors meeting, Apr. 14, 1971, Cannon Mills Company Minute Book, 1950–1971.

14. The Civil Rights Movement, Federal Interference, and the Weakening of Paternalism

1. Minchin, *Hiring the Black Worker*, 45.

2. Rowan, "Negro in the Textile Industry," 20.

3. Minchin, *Hiring the Black Worker*, 21, 68–91.

4. Ibid., 3 and 21.

5. Byerly, *Hard Times Cotton Mill Girls*, 151.

6. Ibid., 156.

7. Ibid., 46.

8. Online at http://www.eeoc.gov./policy/vii.html/.

9. Numan V. Bartley, *The New South, 1945–1980* (Baton Rouge: Louisiana State Univ. Press, 1995), 22; "Washington Outlook," *Textile World*, July 1964, 22.

10. Minchin, *Hiring the Black Worker*, 6 and 29.

11. Ibid., 176 and 178.

12. Byerly, *Hard Times Cotton Mill Girls*, 141.

13. *New York Times*, Oct. 20, 1985, in Minchin, *Hiring the Black Worker*, 81.

14. Timothy Minchin, *From Rights to Economics: The Ongoing Struggle for Black Equality in the U.S. South* (Gainesville: Univ. Press of Florida, 2007), 37.

15. Byerly, *Hard Times Cotton Mill Girls*, 137.

16. Minchin, *Hiring the Black Worker*, 4.

17. Byerly, *Hard Times Cotton Mill Girls*, 139.

18. Ibid., 141.

19. Minchin, *Hiring the Black Worker*, 188.

20. Ibid., 189.

21. Ibid., 194.

22. Ibid.

23. While some historians believe that the labor shortage opened the door to blacks working in the southern textile industry, historian Timothy Minchin argues that of more importance was the effort of the federal government to ensure fair employment practices under the Civil Rights Act of 1964. Minchin, *Hiring the Black Worker*, 268. "Government Pressuring Textile to Upgrade Negroes," *Textile World* 116 (May 1966): 22; "Industry Mounts Program to Woo New Workers," *Textile World* 120 (Jan. 1970): 34.

24. "Late Report—News and Comment," *Textile World* 119 (Jan. 1969):18.

25. Salmond, *Southern Struggles*, 10; Herring, *Passing of the Mill Village*.

26. Herring, *Passing of the Mill Village* 16.

27. Ibid., 10.

28. Smith, *Mill on the Dan*, 320 and 519.

29. Herring, *Passing of the Mill Village*, 10–11.

30. George Griggs to Ed Rankin, memo, Oct. 20, 1983, Series I4, Company Housing Sales 1983 #2, Folder 141, Cannon Collection.

31. Timothy J. Minchin, "Black Activism, the 1964 Civil Rights Act, and the Racial Integration of the Southern Textile Industry," *Journal of Southern History* 55 (Nov. 1999): 820. Attorney Richard T. Seymour represented suing black workers against J. P. Stevens in the case *Lucy Sledge et al. v. J. P. Stevens* in 1970.

32. "Late Report Washington Outlook," *Textile World* (Mar. 1970): 38.

33. Board of Directors meeting, May 1, 1969, Cannon Mills Company Minute Book, 1950–1971; "Cannon Mills: Part of a Nixon Campaign?" *Textile World* 119 (May 1969): 24; Minchin, "Black Activism," 835–36.

34. Minchin, *Hiring the Black Worker*, 135.

35. "Black Plaintiff: Conditions Are Better at Cannon," *Salisbury Post*, Jan. 12, 1982, 1B; "Cannon Mills Agrees to Settlement in 1970 Race Discrimination Suit," *Charlotte Observer*, Jan. 12, 1982, 1A.

36. "Cannon Mills Agrees to Settlement in 1970 Race Discrimination Suit," 1A.

37. Ibid.

38. Ibid.

39. "Black Plaintiff: Conditions Are Better at Cannon," 1B.

40. Minchin, *Hiring the Black Worker*, 193–96.

41. *Equal Employment Opportunity Commission v. Cannon Mills Company*, Suits in Court, Executive Office Series, Box 79, Cannon Mills Collection; Adgie O'Bryant Jr., Trial Attorney for the Equal Employment Opportunity Commission, Suits in Court, Executive Office Series, Box 79, Cannon Mills Collection.

42. Robert J. Lenrow, EEOC Trial Attorney, to Eugene T. Bost Jr., May 10, 1977, Suits in Court, Executive Office Series, Box 79, Cannon Mills Collection; Minchin, *Hiring the Black Worker*, 159.

43. "Cannon: I," *Fortune*, Nov. 1933, 137.

15. Cannon Mills after Charles Cannon

1. "Passing of Mr. Charlie," 22.

2. Harden, "Cannon," Profile 17; "What's Behind the New Look at Cannon," *Textile World* 121 (Oct. 1971): 32; Rankin, *Century of Progress*, 23.

3. John Harden, "Cannon: The Story of Cannon Mills Company—90 Years of Textile Leadership and Innovation, 1887–1977," Cannon Stories, n.p., Cannon Collection.

4. "What's Behind the New Look at Cannon," 36.

5. Ibid., 32.

6. Ibid.; Harden, "Cannon," Profile 17.

7. Harden, "Cannon," Profile 19; "What's Behind the New Look at Cannon," 33.

8. Cannon Mills had a company paper during World War II, but it was replaced by the industry's *Textile Neighbor* during the early 1950s.

9. "What's Behind the New Look at Cannon," 32.

10. Harden, "Cannon," Profile 18–19a.

11. Ibid., Profile 18–19.

12. "What's Behind the New Look at Cannon," 32.

13. Ibid., 2–3.

14. Ibid., 2.

15. Viola A. Safrit to Whom It Concerns, n.d., Executive Office Files Series, Unions, Box 80, Cannon Mills Collection (hereafter cited as Box 80, Cannon Mills Collection).

16. Estelle Spry to Sir or Who Ever This Consurns [*sic*], Aug. 20, 1974, Box 80, Cannon Mills Collection.

17. A 30 Year Employee to Cannon Mills Company, Aug. 15, 1974, Box 80, Cannon Mills Collection.

18. Lynn M. Sloop to Mr. Don Holt, Oct. 1, 1974, Box 80, Cannon Mills Collection.

19. "Cannon Mills, Union Prepare for Showdown in Kannapolis," *Charlotte Observer*, Sept. 1, 1974, 1A.

20. Ibid.

21. 21. Ibid., 20A.

22. Roy Reed, "Cannon Mills Workers Bar the Union Again," *New York Times*, Nov. 22, 1974, n.p., Box 80, Cannon Mills Collection.

23. Don S. Holt to Cannon People, Nov. 5, 1974, Box 80, Cannon Mills Collection.

24. Harold P. Hornaday to Cannon People, Nov. 14, 1974, and Don S. Holt and Harold P. Hornaday to Cannon People, Nov. 16, 1974, both in Box 80, Cannon Mills Collection.

25. F. L. Wilson, Senior Vice President and Director of Manufacturing, to All Cannon Mills Supervisors, Oct. 31, 1974, Box 80, Cannon Mills Collection.

26. Terry Altas, "Cannon Won, but TWUA Displayed Strength," *Charlotte Observer*, Nov. 24, 1974, 12D; Reed, "Cannon Mills Workers Bar the Union Again."

27. Rankin, *Century of Progress*, 24.

28. "Living in the Past: It Has a Great Name and a Heap of Cash, but Cannon Mills Still Lives in a Vanished Era," *Forbes* 115 (June 1, 1975): 46; "Textile World '71–'72 Fact File," *Textile World* 121 (July 1971): 24–25.

29. "Living in the Past," 47.

30. The total consisted of 1,596 company-owned houses in Kannapolis for Plants 1 and 4, 118 for Plant 3, 140 for Plant 12, 473 for the plants in Concord, 94 for Plant 7, 77 for Plant 8, 31 for Plant 11, and 8 for Plant 14. Additional Information Concerning Houses Owned by Cannon Mills Company, Aug. 2, 1978, Folder 138, Company Housing Sales, 1978–79, Cannon Collection. The total number of mill houses was never consistent in company papers.

31. Ibid.

32. Cannon' s share of the sheet market had fallen from 20 percent. "Living in the Past," 46.

33. Kathryn Christensen, "New Era for Textile Firm: Cannon Mills Courts Wall Street," *Charlotte News*, Feb. 24, 1979, 16B; Jack Scism, "Changes at Cannon Mills," *Greensboro Daily News*, Nov. 30, 1980, 1D.

34. "A Rough Year for Cannon Mills," *New York Times*, Dec. 30, 1980, 1D; Christensen, "New Era for Textile Firm."

35. Everette L. Gilliam, "Union Claims Sentiment Strong for Cannon Organization Drive," *Concord Tribune*, July 18, 1980, 1; Gary L. Wright, "Union Taking Sounding Again at Cannon Mills," *Charlotte Observer*, July 18, 1980, 1B.

36. Wright, "Union Taking Sounding Again"; Gilliam, "Union Claims Sentiment Strong for Cannon Organization Drive."

37. "A Rough Year for Cannon Mills"; Scism, "Changes at Cannon Mills." The real reason for Hornaday's resignation was probably due to a business arrangement with Peak Textiles, Inc., of Georgia in 1970 and an unsecured line of credit offered to the textile firm. See both of the above newspaper articles for details.

38. Bill Workman, "1980s Exciting Decade," *Daily Independent*, Aug. 17, 1980, 1A.

39. Bill Workman, "Cannon Is Aware of Changes," *Daily Independent*, Aug. 17, 1980, 1A.

40. Statement from Cannon Mills Company, Oct. 21, 1980, Folder 277, Union (1980), Cannon Collection.

41. W. S. Murdoch to All Members of Management, Aug. 26, 1980, Folder 277, Union (1980), Cannon Collection.

42. Supervisory Training Session, Aug. 27, 1980, Folder 277, Union (1980), Cannon Collection.

43. Bill Workman, "Participation Pleases Loyalty Leaders," *Daily Independent*, Dec. 16, 1980, 1A; Gary L. Wright, "Workers Have 'Loyalty Day' at Cannon Mills," *Daily Independent*, Dec. 17, 1980, 1A.

44. Andrews, *Men and the Mills*, 250.

45. Gary L. Wright, "Cannon Lays Off 8,500 Workers Until March 28," *Charlotte Observer*, Apr. 20, 1982, Folder 112, Cannon Mills—Misc. Clippings, Cannon Collection.

46. Ken Friedlein, "Cannon Trustees Willing to Sell Blocks of Stock," *Charlotte Observer*, Jan. 29, 1982, 1.

16. David Murdock, Modern Management, and the Demise of Paternalism

1. Wright, "Cannon Lays Off 8,500 Workers"; Bill Workman, "Seasonal Slide in Cannon Sales Ends," *Daily Independent*, Aug. 11, 1982, 1A; Steve Matthews, "Next Big Union Battle May Be Shaping Up at Cannon," *Charlotte Observer*, July 30, 1984, Folder 278, Unions (1984–85), Cannon Collection; Andrews, *Men and the Mills*, 250.

2. Andrews, *Men and the Mills*, 251; Rankin, *Century of Progress*, 24; Wright, "Cannon Lays Off 8,500 Workers."

3. Andrews, *Men and the Mills*, 251.

4. Workman, "Seasonal Slide in Cannon Sales Ends"; Wright, "Cannon Lays Off 8,500 Workers."

5. Bob Dennis, "Cannon Sells Fabric Factory," *Charlotte Observer*, Oct. 9, 1982, Folder 112, Cannon Mills—Misc. Clippings, Cannon Collection.

6. Winston Williams, "David Murdock Beats the Union," *New York Times*, Oct. 20, 1985, sec. 3, p. 1.

7. Jan Stucker, "Murdock Reassures Workers," *Charlotte Observer*, July 1, 1982, 1.

8. John Hackman, "Company Loosens Paternalistic Ties to Town It Sired," *Charlotte Observer*, Mar. 20, 1983, 1.

9. Byerly, *Hard Times Cotton Mill Girls*, 6.

10. Hackman, "Company Loosens Paternalistic Ties."

11. Workman, "Seasonal Slide in Cannon Sales Ends."

12. "Cannon Mills Puts Houses Up for Sale," *Daily Independent*, Oct. 18, 1983, 1A; Andrews, *Men and the Mills*, 202.

13. Rankin, *Century of Progress*, 10–11.

14. Hackman, "Company Loosens Paternalistic Ties."

15. Rankin, *Century of Progress*, 11; James Claude Benton, "Union Drive Puts Townspeople at Odds," *Daily Independent*, July 7, 1991, 6A.

16. David H. Murdock to Employees, July 23, 1984, Folder 278, Unions (1984–85), Cannon Collection; Matthews, "Next Big Union Battle May Be Shaping Up."

17. Minchin, *Fighting Against the Odds*, 151. Consultants specializing in union busting became prevalent during the 1970s and 1980s. See Norwood, *Strikebreaking and Intimidation*, 236–38.

18. Leon R. Lackey to Distribution, July 31, 1984, and Lackey to Administrative Department Managers, 31 July 1984; and Ed Rankin to David H. Murdock and Max Messmer, Aug. 24, 1984, all in Folder 278, Unions (1984–85), Cannon Collection.

19. Nancy Peckenham, "Out in the Cold at Cannon Mills," *Nation*, Sept. 16, 1991, 298.

20. Cannon Employee Questions Answered by Mr. Murdock, n.d., Folder 279, Union (1985), Cannon Collection.

21. Rankin, *Century of Progress*, 24. The *New York Times* reported the vote at 5,982 against to 3,530 for the union. See Williams, "David Murdock Beats the Union."

22. David Murdock's Pacific Holding Company retained Wiscassett Mills Company and Beacon Manufacturing Company. Andrews, *Men and the Mills*, 287; Rankin, *Century of Progress*, 24.

23. Karen Haywood, "Kannapolis a 'Money Pump' for Murdock, Study Says," *Salisbury Post*, June 22, 1986, in Series I.4, Murdock Purchase 2, Folder 211, Cannon Collection.

24. Peckenham, "Out in the Cold at Cannon Mills," 298.

25. Ibid., 300; Karen Ferguson and Kate Blackwell, *Pensions in Crisis: Why the System Is Failing America and How You Can Protect Your Future* (New York: Arcade, 1995), 139–40; Glass, *Textile Industry in North Carolina*, 101.

26. Peckenham, "Out in the Cold at Cannon Mills," 300.

27. Buford Henley was the grandfather of the author. Pension check stubs in the possession of the author.

28. Ferguson and Blackwell, *Pensions in Crisis*, 139.

17. Fieldcrest Cannon, Pillowtex, Bankruptcy, and the Return of David Murdock

1. *Moody's*, 1990, 2950; *Moody's*, 1991, 2948.

2. Don R. Smith, "Fieldcrest Says Customers Worry About Union Vote," *Daily Independent*, Aug. 14, 1991, 1A; *Moody's*, 1992, 2978.

3. Smith, "Fieldcrest Says Customers Worry About Union Vote."

4. Benton, "Union Drive Puts Townspeople at Odds," 6A.

5. David Ramsey, "Fieldcrest Will Fight Union," *Daily Independent*, June 13, 1991, 1A.

6. David Ramsey, "Union Files for a Vote at Plants in Two Counties," *Daily Independent*, June 20, 1991, 1A.

7. David Ramsey, "Fieldcrest Plans All-Out Effort to Keep Out Union," *Daily Independent*, June 21, 1991, 1A.

8. Smith, "Fieldcrest Says Customers Worry About Union Vote."

9. Benton, "Union Drive Puts Townspeople at Odds," 6A.

10. "Union Vote at Plants Tentatively Set for Aug. 20–21," *Daily Independent*, July 5, 1991, 1A.

11. David Ramsey, "Union Supporters Claim They Will Win Next Week's Election," *Daily Independent*, Aug. 12, 1991, 1A.

12. Fieldcrest had unionized plants in Eden and Salisbury, North Carolina; Fieldale, Virginia; Columbus, Georgia; and Phenix City, Alabama, covering forty-five hundred workers. Ramsey, "Fieldcrest Will Fight Union."

13. Ramsey, "Fieldcrest Plans All-Out Effort to Keep Out Union," 6A.

14. Ramsey, "Union Files for a Vote at Plants in Two Counties."

15. David Ramsey, "Union Barely Loses; Will Challenge Vote," *Daily Independent*, Aug. 22, 1991, 1A; David Ramsey, "Sorting Out Union Election Results May Take Months," *Daily Independent*, Aug. 23, 1991, 1A; "Union Says It Will Drop Complaints," *Daily Independent*, Oct. 23, 1992, 1A; "Count of Ballots Gives Company Big Margin," *Daily Independent*, Oct. 28, 1992, 1A.

16. Benton, "Union Drive Puts Townspeople at Odds," 6A.

17. Scott Jenkins, "Economic Recruiters Say Union Presence Would Hinder Bid to Attract Industry, Jobs," *Daily Independent*, Aug. 8, 1997, 1A; Shannon Buggs, "Key Vote Ahead at Cannon," *News and Observer*, Aug. 10, 1997, 1A.

18. The union is now called UNITE HERE. See the history of the union at http://www.unitehere.org/about/history.php/.

19. Scott Jenkins, "NLRB Alleges Fieldcrest Trying to Subvert Election," *Independent Tribune*, Aug. 7, 1997, 1A; Buggs, "Key Vote Ahead at Cannon"; Gail Smith and Maki Becker, "Union Tries Again Today at Fieldcrest," *Charlotte Observer*, Aug. 12, 1997, 1A; Stella M. Hopkins, "Union Apparent Loser in Election," *Charlotte Observer*, Aug. 14, 1997, 1A.

20. Scott Jenkins, "Union Loses," *Independent Tribune*, Aug. 14, 1997, 1A; Scott Jenkins and Beth McLaughlin, "Union Cries Foul, Vows Court Battle," *Independent Tribune*, Aug. 14, 1997, 1A; Hopkins, "Union Apparent Loser in Election."

21. "Chuck Hansen: Visionary? Scoundrel? Cowboy? Or Just a Success?" *Independent Tribune*, Dec. 28, 1997, 1A; "Will Moves by Pillowtex Change Bedding Business?" *Independent Tribune*, Dec. 28, 1997, 1A; Marshall Smith, "Union Claims Victory," *Independent Tribune*, June 24, 1999, 6A.

22. *Moody's*, 1995, 3193; *Moody's*, 1997, 3325.

23. *Moody's*, 1999, 6324.

24. Marshall Smith, "Fieldcrest Union Vote Under Way," *Independent Tribune*, June 23, 1999, 1A; Smith, "Union Claims Victory."

25. Ibid.

26. Smith, "Fieldcrest Union Vote Under Way."

27. Smith, "Union Claims Victory."

28. Paul Nowell, "Union Calls Textile Victory Greatest Ever in South," *Independent Tribune*, June 25, 1999, 1A.

29. Ibid., 8A.

30. Marshall Smith, "We Need Each Other," *Independent Tribune*, Nov. 11, 1999, 1A.

31. Marshall Smith, "25-Year War Over," *Independent Tribune*, Feb. 11, 2000, 1A.

32. *Common Threads* 2, no. 8 (Oct. 1997): 1, Cannon Collection; James C. Benton, "Economic Change and the 'City of Loom': Trade Adjustment Assistance in an American Community" (master's thesis, Georgetown Univ., 2008), 85.

33. Smith, "25-Year War Over," 6A; "Threadbare Prospects Loom for Cloth and Clothing Makers," *Business North Carolina* 20 (Feb. 1, 2000).

34. Ben McNeely, Josh Lanier, and Eric C. Deines, "Special Report, Pillowtex Fives Years Later," *Independent Tribune*, July 27, 2008, 4.

35. Ibid., "Pillowtex Relaunches Cannon Brand," *Textile World*, May 2003, http://www.textileworld.com/Articles/2003/May/Textile_News/Pillowtex/.

36. "Pillowtex Relaunches Cannon Brand"; "Pillowtex Emerges from Bankruptcy," *Charlotte Business Journal*, May 28, 2002, http://www.bizjournals.com/charlotte/stories/2002/05/daily3.html/.

37. Benton, "Economic Change and the 'City of Loom,'" 86.

38. Ibid., 87; McNeely, Lanier, and Deines, "Special Report," 8; "Pillowtex Files Chapter 11 Shuts Down Operations," *Textile World*, Sept. 2003, http://www.textileworld.com/Articles/2003/September/Textile_News/Pillowtex/.

39. McNeely, Lanier, and Deines, "Special Report," 8; Benton, "Economic Change and the 'City of Loom,'" 87–88; Minchin, *Fighting Against the Odds*, 179. Figures for the jobs lost vary. Benton used 6,450 and 7,600 for the total lost (139). A report from the University of North Carolina stated that 7,650 were eliminated. Additionally, figures for local losses vary. Benton mentioned 4,250 for Concord, Kannapolis, and Rowan County, while the UNC report stated 4,340. The *Independent Tribune* used 2,592 for the number lost in Cabarrus County and 1,392 in Rowan County. Kannapolis straddles both Cabarrus and Rowan Counties, but two-thirds of the town is in Cabarrus County.

40. Department of Labor, Bureau of Statistics, in McNeely, Lanier, and Deines, "Special Report," 8.

41. Benton, "Economic Change and the 'City of Loom,'" 141.

42. McNeely, Lanier, and Deines, "Special Report," 5; Myra Beatty, Douglas Longman, and Van Tran, "Community Response to the Pillowtex Textile Kannapolis Closing: The 'Rapid Response' Team as a Facilitative Device," 6, unpublished paper, Apr. 2004, University of North Carolina at Chapel Hill

43. Beatty, Longman, and Tran, "Community Response," 4; Rankin, *Century of Progress*, 17.

44. Beatty, Longman, and Tran, "Community Response," 9; McNeely, Lanier, and Deines, "Special Report," 8.

45. Beatty, Longman, and Tran, "Community Response," 7–8; Benton, "Economic Change and the 'City of Loom,'" 89. Benton listed slightly different amounts of aid that was available to Pillowtex workers.

46. Beatty, Longman, and Tran, "Community Response," 9.

47. McNeely, Lanier, and Deines, "Special Report," 8.

48. Ibid., 7–8.

49. Betty Ann Bowser, narrator, "Textile Jobs in Decline," special, PBS, Sept. 23, 2003. Transcript available at http://pbs.org/newshour/bb/economy/july-dec03/textile_9–23.html/.

50. Alan Hodge, "Kannapolis: This Former Cabarrus County Mill Town Is Turning from Textiles to Test Tubes for Its Future," *Our State: North Carolina*, Aug. 2006, 4–5.

51. McNeely, Lanier, and Deines, "Special Report," 9.

52. Ibid.; Rhonda L. Rundle, "Lean Operation: Dole Food Owner Pours His Fortune into Health Ventures," *Wall Street Journal*, July 28, 2006, reprint included in North Carolina Research Campus information packet.

53. "Mrs. Murdock Dies in L.A.," *Daily News Record*, Jan. 14, 1985, 1; Rundle, "Lean Operation."

54. "What People Are Saying About the North Carolina Research Campus," in *A Guide to the North Carolina Research Campus* (n.p.: Salisbury Post, n.d.), 22; McNeely, Lanier, and Deines, "Special Report," 10.

55. McNeely, Lanier, and Deines, "Special Report," 9–10; Rundle, "Lean Operation."

56. Rita Lee, "Kannapolis Gaining State-of-the-Art Research Campus," *Charlotte Medical News*, July 2007, 1 and 12.

57. Ibid., 12.

CONCLUSION

1. Lee J. Alston and Joseph P. Ferrie, *Southern Paternalism and the American Welfare State: Economics, Politics, and Institutions in the South, 1865–1965* (New York: Cambridge Univ. Press, 1999), 2.

2. Salmond, *Southern Struggles*, 10.

BIBLIOGRAPHY

———◆◆)◆◆◆———

Primary Sources

Archives

Center for Advertising History, National Museum of American History, Smithsonian
  Institution, Washington, D.C.
        N. W. Ayers Collection

Foy and Gertrude Hinson History Room, Cannon Memorial Library, Kannapolis Branch,
  Kannapolis, N.C.
        Cannon Collection

Special Collections, Perkins Library, Duke University, Durham, N.C.
        Cannon Mills Collection
        CIO Organizing Committee Papers for North Carolina

Wingate University Library, Wingate, N.C.
        Charles A. Cannon Collection

Newspapers

Charlotte Observer

Columbia (S.C.) *Record*

(Concord and Kannapolis) *Independent Tribune*

Concord Daily Tribune

Concord Standard

Concord Times

Concord Tribune

Daily Charlotte Observer

Greensboro Daily News

Greenville (S.C.) *News*

Kannapolis Daily Independent

New York Daily News Record

New York Times

Raleigh News and Observer
Raleigh Register
Salisbury (N.C.) *Post*

PERIODICALS AND TRADE JOURNALS

Better Homes and Gardens
Business North Carolina
Cannon News
Charlotte Business Journal
Charlotte Medical News
Chesapeake Pilot
Common Threads
Cotton
Forbes
Fortune
Guide to the North Carolina Research Campus
Ladies' Home Journal
Moody's Manual
Niles' Weekly Register
Our State: North Carolina
Southern Textile Bulletin
Textile Neighbor
Textile World
Textile World and Industrial Record
Textile World Journal
Uplift

SECONDARY SOURCES

BOOKS

Alston, Lee L., and Joseph P. Ferrie. *Southern Paternalism and the American Welfare State: Economics, Politics, and Institutions in the South, 1865–1965.* New York: Cambridge Univ. Press, 1999.

Anderson, Cynthia D. *The Social Consequences of Economic Restructuring in the Textile Industry: Change in a Southern Mill Village.* New York: Garland, 2000.

Andrews, Mildred Gwin. *The Men and the Mills: A History of the Southern Textile Industry.* Macon, Ga.: Mercer Univ. Press, 1987.

Arthur-Cornett, Helen. *Remembering Kannapolis: Tales from Towel City.* Charleston, S.C.: History Press, 2006.

Backman, Jules, and M. R. Gainsbrugh. *Economics of the Cotton Textile Industry.* New York: National Industrial Conference Board, 1946.

Bartley, Numan V. *The New South, 1945–1980*. Baton Rouge: Louisiana State Univ. Press, 1995.

Bernstein, Irving. *Turbulent Years: A History of the American Worker, 1933–1941*. Boston: Houghton Mifflin, 1970.

Brandes, Stuart D. *American Welfare Capitalism, 1880–1940*. Chicago: Univ. of Chicago Press, 1976.

Brandis, R. Buford. *The Making of Textile Trade Policy, 1935–1981*. Washington, D.C.: American Textile Manufacturers Institute, 1982.

Byerly, Victoria. *Hard Times Cotton Mill Girls: Personal Histories of Womanhood and Poverty in the South*. Ithaca, N.Y.: ILR Press, 1986.

Cash, Wilbur J. *The Mind of the South*. New York: Alfred A. Knopf, 1941; reprint, New York: Vintage Books, 1991.

Chandler, Alfred D., Jr. *Strategy and Structure: Chapters in the History of the Industrial Enterprise*. Cambridge, Mass.: MIT Press, 1962.

Clark, Daniel J. *Like Night and Day: Unionization in a Southern Mill Town*. Chapel Hill: Univ. of North Carolina Press, 1997.

Cobb, James. *Industrialization and Southern Society, 1877–1984*. Lexington: Univ. Press of Kentucky, 1984.

Cook, John Harrison. *A Study of Mill Schools of North Carolina*. New York: Teachers College, Columbia Univ., 1925.

Cruden, Robert M. *Ministers of Reform: The Progressives' Achievements in American Civilization, 1889–1920*. New York: Basic Books, 1982.

Davidson, Elizabeth H. *Child Labor Legislation in the Southern Textile States*. Chapel Hill: Univ. of North Carolina Press, 1939.

Fantasia, Rick. *Cultures of Solidarity: Consciousness, Action, and Contemporary American Workers*. Berkeley and Los Angeles: Univ. of California Press, 1998.

Ferguson, Karen, and Kate Blackwell, *Pensions in Crisis: Why the System Is Failing America and How You Can Protect Your Future*. New York: Arcade, 1995.

Galambos, Louis. *Competition and Cooperation: The Emergence of a National Trade Association*. Baltimore: John Hopkins Univ. Press, 1966.

Galambos, Louis, and Joseph Pratt. *The Rise of the Corporate Commonwealth: U.S. Business and Public Policy in the Twentieth Century*. New York: Basic Books, 1988.

Gerstle, Gary. *Working-Class Americanism: The Politics of Labor in a Textile City, 1914–1960*. New York: Cambridge Univ. Press, 1989.

Glass, Brent D. *The Textile Industry in North Carolina: A History*. Raleigh: Division of Archives and History, North Carolina Department of Cultural Resources, 1992.

Griffith, Barbara. *Crisis of American Labor: Operation Dixie and the Defeat of the CIO*. Philadelphia: Temple Univ. Press, 1988.

Hall, Jacquelyn Dowd, James Leloudis, Robert Korstad, Mary Murphy, Lu Ann Jones, and Christopher B. Daly. *Like a Family: The Making of a Southern Cotton Mill World*. New York: W. W. Norton, 1987.

Hawley, Ellis. *The New Deal and the Problem of Monopoly: A Study in Economic Ambivalence*. Princeton, N.J.: Princeton Univ., 1966.

Hearden, Patrick J. *Independence and Empire: The New South's Cotton Mill Campaign, 1865–1901*. DeKalb: Northern Illinois Univ. Press, 1982.

Herring, Harriet L. *Passing of the Mill Village: Revolutions in a Southern Institution*. Chapel Hill: Univ. of North Carolina Press, 1949.

———. *Welfare Work in Mill Villages: The Story of Extra-Mill Activities in North Carolina*. Chapel Hill: Univ. of North Carolina Press, 1929.

Hodges, James A. *New Deal Labor Policy and the Southern Cotton Textile Industry, 1933–1941*. Knoxville: Univ. of Tennessee Press, 1986.

Hower, Ralph M. *The History of an Advertising Agency: N. W. Ayer and Son at Work, 1869–1939*. Cambridge: Harvard Univ. Press, 1939.

Hughes, Thomas P. *American Genesis: A Century of Invention and Technological Enthusiasm*. New York: Penguin Books 1989.

Jones, John Philip. *What's in a Name? Advertising and the Concept of Brands*. Lexington, Mass.: Lexington Books, 1986.

Kannapolis: A Pictorial History. Kannapolis, N.C.: City of Kannapolis, 2008.

Kearns, Paul R. *Mullen Leaves and Brown Sugar: Memories to Make Our Hearts Smile*. Barium Springs, N.C.: Mullein Press, 1993.

———. *Weavers of Dreams*. Barium Springs, N.C.: Mullein Press, 1995.

Kennedy, Stephen Jay. *Profits and Losses in Textile: Cotton Textile Financing Since the War*. New York: Harper and Brothers, 1936.

Kerr, K. Austin. *American Railroad Politics, 1914–1920: Rates, Wages, and Efficiency*. Pittsburgh: Univ. of Pittsburgh Press, 1968.

Lahne, Herbert J. *The Cotton Mill Worker*. New York: Farrar and Rinehart, 1944.

Lescohier, Don, and Elizabeth Brandies. *History of Labor in the United States, 1896–1932*. New York: Macmillan, 1935.

Leuchtenburg, William E. *Franklin D. Roosevelt and the New Deal, 1932–1940*. New York: Harper and Row, 1963.

Mann, Michael. *Consciousness and Action Among the Western Working Class*. London: Macmillan, 1973.

Marshall, F. Ray. *Labor in the South*. Cambridge: Harvard Univ. Press, 1934.

Martin, Albro. *Enterprise Denied: Origins of the Decline of American Railroads, 1897–1917*. New York: Columbia Univ. Press, 1971.

McCune, Wesley. *Ezra Taft Benson: Man with a Mission*. Washington, D.C.: Public Affairs Press, 1958.

McHugh, Cathy L. *Mill Family: The Labor System in the Southern Cotton Textile Industry, 1880–1915*. New York: Oxford Univ. Press, 1988.

McLaurin, Melton A. *Paternalism and Protest: Southern Cotton Mill Workers and Organized Labor*. Westport, Conn.: Greenwood Press, 1971.

McLaurine, W. M. *James William Cannon (1852–1921): His Plants, His People, His Philosophy*. New York: Newcomen Society of North America, 1951.

Michl, H. E. *The Textile Industry: An Economic Analysis*. Washington, D.C.: Textile Foundation, 1938.

Minchin, Timothy J. *Fighting Against the Odds: A History of Southern Labor Since World War II*. Gainesville: Univ. Press of Florida, 2005.

———. *From Rights to Economics: The Ongoing Struggle for Black Equality in the U.S. South*. Gainesville: Univ. Press of Florida, 2007.

———. *Hiring the Black Worker: The Racial Integration of the Southern Textile Industry, 1969–1980*. Chapel Hill: Univ. of North Carolina Press, 1999.

————. *What Do We Need a Union For? The TWUA in the South, 1945–1955*. Chapel Hill: Univ. of North Carolina Press, 1997.

Mitchell, Broadus. *The Rise of the Cotton Mills in the South*. Baltimore: Johns Hopkins Univ. Press, 1921; reprint, New York: Da Capo Press, 1968.

Mitchell, George Sinclair. *Textile Unionism and the South*. Chapel Hill: Univ. of North Carolina Press, 1931.

Moore, James Lewis, and Thomas Herron Wingate. *Cabarrus Reborn: A Historical Sketch of the Founding and Development of Cannon Mills Company and Kannapolis*. Kannapolis, N.C.: Kannapolis Publishing, 1940.

Morrison, Joseph L. *Governor O. Max Gardner: A Power in North Carolina and New Deal Washington*. Chapel Hill: Univ. of North Carolina Press, 1971.

Murchison, Claudius T. *King Cotton Is Sick*. Chapel Hill: Univ. of North Carolina Press, 1930.

Norwood, Stephen H. *Strikebreakers and Intimidation: Mercenaries and Masculinity in Twentieth-Century America*. Chapel Hill: Univ. of North Carolina Press, 2002.

Novick, David, Melvin Anshen, and W. C. Truppner. *Wartime Production Controls*. New York: Columbia Univ. Press, 1949.

Peterson, Trudy Huskamp. *Agricultural Exports, Farm Income, and the Eisenhower Administration*. Lincoln: Univ. of Nebraska Press, 1979.

Pope, Liston. *Millhands and Preachers: A Study of Gastonia*. New Haven, Conn.: Yale Univ. Press, 1942.

Powell, William S. *North Carolina Through Four Centuries*. Chapel Hill: Univ. of North Carolina Press, 1989.

Rankin, Edward L., Jr. *A Century of Progress: Fieldcrest Cannon, Inc. Salutes cannon mills company and Its Employees, Past and Present*. N.p.: Fieldcrest Cannon, 1987.

Rodgers, Daniel T. *The Work Ethic in Industrial America, 1850–1920*. Chicago: Univ. of Chicago Press, 1978.

Roscigno, Vincent J., and William F. Danaher. *The Voice of Southern Labor: Radio, Music, and Textile Strikes, 1929–1934*. Minneapolis: Univ. of Minnesota Press, 2004.

Salmond, John. *Gastonia 1929: The Story of the Loray Mill Strike*. Chapel Hill: Univ. of North Carolina Press, 1995.

————. *Southern Struggles: The Southern Labor Movement and the Civil Rights Struggle*. Gainesville: Univ. Press of Florida, 2004.

Schapsmeier, Edward L., and Frederick H. Schapsmeier. *Ezra Taft Benson and the Politics of Agriculture: The Eisenhower Years, 1953–1961*. Danville, Ill.: Interstate Printers and Publishers, 1975.

Slide, Anthony. *American Racist: The Life and Films of Thomas Dixon*. Lexington: Univ. Press of Kentucky, 2004.

Smith, Robert Sidney. *Mill on the Dan: A History of Dan River Mills, 1882–1950*. Durham, N.C.: Duke Univ. Press, 1960.

Stover, John Ford. *The Life and Decline of the American Railroad*. New York: Oxford Univ. Press, 1970.

Thompson, E. P. *The Making of the English Working Class*. New York: Vintage Books, 1966.

Thompson, Holland. *From the Cotton Field to the Cotton Mill*. Norwood, Mass.: Norwood Press, 1906.

Tindall, George B. *The Emergence of the New South, 1913–1945*. Baton Rouge: Louisiana State Univ. Press, 1967.

Tippett, Tom. *When Southern Labor Stirs*. New York: Jonathan Cape and Harrison Smith, 1936.

Utley, R. G., and Scott Verner. *The Independent Carolina Baseball League, 1936–1938*. Jefferson, N.C.: McFarland, 1999.

Vatter, Harold G. *The U.S. Economy in World War II*. New York: Columbia Univ. Press, 1985.

Woodward, C. Vann. *Origins of the New South, 1877–1913*. 1951. Reprint, Baton Rouge: Louisiana State Univ. Press, 1971.

Wright, Gavin. *Old South, New South: Revolutions in the Southern Economy Since the Civil War*. New York: Basic Books: 1986.

Young, James R. *Textile Leaders of the South*. Columbia, S.C.: R. L. Bryan, 1963.

ARTICLES

Brody, David. "The Rise and Decline of Welfare Capitalism." In *Change and Continuity in the Twentieth-Century: The Twenties*, edited by John Braeman, Robert H. Bremner, and David Brody, 148–78. Columbus: Ohio State Univ. Press, 1968.

Clune, Erin Elizabeth. "From Light Copper to the Blackest and Lowest Type: Daniel Tompkins and the Racial Order of the Global South." *Journal of Southern History* 76, no. 2 (May 2010): 282–91.

Collins, Herbert. "The Idea of Cotton Textile Industry in the South, 1870–1900." *North Carolina Historical Review* 34 (July 1957): 358–92.

Crawford, Margaret. "Earle S. Draper and the Company Town in the American South." In *The Company Town: Architecture and Society in the Early Industrial Age*, edited by John Garner, 139–72. New York: Oxford Univ. Press, 1992.

Davenport, F. Gavin, Jr. "Thomas Dixon's Mythology of Southern History." *Journal of Southern History* 36, no. 3 (Aug. 1970): 350–67.

Dinius, Oliver J., and Angela Vergara. "Company Towns in the Americas: An Introduction." In *Company Towns in the Americas: Landscape, Power, and Working-Class Communities*, edited by Oliver J. Dinius and Angela Vergara, 1–20. Athens: Univ. of Georgia Press, 2011.

Donajgrodzki, A. P. "Introduction." In *Social Control in Nineteenth Century Britain*, edited by A. P. Donajgrodzki, 9–26. Totowa, N.J.: Rowman and Littlefield, 1977.

Downs, Gregory P. "University Men, Social Science, and White Supremacy in North Carolina." *Journal of Southern History* 75, no. 2 (May 2009): 267–304.

Freeze, Gary Richard. "Patriarchy Lost: The Preconditions for Paternalism in the Odell Cotton Mills of North Carolina, 1882–1900." In *Race, Class and Community in Southern Labor History*, edited by Gary M. Fink and Merle E. Black, 27–40. Tuscaloosa: Univ. of Alabama Press, 1994.

Galambos, Louis. "The Cotton-Textile Institute and the Government: A Case Study in Interacting Value Systems." *Business History Review* 38 (Summer 1964): 186–213.

Hagedorn, Homer J. "A Note on the Motivation of Personnel Management: Industrial Welfare 1885–1910." *Explorations in Entrepreneurial History* 10 (Apr. 1958): 134–39.

Hodson, Randy. "Management Citizenship Behavior: A New Concept and an Empirical Test." *Social Problems* 46, no. 3 (1999): 460–78.

Koh, Sung Jae. "A History of Cotton Trade Between the United States and the Far East." *Textile History Review* 4 (July 1963): 134–49.

Lazonick, William. "Industrial Relations and Technical Change: The Case of the Self-Acting Mule." *Cambridge Journal of Economics* 3 (1979): 231–62.

———. "The Subjection of Labour to Capital: The Rise of the Capitalist System." *Review of Radical Political Economics* 10 (Spring 1978): 6–9.

Lears, T. J. Jackson. "The Concept of Cultural Hegemony: Problems and Possibilities." *American Historical Review* 90 (June 1985): 567–93.

———. "From Salvation to Self-Realization: Advertising and the Therapeutic Roots of the Consumer Culture, 1880–1930." In *The Culture of Consumption: Critical Essays in American History, 1880–1980*, edited by Richard W. Fox and T. J. Jackson Lears, 101–41. New York: Pantheon Books, 1983.

Minchin, Timothy J. "Black Activism, the 1964 Civil Rights Act, and the Racial Integration of the Southern Textile Industry." *Journal of Southern History* 55 (Nov. 1999): 809–44.

Nelson, Daniel, and Stuart Campbell. "Taylorism Versus Welfare Work in American Industry: H. L. Gantt and the Bancrofts." *Business History Review* 46 (Spring 1972): 1–16.

Nolan, Dennis R., and Donald E. Jones. "Textile Unionism in the Piedmont, 1901–1932." In *Essays in Southern Labor History: Selected Papers, Southern Labor History Conference, 1976*, edited by Gary Fink and Merl Reed, 49–68. Westport, Conn.: Greenwood Press, 1976.

Rimlinger, Gaston V. "Welfare Policy and Economic Development: A Comparative Historical Perspective." *Journal of Economic History* 26 (Dec. 1966): 556–71.

Rowan, Richard. "The Negro in the Textile Industry." In *Negro Employment in Southern Industry: A Study of Racial Policies in Five Industries*, edited by Herbert R. Northrop, Richard L. Rowan, Darold T. Barnum, and John C. Howard, 7–115. Philadelphia: Industrial Research Unit, Wharton School of Finance and Commerce, Univ. of Pennsylvania, 1970.

Roy, Donald F. "Change and Resistance to Change in the Southern Labor Movement." In *The South in Continuity and Change*, edited by John C. McKinney and Edgar T. Thompson, 225–47. Durham, N.C.: Duke Univ. Press, 1965.

Rule, John. "The Property of Skill in the Period of Manufacture." In *The Historical Meaning of Work*, edited by Patrick Joyce, 99–118. Cambridge: Cambridge Univ. Press, 1987.

Schulman, Michael D., and Cynthia Anderson. "The Dark Side of the Force: A Case Study of Restructuring and Social Capital." *Rural Sociology* 63 (Sept. 1999): 351–72.

Schulman, Michael D., and Jeffrey Leiter. "Southern Textiles: Contested Puzzles and Continuing Paradoxes." In *Hanging by a Thread: Social Change in Southern Textiles*, edited by Jeffrey Leiter, Michael D. Schulman, and Rhonda Zingraff, 3–17. Ithaca, N.Y.: ILR Press, 1991.

Sewell, William H., Jr. "How Classes Are Made: Critical Reflections on E. P. Thompson's Theory of Working-Class Formation." In *E. P. Thompson: Critical Debates*, edited by Harvey J. Kaye and Keith McClelland, 50–77. Oxford: Basil Blackwell, 1990.

Sitterson, J. Carlyle. "Business Leaders in Post-War North Carolina, 1865–1900." In *Studies in Southern History*, edited by J. Carlyle Sitterson, 111–21. Chapel Hill: Univ. of North Carolina Press, 1957.

Stewart, Peter. "Paternalism in a New England Mill Village." *Textile History Review* 6 (Apr. 1968): 59–65.

Thompson, E. P. "Time, Work-Discipline, and Industrial Capitalism." *Past and Present* 35 (1967): 56–97.

Thompson, F. M. L. "Social Control in Victorian Britain." *Economic History Review* 34 (May 2, 1981): 189–208.

Usselman, Steve. "James William Cannon." In *American National Biography*, edited by John A. Garraty and Mark C. Carnes, 335–36. New York: Oxford Univ. Press, 1999.

Zahovi, Gerald. "Negotiated Loyalty: Welfare Capitalism and Shoeworkers of Endicott Johnson, 1920–1940." *Journal of American History* 70 (Dec. 1983): 602–20.

Theses and Dissertations

Brewington, Paulette F. "The 'Colored Page': A History of African-American Communities of Centerview, Bethel, Texas, and Happy Holler in Kannapolis, North Carolina: An Account Based on Oral Narratives and Other Sources." Master's thesis, North Carolina A&T Univ., 1996.

Freeze, Gary Richard. "Master Mill Man: John Milton Odell and Industrial Development in Concord, North Carolina, 1877–1907." Master's thesis, Univ. of North Carolina at Chapel Hill, 1980.

———. "Model Mill Men of the New South: Paternalism and Methodism in the Odell Cotton Mills of North Carolina, 1877–1908." Ph.D. diss., Univ. of North Carolina at Chapel Hill, 1987.

Richards, Paul David. "The History of the Textile Workers Union of America, CIO, in the South, 1937 to 1945." Ph.D. diss., Univ. of Wisconsin–Madison, 1978.

Siniavsky, Boris. "The Cotton-Textile Institute, Inc., a Stabilizing Agency in the Cotton Textile Industry." Master's thesis, Univ. of North Carolina at Chapel Hill, 1931.

Electronic Sources

Library of Congress. American Life Histories: Manuscripts from the Federal Writers' Project, 1936–1940. http://memory.loc.gov/ammem/wpaintro/wpahome.html/.

National Archives and Records Administration. Administrative History, Records of the Office of Price Stabilization. http:/www.archives.gov/research/guide-fed-records/groups/295.html/.

UNITE HERE. UNITE HERE Historical Timeline. http://www.unitehere.org/about/history.php/.

INDEX

Boston, 7, 13
Boyle, J. J., 70
brand loyalty, 14, 69, 76, 107, 122
Brandes, Stuart, 79, 140
Brazil, 24
Broad, Molly, 209
Broome and Wellington, 206
Brown, A. Luther, 70
Brown, Bachman, 197, 203
Brown v. Board of Education, 175
Brown, Eural, 181
Brown Manufacturing Company, 145
Bruere Board, 93, 96, 98
Bruere, Robert, 93
Buck Creek Cotton Mill, 50
Buncombe County, NC, 86
Bureau of the Census, 164
Bureau of Internal Revenue, 85, 86
Bureau of Labor, 38, 130
Burlington Industries (Burlington Mills), 170, 177, 179, 180, 186, 194

Cabarrus Cotton Mills, 11, 56, 66, 71
Cabarrus County Board of Commissioners, 16
Cabarrus County Board of Education, 28
Cabarrus County Department of Social Services, 207
Cabarrus County Tuberculosis Association, 80
Cabarrus Memorial Hospital, 173, 207
Caldwell, Ida Mae, 178
Calloway, Fuller, 43
Camp Elliot, 82
Campbell, Jay, 182
Cannapolis, 16
Cannon, Charles Albert,
—advertising, 69, 87, 108, 119, 102
—General Strike of 1934, 94, 98
—imports, 146-48, 163-65
—New York Stock Exchange, 159, 160
—paternalism, 57, 76, 84, 96, 128, 129, 131, 136, 139, 141, 166, 182, 196
—unions, 57, 75, 124, 126, 131, 141
—two priced cotton, 150, 159, 164, 168
—welfare work, 79-82, 84
Cannon, Charles Albert, Jr., 111
Cannon, Corine Lythe, 176
Cannon, David, 5-7, 11-13
Cannon, Eliza Long, 4

Cannon, Eugene Thomas, 66, 74, 113
Cannon, James William, 5, 21; advertising, 69; paternalism, 6-8; welfare work, 79
Cannon, James William, Jr., 13, 40, 60, 61
Cannon, Joseph Franklin, 40, 66, 74; dispute with J. W. Cannon (father), 228n6; drinking problem, 227n7
Cannon, J. Harry, 114, 134
Cannon, Junius Ross, 61, 66, 74
Cannon, Katie Geneva, 31; claimed that her family had been slaves to the Cannon family, 223n32
Cannon, Martin Luther, 42, 61, 66, 74, 95, 113, 146
Cannon, Mary Ella, 6, 60, 61
Cannon, William C., 113, 160, 190
Cannon Cloth, 10, 11, 14
Cannon Foundation, 207
Cannon Group, 53, 60, 69, 72; profits in the 1920s, 73; welfare work, 84
Cannon Manufacturing Company, and Cannon Cloth, 10; donation of land for black school, 28; family control of, 60; John Odell president, 12; Knights of Labor, 9; organized, 7; trademark, 69; welfare work, 79-80
Cannon Mills, 40
—advertising during WWII, 105
—consolidation to create, 69
—demolition of smoke stacks, 210
—General Strike of 1934, 94
—laws suits for racial discrimination under the Civil Rights Act of 1964, 177, 179
—loyalty banquets, 83
—plant designations, 71
—sale of mill houses, 196
—target of Operation Dixie, 124
—three stages of management, xiv
—*United States v. Cannon Mills*, 181
—union vote of 1974, 189; of 1985, 197
—vertical integration, 70
Cannon Mills Band, 44
Cannon Mills, Inc. (sales agent for the Cannon Group), 13, 56; sales agent for other mills, 220n55; sales agent for other mills the Cannon family controlled, 232n55
Cannon myth, 128-29, 140-41, 214
Cannonville, 8, 16, 20; annexed by Concord, 219n24
Cannon Rug Company, 210
Cannon Village, 196